Exploiting the Wilderness

Exploiting the Wilderness

An Analysis of Wildlife Crime

GREG L. WARCHOL

TEMPLE UNIVERSITY PRESS
Philadelphia • *Rome* • *Tokyo*

TEMPLE UNIVERSITY PRESS
Philadelphia, Pennsylvania 19122
www.temple.edu/tempress

Photographs by Greg L. Warchol

Library of Congress Cataloging-in-Publication Data

Names: Warchol, Greg L. (Gregory L.), 1961– author.
Title: Exploiting the wilderness : an analysis of wildlife crime / Greg L.
  Warchol.
Description: Philadelphia, Pennsylvania : Temple University Press, 2017. |
  Includes bibliographical references and index.
Identifiers: LCCN 2017012895 (print) | LCCN 2017014178 (ebook) | ISBN
  9781439913666 (hardback : alk. paper) | ISBN 9781439913673 (paper : alk.
  paper) | ISBN 9781439913680 (e-book)
Subjects: LCSH: Wildlife crimes. | Wildlife conservation—Law and
  legislation—Criminal provisions. | Wild animal trade—Law and
  legislation—Criminal provisions. | Endangered species—Law and
  legislation—Criminal provisions. | Offenses against the environment. |
  BISAC: LAW / International. | NATURE / Animals / Wildlife.
Classification: LCC K3525 .W37 2017 (print) | LCC K3525 (ebook) | DDC
  364.1/45—dc23
LC record available at https://lccn.loc.gov/2017012895

Printed in the United States of America

9 8 7 6 5 4 3 2 1

To my South African friends

Willie Clack, Simon Pillinger, and Louis Breytenbach

Contents

Preface

The origins of this work date to 2001, when I began my research on the illegal wildlife trade. It was a new area of concern for me, given the extent and impact of the illegal market for wildlife and my interest in conservation and criminology. The illegal trade is a multi-billion-dollar transnational criminal activity that involves wildlife taken from source nations and trafficked to consumer markets around the world. Its impact on many species has been devastating, nearly rendering some extinct. Yet what was surprising was how few criminological studies had focused on the illegal trade. When I began to prepare a literature review on the subject, I found that just a handful of articles on the illegal wildlife trade had been published in criminology or criminal justice journals. Rather, most of the research had been conducted by scholars in the fields of biology, conservation, and environmental studies, often with a focus on species survivability, habitat, and management. While this presented a challenge in building background material for a new study, it also presented the rare opportunity to break new ground. Working with a colleague in my department, Dr. Linda Zupan, and another from the University of South Africa, Professor Willie Clack, I collaborated on a research proposal that focused on the illegal trade in South Africa and Namibia. Once the project was approved and funded, we established contacts in the two nations. Our goal was to identify as many individuals and groups who were knowledgeable about the illegal wildlife trade as possible in order to assemble a sample of interview subjects.

In South Africa, Willie Clack took on the task of making cold calls to researchers, practitioners, and conservationists familiar with the illegal trade. I followed suit by writing a series of letters requesting assistance from conservation groups, law enforcement agencies, wildlife departments, and the U.S. embassies in both countries. The first promising contact came when a U.S. State Department Foreign Service officer called us from the embassy in Johannesburg to offer help. She arranged for us to meet at the U.S. embassy with staffers familiar with international law enforcement issues, including the illegal wildlife trade, when we arrived in South Africa. Even more important, the embassy staff connected us with other groups for our interviews. Several other organizations and agencies in South Africa and Namibia also later responded to my letters. However, it was Willie Clack who hit pay dirt! Clack's cold call to a Simon Pillinger, of Strategic Wildlife Consultants in Durban, South Africa, landed the best in-country contact we could have ever anticipated. Pillinger had decades of service with Natal Parks and was one of the principals behind the efforts to recover the African rhinoceros populations after their numbers were decimated by massive poaching. Pillinger knew virtually everyone involved in wildlife conservation in southern Africa and East Africa, and those he did not know personally he still knew how to contact. Interviews with such individuals as Ted Reilly of Big Game Parks, Swaziland; Ian Manning in Zambia; Section Ranger Johann Oelofse of Kruger National Park; and the director of Tanzania's National Parks became just a phone call away. Pillinger provided a key that unlocked the wildlife research kingdom, facilitating years of work in Africa. Pillinger also introduced me to wildlife consultant Louie Breytenbach of South Africa, a former police officer whose vast knowledge of the smuggling routes and techniques used in southern Africa were a great help in the years that followed.

My field research commenced in 2002 with a month-long trip to South Africa and Namibia to examine the nature of the illegal wildlife trade in the two nations. South Africa had always experienced poaching, but its modern transportation and banking infrastructure allowed it to become a major transshipment point for illegal wildlife products from other parts of the continent that were destined for overseas markets. This first venture was a terrific introduction to the universe of wildlife trafficking and Africa. Willie Clack, Simon Pillinger, Louie Breytenbach, and I were able to meet and interview individuals at South African National Parks, TRAFFIC East and Southern Africa, the U.S. State Department, the World Wildlife Fund, the Harnas Wildlife Center, and the South African Police Service Endangered Species Protection Unit, as well as field rangers, academics, and customs and South African Revenue Service anti-smuggling officers. When I returned to the States, I analyzed the results and published them in a journal article the following year.

This first venture was soon followed by several additional field visits to the region that included work with Clack, Breytenbach, and Pillinger in Botswana, Swaziland, and Zambia. In addition to collecting data about the illegal trade, I began to focus on specific wildlife crimes, including rhinoceros poaching and the poaching of protected species for use in traditional medicines. This second series of research initiatives led to a larger study in Tanzania, Zambia, Malawi, and Mozambique, specifically concerning the poaching and trafficking of ivory and rhinoceros horn. More recently, I made several visits to Kenya, in East Africa, to gather data on the illegal trade in that region and to prepare the groundwork for future projects.

Although working on overseas research projects in the field can be quite challenging, with the researcher away from home for weeks at a time and often unfamiliar with the culture, language, and people of each area, the experience is invaluable. I learned more than a few words of Afrikaans and Swahili, became accustomed to eating sausage rolls and biltong while I was on the road, and survived Zambezi River crossings in rickety ferry boats, charges by irritated elephants in Chobe National Park, and high-speed drives down rutted dirt tracks in beat-up trucks to reach a border crossing before it closed. I had the considerable benefit of working with three outstanding individuals from South Africa, who used their insider status to help me obtain numerous forms of access. Without their efforts, my overseas field research would not have been possible. After I entered each country, I met up with Clack, Pillinger, and Breytenbach. We generally traveled by truck or plane to various locations for interviews that we had scheduled on the basis of our research questions. We also gathered as many secondary documents and reports as we could from the various organizations. These materials, which were sometimes hard to come by (many of which are referenced herein), became invaluable resources for clarifying and validating information from the interviews and as secondary sources of statistical data. I also made it a point to take roughly a thousand photographs on each trip as an additional source of data and for use in presentations. Before I moved to digital photography, I often returned from Africa with some fifty rolls of exposed slide and print film, a very dusty Nikon F100, and my always reliable F3, along with several notepads loaded with interview field notes. Recognizing the importance of reviewing field notes after each day of travel and interviews, we often gathered after dinner to discuss the day's work and verify the information recorded in our notes. We found that we were absorbing a lot about the countries that we were fortunate to be spending time in. With each visit, we reaped the benefit of learning more about each nation's culture, how its institutions functioned, the nature of its people, and its geography. One unexpected benefit of being an American academic was that it seemed to open many doors during my research. Interviewees eagerly complied, and I was granted exceptional access to people and places.

Over the years, this research evolved from the first descriptive study of the wildlife trade in southern Africa to studies focused on the illegal trade in traditional medicines, bushmeat poaching, abalone poaching in the Western Cape, elephant and rhinoceros poaching and trafficking, field ranger training and operations, and wildlife trafficking methods and routes. The research took my colleagues and me to nearly thirty different game reserves in nine countries, border stations known for wildlife smuggling, game departments, illegal ivory dealers, harbors, airports, wildlife markets in remote villages and large cities, professional hunting operations, and police storage rooms loaded with confiscated ivory and rhinoceros horn. We conducted hundreds of interviews with individuals involved in all aspects of conservation law enforcement, ranging from game scouts to heads of national wildlife departments. We were able to speak with individuals selling illegal wildlife products, poachers, corrupt field rangers, judges, prosecutors, private investigators, and professional hunters involved in anti-poaching efforts.

The results of subsequent research trips were also published in various journals and became the basis for three new wildlife conservation courses at my university. I presented the findings at numerous national criminal justice and criminology conferences, where, when I first began, my paper was frequently the only one on the subject. In recent years, interest in this area has increased to the point where it is not unusual for several conference panels to be dedicated to papers on the subject. The idea for a book on the illegal wildlife trade came from a call from Temple University Press editor Aaron Javsicas just before the opening of the American Society of Criminology Conference in 2014. This work, which is based on my own field research and that of many others, is designed as an introduction to the illegal wildlife trade. In several places herein, I reference interviews conducted (personal communications) or my own past studies to highlight specific topics. The illegal trade in wildlife is an extensive transnational criminal activity that involves nearly every protected species that has a value and consumers in both the developed and the developing worlds. The primary focus of this book is wildlife crime in Africa. Given the global nature of this illegal trade, I have included some research describing various aspects of wildlife crimes in Asia, Europe, and the United States.

Chapter 1 provides a description of the illegal wildlife trade, some of the major species that are illegally hunted and trafficked, and the structure of the market for these products. Chapter 2 addresses the national and international efforts to prevent the illegal trade in wildlife. The chapter covers selected U.S. and African laws and international treaties and agreements, along with the role of nongovernmental organizations in wildlife conservation. Chapter 3 examines offenders in the illegal trade, including various types of poachers and middlemen involved in illegally hunting and facilitating the movement of wildlife from source to consumer. The chapter also examines the impact of corruption on wildlife crime. Chapter 4 explores the reasons why the crime occurs, describing first the impact of the colonial period and its aftermath on the use of wildlife in Africa. Findings from both the descriptive and explanatory research applying criminological theory to the study of offenders follow. This combined information furthers an understanding of the causes of the illegal trade in wildlife. Chapter 5 focuses on the end user, or consumer, of illegally harvested and trafficked wildlife products, without whom poachers would have little incentive to hunt protected wildlife. Chapter 6 turns to the subject of the agencies charged with protecting wildlife. Examples from the United States and Africa illustrate the operations and compare and contrast American game wardens and African field rangers. The chapter also examines the militarization of ranger forces in Africa and the need for dedicated environmental courts, or *green courts,* for wildlife crimes. Chapter 7 looks at a selection of current and future efforts to protect wildlife. It describes the value of community-based conservation programs in Africa and contemporary efforts to apply modern predictive analysis techniques and new surveillance technologies to the prevention of poaching. The chapter closes by addressing the question of the legal commercialization of protected wildlife as a means of reducing the illegal wildlife trade.

Terms and Abbreviations

bushmeat: In Africa and Asia commonly refers to wild game meat

CITES: United Nations Convention on International Trade in Endangered Species

conflict animal: Wild animal that represents a threat to human life, livestock, or agriculture

curio market: Gift or souvenir shop

drone: Unmanned aerial vehicle

EIA: Environmental Investigation Agency

ESA: U.S. Endangered Species Act of 1973

ESPU: Endangered Species Protection Unit

hanko: Small rectangular or cylindrical ivory block

inyanga: South African traditional medicine healer or doctor; often acts as an herbalist

IUCN: International Union for Conservation of Nature

KWS: Kenya Wildlife Service

Lacey Act: First U.S. wildlife protection legislation, passed in 1900

MIKE: Monitoring the Illegal Killing of Elephants

muti: In South Africa refers to traditional medicine

NGO: Nongovernmental organization

PAWS: Protection Assistant for Wildlife Security

pre-ban ivory: Legal ivory that predates the international ivory ban of 1989

predictive analysis anti-poaching: Contemporary data-driven technique used to design ranger patrols on the basis of the most likely areas for poaching

protected area: Refers, in general, to a national or provincial park or private game reserve

sangoma: South African traditional medicine practitioner who acts as a diviner of the ailment

SAPS: South African Police Service

snare: Simple wire noose commonly used by poachers to trap wildlife

TAM/TCM: Traditional Asian medicine/traditional Chinese medicine

TRAFFIC: Monitoring agency for the trade in wildlife

USCBP: U.S. Customs and Border Protection

USFWS: U.S. Fish and Wildlife Service

WCS: Wildlife Conservation Society

WWF: World Wildlife Fund

Exploiting the Wilderness

I

The Illegal Trade in Wildlife

An Overview

The Illicit Trade

On the outskirts of the remote town of Pemba in far northern Mozambique, we stopped at a small roadside curio shop offering an array of items for tourists. In plain view on the display tables were numerous ivory bracelets and carvings of animals, people, and religious figures. Out of curiosity we asked the owner what other ivory items he had available. He hesitated briefly to assess our motives and then, believing we might be free-spending tourists, left for the storeroom and soon returned with a raw elephant tusk, dirty brown in color and about thirty inches long. Even knowing we were foreign visitors, he offered to sell it to us "as is" for about $70 USD. We declined and, while leaving, spotted two young men working in an outdoor area adjacent the shop. One man was using basic hand tools to carve an ivory tusk into an ornate and finely detailed object of art to be offered to tourists. I saw this scene repeatedly during my research work in East Africa and southern Africa over fourteen years. Ivory of questionable origins and illegally harvested endangered plants, mammals, reptiles, birds, and even insects were easily found for sale in both cities and rural areas. Little or no effort was made to conceal these natural resources from interested buyers. If such items were not visible, simply asking the proprietor of a shop about them would result in numerous illegal items being offered for sale. Seeing such items, foreign tourists might view them as legal to buy and transport home. Local police were often reluctant to confiscate the items, knowing they would just be replaced later by more poaching. This was just one part of the illegal global trade in wildlife.

Nearly any protected species that can be used for food, clothing, decorative objects, medicine, a fuel source, building material, or a collection specimen is subject to being poached and traded in this illegal market. A comprehensive description of the multi-billion-dollar global illegal trade in wildlife would require many volumes, but the goal of this work is to provide the reader with a sound overview of the trade, including a description of some of the main species being exploited; the participants and their motivations and operations; explanations of participants' behavior; legislative and law enforcement efforts to control and prevent wildlife poaching and trafficking; and contemporary conservation initiatives. This work draws considerably from my research in East Africa and southern Africa. However, I also provide numerous examples of wildlife crimes in other regions of the world to illustrate the extent of the problem and allow for contrasts and comparisons. The objective of this first chapter is to examine the structure and operation of the illegal trade in wildlife.

Wildlife is illegally harvested either because it cannot be obtained legitimately or because consumers cannot afford to purchase the products. The chapter begins by examining the nature and extent of the illegal trade with a primary though not exclusive focus on Africa, the locations of many species that are exploited in this illegal market and the area of my extensive research. Next is a description of some of the major species that are illegally taken from the wild and sold or consumed. It is not possible in this book to list every species, so I examine instead a select wildlife whose survival is imperiled due to heavy pressure from poachers to meet consumer demand. While many illegally harvested products from endangered and threatened wildlife are consumed in their source countries, others are smuggled overseas to consumer nations, where they are prized as medicines or decorative items. Common among these are elephant ivory, rhinoceros horn, tiger pelts and body parts, and marine, bird, and reptile species. The chapter concludes with a description of the organization and functioning of the illegal transnational markets that move wildlife products from their source countries to the end user or consumer markets.

Defining the Trade in Wildlife: Legal and Illegal Components

Natural resources, which include flora and fauna, represent an important national asset for a country as marketable commodities and as part of its national heritage and identity (Warchol and Kapla 2012; World Bank 2013).

The transnational illicit wildlife trade is an extensive and highly lucrative type of natural resource offense. The species exploited in this trade include rare and endangered mammals, marine life, reptiles, insects, birds, and timber and other plants (TRAFFIC 2008). The trade is driven by demand for products that cannot be obtained legally or at low cost, combined with weak levels of enforcement that make apprehension of offenders unlikely (Albanese 2011). While many researchers and the media have focused considerable attention on the plight of rhinoceroses, elephants, and tigers, whose exploitation has accelerated dramatically in recent years (Lo and Edwards 2015; Orenstein 2013; Rademeyer 2012; Swails and Magnay 2014), these species represent a small fraction of the total number of plants and animals illegally taken or killed and trafficked, both in their source countries and internationally. The trade typically includes millions of birds and reptiles shipped live to supply pet dealers with rare species; smaller mammals, both common and endangered, hunted as a source of bushmeat to meet the demand for protein; timber species harvested for home and commercial furnishings; plants collected for use in traditional medicines and in decorative landscaping; and marine life, including shark fin, beluga caviar, and abalone, harvested for use in exotic cuisine (Warchol, Zupan, and Clack 2003; TRAFFIC 2016c).

Participants in the illegal trade include individual actors and informal and formal criminal networks (Albanese 2011; Knecht 2006; Warchol and Johnson 2009) with various motivations. Furthermore, military and insurgency forces exploiting destabilized conflict zones and more recently terrorist groups in search of revenue sources have long been documented as involved in the illegal wildlife trade (Orenstein 2013; Venter 2003). Though some poaching is for individual subsistence, other offenders are motivated by the economic value of the illegal global trade in wildlife. While it is very difficult to put a precise value on an illegal enterprise, the illicit trade is clearly a multi-billion-dollar international business (U.S. Fish and Wildlife Service [hereafter USFWS] 2016), estimated at $50 to 150 billion annually if illegal fishing and timber harvesting are included (United Nations Environment Programme 2014). This offense ranks among the top three or four types of transnational crime, behind narcotics and weapons trafficking (Lo and Edwards 2015; TRAFFIC 2016a). The profits are strong motivators for the various actors in this trade—that is, poacher, middleman, and retailer. A poacher can earn a small profit, but the value of wildlife increases as it moves from middleman to retailer (Broad, Mulliken, and Roe 2005; Warchol, Zupan, and Clack 2003).

Beyond the peril to the survival of the species, the illegal trade represents a threat to the financial stability and potentially the security of nations dependent on natural resources for their economic growth. This is certainly the

Raw elephant tusk in curio shop near Pemba, Mozambique, offered to the author for about $70 USD. The legality of its origins is unknown.

case in the developing world, where many nations rely on their wildlife as a major part of their economy. These resources include timber, other plants, marine life, birds, and mammals that are used for building materials, food, medicines, decorations, clothing, and tourist attractions. The significance of this resource is illustrated by the value of the *legal* global trade in wildlife—live animals and plants, as well as wildlife products—estimated at $323 billion USD (TRAFFIC 2016a). Demand for wildlife generally increases with the growth of human populations, causing additional pressure on these resources. However, as with other types of valuable products, this resource is also illegally exploited as part of the transnational trade in wildlife, an extensive and highly lucrative type of natural resource offense.

Countries dependent on eco-tourism revenue (Chamley 2005; Frost and Bond 2007) or on marketable commodities for the domestic and international trade, such as timber and marine life (World Bank 2013), are seriously affected by natural resource crimes. In developing nations such as Kenya, Zimbabwe, or Botswana, environmental tourism constitutes a significant part of the economy (Donovan 2013). Game reserves, both public and private, attract international and domestic visitors for photo safaris, employ local residents, and generate tax revenue. Species decline due to illegal hunting, and incidents of tourists on safari spotting animal carcasses attributed to poaching and news reports of violent encounters between field rangers and poachers in the game reserves diminish the lucrative eco-tourism industry. One part of wildlife tourism, the trophy hunting industry, provides an estimated $120 million USD annually in South Africa (Statistics South Africa 2015) and makes up nearly 10 percent of total GDP in Tanzania and Namibia (Donovan 2013). Finally, cross-border military and insurgency poaching operations represent a threat to several East African nations targeted for their wildlife resources (National Public Radio 2003; Vira and Ewing 2014; Warchol, Zupan, and Clack 2003).

The Major Species under Threat

The illegal trade in wildlife involves the full range of protected flora and fauna species, both common and endangered. This section describes the different species that are trafficked in the illegal wildlife trade, primarily focusing on Africa but with references to regions in Asia, Europe, and South America. Illegal timber harvesting and commercial fishing are not included in this work. While these two aspects of the illegal trade constitute the largest and most lucrative part due to the sheer volume of product, their harvesting often involves nation-states and/or corporations exploiting the resource via large-scale illicit commercial fishing and timbering operations. The focus here is rather directed toward the activities of individuals, informal networks, and criminal syndicates that target a range of animals and plants for personal use and profit.

Elephant and Rhinoceros

African elephants are unique among the various species of animals, having been used by humans for decoration, warfare, entertainment, and food for thousands of years (USFWS 2001). Around 3000 BC, their habitat included the whole of Africa, from the southern Cape to as far north as Egypt, where they were both captured for domestication and hunted for their ivory. The appreciation of and resulting demand for ivory dates back to at least 1000 BC. African elephants were also used for military purposes, most notably by Alexander the Great and the Carthaginian general Hannibal. Around 45 BC, the Romans commonly used elephants in addition to rhinoceros and other African animals in ceremonies and war games for popular entertainment. By about AD 500, the once large populations of North African elephants were greatly reduced in number by both overhunting and the encroachment of the Sahara Desert (Meredith 2003).

With the development of the slave trading routes into East Africa by Arabs and Persians (one center of which was the island of Zanzibar, off the coast of Tanzania), elephant hunting for ivory steadily increased to meet the

Elephants on an afternoon walk in Chobe National Park, Botswana.

demand, primarily in India and China though not the Middle East. Starting in the 1400s and lasting for centuries, pressure on elephant populations slowly increased as European explorers opened up more of Africa and exploited its natural resources, with perhaps the most notorious example being Belgium's King Leopold in the Congo Free State in the late 1800s. While indigenous Africans mainly hunted elephants as a source of food, Europeans desired the ivory as a decorative object.

Sometimes referred to as *white gold,* an elephant tusk is essentially a long dentine tooth, though only the tip has enamel. The tusk may be partly covered with a type of light brown bark, which is removed to facilitate carving. The ivory varies in hardness, color, and translucency, depending on the species of elephant (Jackson 2003). Ivory has been worked into a variety of objects, including ornate religious carvings, bracelets, piano keys, billiard balls, knife handles, combs, statues, table legs, ink pens, and bird cages, just to name a few. A common use of ivory in modern-day Japan—the largest market for ivory for most of the twentieth century until the expansion of China's economy—is for the manufacture of *hankos* (Orenstein 2013). A *hanko* is a small rectangular ivory block or cylinder, the bottom of which contains a person's or company's individual seal or signature (Jackson 2003).

Ivory became so popular in the 1800s that today's writers refer to it as the "plastic of the era" (Meredith 2003, 107). As demand steadily increased into the twentieth century, there was a corresponding decline in elephant populations. The amount of ivory exported from Africa reached a peak in 1914 at 1,000 metric tons, potentially representing the killing of as many as 50,000 elephants. Although ivory exports rapidly declined during and after World War I, they subsequently increased slowly but steadily, reaching nearly 28 metric tons in 1950, 485 metric tons in 1964, and a staggering 1,263 metric tons in 1973, when ivory attained the status of an investment commodity under unstable global economic conditions (Jackson 2003). Retail ivory prices climbed from $7.50 per kilogram in 1970 to $78 per kg in 1978, then to $150 per kg in Africa in 1989 (USFWS 2001). With a single elephant yielding about 10 kg of ivory, each one killed provided about $1,500 in the consumer market (Vira and Ewing 2014).

As ivory increased in value during the economic recessions of those years, the final chapter in the colonial period of Africa was written as the European powers willingly or unwillingly gave up control of their colonial holdings. While some transitions were peaceful, others involved violent liberation struggles sometimes defined by Cold War politics, bringing political instability not only to the subject country but often also to its neighbors. Warring factions, now well armed with military weapons provided by communist-bloc (especially China) and pro-Western nations, soon realized that natural resources, including ivory, could be used to fund their cause and enrich corrupt officials. These factors contributed to large increases in poaching well into the late 1980s as ivory was used in part to finance the conflicts in Africa. What made this period especially devastating to elephant populations was the capacity of military units to poach large numbers of animals. Unlike individuals or small gangs of poachers, military units had the weaponry and transportation capability to take and move large quantities of ivory from the bush to ports for export to consumer nations (Vira and Ewing 2014). This tactic would define the industrial-scale poaching of the postcolonial era.

African elephant populations were estimated to be at about 1.3 million in 1979 and already in decline. By 1989, approximately 700,000 of them had been killed by poachers (Jackson 2003). Certain countries were hit exceptionally hard, while others, such as South Africa, Botswana, and Zimbabwe, were spared the brunt of massive poaching. Kenya's Tsavo National Park alone lost half of its population of 30,000 elephants in two years, while Uganda's total population fell from 60,000 to 6,000 by the mid-1970s (Meredith 2003). Between 1981 and 1987, Zambia's elephant herd of 160,000 was reduced by poachers to 43,000. Tour operators and professional hunters often commented on hearing constant volleys of automatic weapons fire in Zambia's Luangwa Valley from poachers operating with near impunity. Suffering a similar fate in the same time period, Mozambique's elephant population was reduced to about 18,600 from an estimated 54,800 in 1981 by poaching (Jackson 2003). Forest elephants of Central Africa tended to fare better, since they were harder to locate than the savannah elephants found farther south. The situation would finally be checked with the 1989 decision to place all African elephants on Appendix I of the 1975 Convention on International Trade in Endangered Species (CITES), banning the global trade in ivory and elephant products (Thornton 1997).

The CITES agreement, which currently has 182 member nations, including the United States, was designed to regulate the trade in wildlife. In Appendix I, the member nations (known as Parties) agree to enforce its provisions by banning international commercial trade of plant and animal species threatened with extinction. The Parties via Appendix II also agree to regulate the trade via the use of CITES permits for other species that may become extinct if their trade is not controlled. Finally, Appendix III lists the species that are subject to regulation in a particular member nation and for which assistance is needed by other Parties to control cross-border trafficking (CITES 2016a, 2016b). Elephants were listed in 1989 as threatened with extinction, and the commercial trade in elephants was prohibited. It was contended by the U.S. Fish and Wildlife Service that had this listing not been done, "the African elephant would have been annihilated throughout most of its range by the end of the 20th century" (2001, 5).

Related to the CITES up-listing strategy was a public relations effort to develop an anti-ivory sentiment among consumers to further decrease demand and reduce prices. This included the distribution of graphic images of slaughtered elephants, echoing the anti-fur campaigns of the 1990s in the United States. One of the most dramatic public relations events was carried out by Richard Leakey, director of the Kenya Wildlife Service, and Kenyan president Daniel Moi when they publicly burned a massive pile of more than two thousand elephant tusks in July 1989. Leakey and Morell (2001) estimated that more than 850 million people saw the event on television or in the print media and were now aware of the plight of African elephants. Complementing these efforts were successful management practices and aggressive anti-poaching efforts, including Kenya's "shoot on sight" directive against armed poachers. Combined, these resulted in population increases in certain East African and southern African nations to the point where some have argued that elephants should be down-listed to a CITES II species. However, the situation is grim in other African countries, where poaching is common for both ivory and wild game meat (USFWS 2001).

Although the 1990s marked a period of recovery for elephants in Africa, two developments occurred near the end of the decade that would contribute to a resurgence in poaching. In June 1997, at the CITES conference in Harare, a proposal was made by Zimbabwe, Namibia, and Botswana, which had been spared the massive poaching of the previous decades, to down-list elephants to a CITES II category, thereby allowing a renewed trade in ivory that would include a one-time sale of ivory stocks to Japan. Concerns that the sale would foster poaching by stimulating demand for ivory resulted in the establishment of new safeguards to protect existing elephant populations and the inauguration of the MIKE program (Monitoring the Illegal Killing of Elephants) to monitor the trade in ivory. However, the Environmental Investigation Agency's early analysis found these programs to be weak and ineffective at attaining their goals. It argued that if the sale was approved, which it eventually was, the new monitoring system would be unable to accurately determine if there was an increase in poaching linked to the ivory trade (EIA 2000). The down-listing of elephants and the ivory sale served to stimulate demand for additional ivory in the retail markets of China and Japan. The other development during this time was the rapid expansion of China's middle class as China opened its markets to foreign investment and new trade deals. As a consequence, consumer interest increased in luxury and status items, including ivory.

The EIA's predictions were correct: elephant poaching began to steadily increase in most of the elephant range states. Corresponding to more poaching were increases in ivory seizures by customs officials in both elephant range states and consumer nations. By the late 1990s, evidence of significantly increased poaching was uncovered in Zimbabwe, Zambia, and Tanzania. Renewed poaching would soon be found in other African states. In 2002, Tanzanian authorities seized a shipment of 1,255 ivory pieces in the capital of Dar es Salaam; additional seizures followed, also in Tanzania. The Kenya Wildlife Service concluded that its severe loss of elephants due to poaching was a by-product of lifting the ban on ivory. Tsavo National Park, located in southern Kenya, lost nearly 90 percent of its elephant population in 1980s, experienced a recovery during the ban, and then saw its progress reversed after the down-listing (EIA 2000). Poaching was not limited to East Africa, nor was it being done just by government military units in destabilized nations, as it increased in both Chad and Congo (Fay 2011). The latter had a population of more than 11,000 elephants in the 1980s but reported fewer than 1,800 remaining animals by the early 2000s. Improvements in transportation, communication, and banking infrastructure due in part to globalization facilitated the growth of transnational crime enterprises, including wildlife traffickers (Vira and Ewing 2014). These new syndicates, combined with insurgency units and, recently, terrorist groups, fostered the second wave of elephant poaching in Africa. News reports indicated that more sophisticated poaching operations were now involved, employing modern military weapons such as rocket-propelled grenades, helicopters, and automatic rifles to bring down entire herds of elephants. The guerrilla group known as the Lord's Resistance Army, under Joseph Kony, sought out ivory as a source of funding for its military operations. Reports noted that nearly 100 elephants were being killed per day in Central Africa, totaling an estimated 35,000 lost in 2012. The result was a 50 percent decline in the population over a thirty-year period. Poaching has also been linked to the insurgencies in neighboring Sudan and Uganda, where ivory was sold by combatants to purchase weaponry. In Chad and Cameroon in north-central Africa, elephant massacres of hundreds of animals were being reported in 2013 and attributed to groups armed with military weapons (Fay 2011; Vira and Ewing 2014).

The rhinoceros has less of a storied relationship with humans than the elephant. Two species exist in Africa: the smaller black rhino and larger white. There are three Asian species—the Javan, Sumatran, and greater one-horned—all of which are endangered (World Wildlife Fund [hereafter WWF] 2016a, 2016b). Initially viewed as pests by farmers or as trophies for hunters, the once large populations of rhinoceros were first dramatically reduced in the nineteenth century. The World Wildlife Fund (2016a) reported that as many as one million white and black rhino may have existed in the mid-1800s. The population of black rhino declined due to excessive hunting to an estimated 65,000 in 1970. The southern subspecies of Africa's white rhino fared even worse with only 50–200 surviving by the first half of the 1970s (USFWS 2004). By the early 1970s, rhino were being killed for their horns, which would bring both species close to extinction. Complicating efforts at conservation was the nature of the trade in rhino horn and its application by consumers.

Unlike ivory, rhinoceros horn was not widely used as a decorative object—with one exception. The highly polished horns were used to produce handles for ceremonial daggers in the Middle East, notably in Yemen. However, with the advent of high-quality synthetic materials, this application for the horns is not a significant current threat to the species (Leakey and Morell 2001). What remains a major problem is the other traditional use of rhinoceros horn—as an ingredient in natural Asian medicines for a variety of ailments. The horn is ground into a powder, mixed with other natural ingredients and even pharmaceuticals, and dispensed by traditional healers in Asia and in Asian communities in the West to consumers for a variety of maladies. During the early 1990s, Taiwan was a major center for rhinoceros horn trafficking. Its stockpile was estimated at nine tons, with a street value of $50 million USD, representing about 3,700 dead rhino (Davies 2005; EIA 1993). The very fact that its use is rooted in centuries of tradition, myth, and mystical beliefs means that a media campaign to shame users would be of questionable value (Leakey and Morell 2001). This problem is compounded by the high value of horns in Asia. Ben Davies (2005) states, "Of all the illegal forms of wildlife trade, the trafficking of rhino horn is the world's most lucrative, secretive, profitable and dangerous. Driven by the horn's extraordinary value

Southern white rhino in Hluhluwe-Imfolozi Park, KwaZulu Natal, South Africa. After massive poaching dramatically reduced Africa's rhino population—again heavily targeted by poachers beginning in about 2007—the park became the site of a vital rhino conservation program.

(in some cases it's worth more than five times its weight in gold), it has long been the domain of powerful international syndicates" (132).

The black rhino was hit the hardest, first by excessive legal hunting and then by poaching. As a result of rampant poaching for horn, its population further declined to about 2,300 in 1996, representing a 96 percent decrease in just twenty-two years. It lost a larger percentage of individuals than any other species in the last one hundred years (USFWS 2004). Individual country data further illustrate the impact of poaching. In the early 1970s, an estimated 50,000 black rhino lived in Zambia's Luangwa Valley. By 1981, the population in this region had been reduced to about 2,000, and by 1992, it had further declined to about a dozen (Gibson 1999). Zimbabwe offered an interesting case study in which black rhino conservation was a success during the 1970s and 1980s, when the population grew to more than 1,700 (about half of the world's population at the time). However, Zimbabwe's political and economic problems in the 1990s resulted in international economic sanctions, a collapsing economy, and social turmoil. The economic sanctions prevented foreign donors from contributing to wildlife conservation projects, including rhino protection. Some rhino conservation areas, now devoid of enforcement, were quickly targeted by poachers (African Wildlife Foundation 2005).

REMAINING AFRICAN AND ASIAN RHINOCEROS SPECIES			
Species	Current Habitat Locations by Nation	Estimated Population	Main Threats to Survival
Southern White Rhinoceros	South Africa, Botswana, Kenya, Namibia, Zambia, Zimbabwe, Swaziland, and Uganda	19,600–21,000	Poaching
Northern White Rhinoceros	Extinct in the wild, remaining animals in Kenyan conservancy	3	Poaching and extremely small captive population
Black Rhinoceros	South Africa, Namibia, Swaziland, Kenya, Tanzania, Zimbabwe, Zambia, Botswana, and Malawi	5,000–5,400	Poaching
Javan Rhinoceros	Indonesia	58–61	Poaching, habitat loss owing to development, and small population
Sumatran Rhinoceros	Indonesia and Malaysia	Fewer than 100	Poaching and habitat loss owing to development
Greater One-Horned Rhinoceros	India and Nepal	3,333	Poaching, habitat loss owing to development, and human-wildlife conflict

Source: Save the Rhino, Poaching Statistics, 2016. Available at https://www.savetherhino.org/rhino_info/poaching_statistics (accessed June 11, 2016).

In another example, after being hunted to extinction in Swaziland, a few rhino were successfully reintroduced in the mid-1960s and the population increased to well over 100 by the late 1980s. However, between 1988 and 1992, the so-called rhino wars began as Zimbabwean poaching gangs crossed into Swaziland, killing an average of one rhino on the reserves every two weeks and in some instances three per day. Initially, Swazi police were ill-prepared to deal with the problem. Claims of corruption in the judiciary and game ranger service only complicated efforts to end the poaching and prosecute offenders. The poaching finally stopped following new national legislation carrying severe penalties, the introduction of a British SAS detachment to assist local law enforcement, and the deaths of more than three hundred poachers (Reilly 2004).

As a result of extensive conservation efforts since the early 1990s, black and white rhinoceros populations have rebounded somewhat in Africa, though they are nowhere near their numbers from the mid-1960s. Current-ly, there are about 20,000 southern white rhino; however, 95 percent of them live in South Africa on public and private game reserves. There are only about three northern white rhino, all of which are in captivity (WWF 2016a). African black rhino currently number about five thousand. The recovery of the rhinoceros was the result of strong law enforcement and management practices (USFWS 2004). This success does not mean that the pressure from poachers has diminished, however. The Tanzanian government, for instance, has constant surveillance of its small rhino herd, located in the Ngorongoro Crater Conservation Area near the Serengeti. Rhino poaching continued in South Africa but remained at relatively low levels that did not threaten the survival of the species. But this situation would change by the early 2000s, owing to the emergence of a new market for horn.

By the early 2000s, increased prosperity in Vietnam among the middle and upper classes, combined with demand for luxury goods and a belief in the medicinal powers of rhinoceros horn, fostered demand for the product. Julian Rademeyer's (2012) investigation found that while the horn has no significant medicinal properties, the myth was still heavily promoted in Vietnam, stimulating demand for the horn. The initial efforts to obtain horn for the Vietnamese market consisted of what was termed *pseudohunting*. Commonly, young Vietnamese women without hunting experience, including prostitutes from low-income areas, were recruited by syndicates for a modest price to go to South Africa for a legal rhino hunting safari with the sole objective of obtaining the horn as a trophy. Once taken back to Vietnam, the rhino horn would quickly disappear into the marketplace, where it was sold at extremely high prices to willing buyers. Although hunting rhino and keeping the horn as a trophy was legal in South Africa, the sale of it as a commodity was illegal under CITES. Between 2003 and 2010, nearly four hundred pseudohunts occurred, with the Vietnamese dominating the legal rhinoceros hunting business in South Africa.

Paralleling this development was a dramatic increase in rhinoceros poaching, primarily in South Africa but also in neighboring Swaziland. South Africa's Kruger National Park, which maintained large populations of rhinoceros, was heavily targeted by poaching syndicates. World Wildlife Fund (2016c) concluded that poaching increased 9,000 percent in South Africa from a loss of 13 animals in 2007 to 1,215 animals by 2014. Between 2013 and 2014, rhino poaching in South Africa increased 21 percent with 1,004 killed in 2014 and another 1,215 in 2015. In Kruger Park, 827 rhinoceros were killed in 2014. While smaller populations of rhinoceros exist in Asia, they have also been under steady poaching pressure, though not as severe as in Africa. This is partly function of their low numbers and the relative difficulty of locating the animals in remote regions of national parks. About 3,500 greater one-horned rhino, fewer than 100 Sumatran rhino, and about 65 Javan rhino survive (WWF 2016b).

The Bushmeat Trade in Africa

Wildlife in Africa is also commonly hunted as bushmeat. The term *bushmeat* refers to wild game, and the bushmeat trade is defined as the hunting of wildlife specifically for human consumption (Robinson and Bennett 2004). Bushmeat hunting is not focused on a single species; rather, it includes a wide range of wildlife—mammals, reptiles, and some insects. There is both a legal and an illegal component, the latter occurring on protected areas or involving prohibited species. Bushmeat had long been carried out at sustainable levels in rural Africa, arguably since the dawn of civilization (TRAFFIC 2002a). Until the late twentieth century, hunting for bushmeat was not a major conservation issue because Africa had large wildlife populations and relatively low human populations. However, from 1900 to 2000, the population of Africa increased eightfold to approximately 800 million; at the same time, wildlife habitat (and hence the size of wildlife populations) significantly declined (Bushmeat Crisis Task Force [hereafter BCTF] 2008). Interestingly, increases in bushmeat consumption were found to correspond to increases in wealth, with large volumes of bushmeat shipped to urban centers.

The origins of the bushmeat trade in several Central African nations (including the Congo, Cameroon, and Gabon) have been traced to the opening of forests for logging and mining operations, which, in turn, fueled the demand for inexpensive sources of protein for the workers (TRAFFIC 2002a). Capitalizing on the profit potential beyond feeding the laborers, hunters began to harvest more game to sell in neighboring settlements. More problematic was that hunters often remained in the forests long after the logging or mining operations ceased in order to hunt what had now become a valuable commodity, in demand in both rural and urban areas (Adams and McShane 1992; Warchol and Johnson 2009). These developments led to further social changes, making the bushmeat trade a socially acceptable but environmentally harmful practice. Beginning in the late 1980s, hunting for wild game in Central Africa and western Africa was no longer limited to in-season harvesting (Adams and McShane 1992), which hindered animal population recovery, nor were considerations made for gender selection or take-off quotas (Burgener, Snyman, and Hauck 2001). While much bushmeat hunting on unprotected lands was not illegal, once local game was exhausted, hunters often became poachers, illegally entering the public and private wildlife reserves for new sources of game (Pillinger 2003).

In regions of Africa, the illegal bushmeat trade includes poaching for subsistence and an extensive small- and large-scale illegal commercial industry (BCTF 2008). The illegal commercial trade common in Central Africa and West Africa eventually expanded into South Africa, targeting its extensive number of game reserves, both public and private (Pillinger 2003).

As a result, the hunting of wildlife for food has been determined by some to be the most significant threat to biological diversity (BCTF 2008), increasing to the point where millions of tons are harvested annually. One of the most comprehensive studies of this problem concluded that the combination of poverty, limited economic opportunities, and increasing human populations has led to the bushmeat trade being the most serious threat to southern African wildlife, including on protected areas (TRAFFIC 2002a).

Asian and African Big Cats

Perhaps best known among the cat species illegally hunted and trafficked within the wildlife trade is the tiger (*Panthera tigris*). It is believed there are populations of tigers in regions of thirteen nations: India, China, Russia, Nepal, Myanmar, Laos, Thailand, Indonesia, Bangladesh, Bhutan, Malaysia, and possibly Cambodia and Vietnam (International Union for Conservation of Nature [hereafter IUCN] 2015b). Tiger populations have declined by 97 percent since 1900, from an estimated 100,000 to about 3,400 animals remaining in the wild in 2016. Furthermore, the historical tiger range has declined over time by 93 percent, with the remaining populations surviving in small and isolated habitats, making them more vulnerable to poaching (WWF 2016e). When dangerous game hunting was considered high sport, in the late nineteenth and early twentieth centuries, tiger populations were dramatically reduced. In the fifty-year period between 1875 and 1925, an estimated 80,000 tigers were taken by hunters in India (Davies 2005).

While the age of legal tiger hunting is long over, tiger populations currently face three other threats to their survival in the wild: habitat loss, retaliatory killing, and poaching. Tigers require a large range with essential prey animals and habitat to survive. However, in parts of their home ranges there have been reductions in their common prey animals along with habitat destruction due to development (EIA 2006). The expansion of logging and mining operations in developing countries that are tiger range states with affected habitat brings to light the conflict between economic progress and conservation. Currently, of the original nine subspecies of tigers, three have become extinct because of hunting, habitat loss, and disease. Conflicts between humans and tigers after the animals kill livestock have also contributed to their decline. High rates of retaliatory killings by affected residents living in proximity to tiger populations in Bangladesh and India occurred between 2000 and 2010, further reducing the population (IUCN 2015b). While habitat loss owing to commercial and agricultural development has contributed to the decline of the species in recent decades in India, home to the majority of the world's remaining tigers, tiger losses since the early 1990s are attributed mainly to demand for their body parts for traditional medicines and their pelts for status objects. Davies (2005) found that nearly every part of the tiger has a medicinal use, from the whiskers to the claws, with the principal consumer market being in Asia. Tiger claws sold for $150 USD in the late 1990s, and a drug manufacturer in Japan produced a tiger penis pill that sold for $27,000 USD per bottle. Highly desired tiger bones, believed to have anti-inflammatory properties, are marketed as a cure in China (IUCN 2015b). Tiger pelts are also a sought-after luxury item in some Asian nations.

High demand for the skins of tigers, along with those of the Asian leopard (*Panthera pardus*) and snow leopard (*Uncia uncia*), have help foster the creation of wildlife trafficking syndicates. Smugglers using ancient trading routes move contraband pelts to markets in China, Nepal, and India (EIA 2006). Syndicates rely on locals, who often operate in transient gangs with deep knowledge of tiger habitat and behavior in their ranges. One unique difference is that unlike elephant and rhinoceros poachers, tiger poachers generally avoid using firearms to kill the animals in order to protect the valuable pelt. Rather, they are more likely to employ jaw traps or poison. Once caught, the tigers are quickly processed and sold to smugglers, who move the animal parts out of the country. Although the tiger population has declined dramatically in the last 115 years, there is some positive news. Reports indicate that tiger numbers in India, Russia, and Nepal have increased because of successful conservation efforts. In 2010, the thirteen tiger range states committed to an initiative called TX2, the goal of which is to double wild tiger populations by the year 2022 (WWF 2016e).

Other species poached and trafficked for the illegal wildlife trade were large African cats. My field research in South Africa and Namibia revealed that poaching of most African cats in these countries can be attributed to three general reasons. The illegal killing of cheetahs, leopards, and lions was frequently done by farmers protecting their livestock from the actual or perceived threat posed by these predators. Second and less common, though still a problem, was the threat posed by demand for African cats for the pet and hunting business. Cheetah cubs were taken live after their mothers were killed. A small number of these animals were illegally sold and exported for the exotic pet trade, one destination being the Middle East. A small number of adult cheetahs and leopards were captured alive and sold to game farms to be hunted (Warchol, Zupan, and Clack 2003).

Finally, African cats are also poached for their body parts for use in *muti*, or traditional African medicine. This finding was confirmed during a visit I made to the traditional market in Durban, South Africa, with an official from KwaZulu Natal Wildlife Conservation. At the market we observed, on prominent display, leopard paws for sale as talismans against bad luck and numerous pelts and bones from leopards and other African cats for use in holistic remedies and for traditional African clothing for *sangomas* (tradi-

Lioness in Kenya's Masai Mara National Park. Lions have been regularly targeted as conflict animals, when they represent a real or perceived threat to local farmers and their livestock, and for body parts used in traditional medicines.

tional African healers). Even though the legality of these items was in doubt, the wildlife authorities would not consider confiscation. When questioned on the subject, the officials responded that if the illegally harvested wildlife body parts were confiscated from the market, they would only be restocked in a few days or a week, resulting in the deaths of many more protected animals. Given that these items sell rather slowly, leaving these products in the market was considered the lesser of the two evils (Warchol, Zupan, and Clack 2003). Interestingly, the use of African wildlife for traditional medicines has of late expanded into Asia. The difficulty of obtaining tiger parts has led to the development of a new market for African lion bones as a substitute in the traditional Asian medicine trade. This trade, which principally originates in South Africa, includes both a legal and illegal component because of the private ownership of captive lions and the lion's status as a CITES II species (TRAFFIC 2015b). While wild lion bones and other body parts cannot be exported for commercial purposes, South Africa's commercial breeding operations are allowed an export quota for these products. The inability to determine if the products are from wild or captive lions complicates efforts at enforcement. A proposal by nine African countries to up-list lions to Appendix I to end the bone trade failed at the September–October 2016 CITES meeting. With about 30,000 wild lions remaining in Africa, their survival may be in additional jeopardy if the trade expands to other range states (Animal Defenders International 2016).

Birds and Reptiles

Elephant, rhino, and large cats are poached and trafficked in Africa and Asia, but they constitute a minority of the species in the illegal wildlife market. Rather, the illicit wildlife trade includes a thriving global business in reptiles and birds. Given the volume of animals and the numerous source and consumer nations involved, it is impossible to place an accurate estimate on the total number of reptiles and birds that are illegally taken from the wild and traded in consumer markets. Yet a sense of the scale of the trade can be found in seizures by police and counts of protected animals found at retail markets. In southern Africa alone, reptiles are poached for resale by local pet shop owners, exported to U.S. and European buyers of exotic live wildlife (who commonly purchase via the Internet), and even trafficked to Asia for use in exotic cuisine. Reptile collectors and pet shop owners from Germany, the Netherlands, and the Czech Republic have often been apprehended by South African and Namibian police with the illegally obtained protected reptiles in their possession. Research indicates that South Africa is also a major importer of illegally caught snakes and other reptiles from various African nations to supply its domestic pet trade (Warchol, Zupan, and Clack 2003).

The illegal trade in birds is also multinational with high demand for live animals, primarily as pets. There is internal trafficking of native wild birds within countries for their domestic markets and international trafficking of species from source to consumer nations. A study of the domestic bird trade in Indonesia found over 19,000 wild-caught native birds offered for sale in its three largest bird markets. Demand for the species is due to long-held cultural reasons for keeping rare avians and songbirds in Indonesia. It was found that 98 percent of the birds were native species, making their capture and sale illegal (Chng et al. 2015). A recent analysis of the international trade found that Singapore serves as a major conduit for exotic birds, including CITES I and II species sourced from parts of Africa, the South Pacific, Europe, and Asia. Dubious figures reported on shipping data and problems with CITES permits in the country have raised serious questions about the legality of a segment of the bird trade (Poole and Shepherd 2016). Similarly, research in Brazil described a dynamic and widespread illegal trade in domestic birds in all parts of the country. Nearly three hundred different species were found to be illegally traded, including some listed as critically endangered, endangered, or vulnerable on the IUCN Red List (Alves, Lima, and Arujo 2013). A somewhat surprising example of a regional domestic trade was found in the European Union. TRAFFIC (2008) reported on a trade in birds in southeastern and central Europe controlled by organized crime. Native birds were hunted in southeastern Europe and smuggled through Hungary and Croatia to Italy and Malta for resale as a delicacy food.

The trade in birds also constitutes a major segment of the illegal wildlife market in South Africa and Namibia. Like the market for reptiles, the trade in birds is highly specialized and dominated by collectors, breeders, and dealers in rare and exotic species. South Africa is classified as both an exporter and importer of birds. In addition to the export of native birds, large numbers of rare African birds from other nations are illegally imported to South Africa for the pet trade and/or for eventual transshipment overseas. My research determined that the bird trade is far more organized than the illegal market in ivory, rhino horn, or African cats. Networks of bird breeders and collectors rely on verbal agreements, e-mail, and Internet sites to buy, sell, or trade birds. While many birds poached from the wild remain in-country to meet domestic demand, large numbers are exported to Europe, Asia, and the United States by air to fill orders from overseas collectors. The situation in southern Africa had become so serious that the very rare specimens were often found only in private ownership and not in zoos or aviaries, which were targeted by enterprising poachers (Warchol, Zupan, and Clack 2003).

Flora and Marine Life

Excluding large-scale illegal timber and fishing operations, poaching of plants and marine species by individuals and criminal networks is another common part of the global illegal wildlife trade. Plant species are illegally harvested for ornamental and medicinal use and, to a lesser extent, for scientific collections. One example of a valuable plant species targeted by poachers is the cycad. Cycads, a palm tree of prehistoric origins, are popular ornamental trees with homeowners and collectors in South Africa and are also used in the traditional medicine trade. With demand outstripping legal supply, poaching and theft of valuable cycads from protected nature reserves, public parks, landscape nurseries, and private homes has become rampant. Immature trees have even been stolen to fuel domestic demand for exotic plants. Furthermore, cycad root balls and sections have also been found for sale at the Durban, South Africa, traditional market for use as a home remedy (Warchol, Zupan, and Clack 2003). Unusual cases of academics and scientists poaching plant specimens that are rare and difficult to legally obtain for private collections were found in a nature reserve in the Western Cape of South Africa, where well-known foreign scientists were apprehended with protected flora (Herbig and Warchol 2011). The illegal plant trade is not limited to southern Africa. It also occurs with regularity within the United States and Europe. World Wildlife Fund (2003) has described an unsustainable trade in cacti and other desert plants harvested from parts of northern Mexico and the southwestern United States and smuggled to Europe and Japan, where demand is high. Wild ginseng and Venus flytraps are also poached in the United States for use as both medicines and decorations (Vallery 2015).

Another large part of the illegal wildlife trade involves marine species. While some fish poaching is done by individuals fishing without a license or exceeding their limit for common species, another aspect involves larger amounts of protected species being illegally harvested for profit. Aside from the industrial-level, illegal ocean-fishing operations, marine species poaching is done by small criminal networks seeking valuable protected species for either resale or export. World Wildlife Fund (2016d) notes that illegal fishing is a major contributor to overfishing and habitat destruction and also may pose a threat to food security. Marine life poaching in South Africa includes the extensive overfishing of a variety of species, with abalone, a protected rare shellfish found around the Cape, being the most high-profile animal. Abalone is a very popular and expensive delicacy in seafood restaurants in South Africa and Asia. However, the poaching of abalone is widespread, both to meet the increasing demand in South Africa and Asia and as an easy source of income for local fishermen. While obviously detrimental to the desired protected species, illegal fishing activities result in two additional environmental problems. One is the issue of *bycatch*, or the accidental capture of other species, including protected wildlife such as the various sea turtle species or the vaquita porpoise near Mexico. Finally, illegal fishing methods, including the use of poisons or even explosives, destroy not only marine life but also marine habitats (WWF 2016d).

The Great Apes

While smaller species of primates are commonly consumed in the bushmeat trade in Asia and Africa, the great apes of Central Africa, a protected species, are also subject to poaching. There are four subspecies of great apes, all of which are either endangered or critically endangered. These primates are forest dwellers indigenous to several Central African nations, including Rwanda and Democratic Republic of Congo (DRC). The threats to their survival come from demand for bushmeat, with just one large animal providing a considerable amount of protein for human consumption; habitat loss caused by the expansion of logging and mining operations; the pet trade; and demand for wildlife body parts for use as decorative items. Contributing to gorilla poaching has been the impact of war and extreme poverty, leading to the hunting of more wildlife in national parks for food. Congo's Virunga National Park, the oldest national park in Africa and often considered the most spectacular because of its geography and biodiversity, is home to an estimated 200 of the world's remaining 720 mountain gorillas (Jenkins 2008). These animals have been targeted by poachers for both food and body parts. In the latter case, the animal's hands and head are taken and the body is left to rot. If an infant is present, it is often taken alive and sold into the wildlife pet trade as an exotic species. In DRC's Kahuzi-Biega National Park, rampant commercial and subsistence poaching has reduced the gorilla population by 50 percent (Yamagiwa 2008). Given the small size of these populations, the impact of poaching even modest numbers is a significant threat to their survival.

A Model of the Illicit Market
for Wildlife Products

Globalization and Organized Crime

Illegally obtained wildlife is traded in a global, multi-billion-dollar marketplace that encompasses the developed and developing world. An understanding of the origins of this market and how it functions can help us identify future trends and create solutions to the problem of wildlife trafficking. The wildlife trade is driven by a demand for products that cannot be obtained legally, such as tiger parts or rhino horn, or at an affordable price, such as cycads or abalone. The source countries are generally though not exclusively found in the developing world. The consumers or end users are located both in the source nations, supporting a domestic illegal wildlife trade, and in the developed world. As a result, the trade is both local and international, the latter representing a type of transnational crime.

The transnational crime literature (Albanese 2011; Shelly 1996; Williams 1984) provides a basic model of the structure of illegal markets that guides this book's description of the distribution chain of wildlife products and the consumer market. Organized crime is identified by the United Nations Convention against Transnational Organized Crime as a specifically structured group of three or more actors existing for a period of time with the aim of committing one or more serious crimes or offenses for financial or material gain (Gastrow 2003). In Africa, for example, some organized crime groups were structured on ethnicity, while others were formed on family or kin connections (Grobler 2003). Finally, organized crime relies on a market of consumers who desire goods and services but cannot purchase them legally or inexpensively.

Illegal markets are typically centered in urban areas because of the need for modern and reliable infrastructure to facilitate the trade in products. This infrastructure includes extensive transportation networks of air and sea ports and roads. Also required is access to financial institutions to move money and sometimes launder illegally obtained funds. The illegal wildlife trade in southern Africa is a major market within the continent. The commodities illegally traded in these markets include not only wildlife but also vehicles, narcotics, firearms, diamonds, and migrants. Oftentimes wildlife products are trafficked by the same individuals who deal in the above-mentioned commodities over the same smuggling routes and sometimes to the same end user destinations using the same network of contacts (Venter 2003). Wildlife is typically viewed as one of many lucrative goods in high demand. South Africa has long been the center of the continent's illegal wildlife trade simply due to its extensive and modern transportation and banking infrastructure and long-established criminal syndicates.

Globalization, a term commonly used today in discussions of the twenty-first-century economy both negatively and positively, has inadvertently played a critical role in the establishment and facilitation of the illegal trade in wildlife. Globalization developed quickly after the fall of Communism and the subsequent opening of markets in nations transitioning away from a state-controlled economic system to a free market of varying degrees, which included the removal of trade barriers to enhance development. With globalization, national borders that were once fully or partially closed to foreign trade were now open to the movement of goods, services, labor, and money (Albanese 2011; Williams 1997). Globalization also created business opportunities in the developing world. One prime example is the extensive financial investment made by China in Africa over the last two decades. China's need for natural resources to fuel its domestic economy brought Chinese businesses to Africa. With the legitimate businesses has also come a criminal element, in this case improved opportunities for obtaining wildlife products from the source. Africa was especially prone to the problems associated with increased global trade because of dramatic political changes in the twentieth century. In the aftermath of the colonial era came a period of transition to new models of governance. This period coincided with political and military interventions on the continent by both sides in the Cold War as they attempted to influence the direction of liberated nations. During this time, some countries embraced Marxist economic systems that eventually stagnated growth. As such countries moved away from this model in the wake of the end of the Cold War, the next period of transition unfortunately included poor management of natural resources, corruption, and struggles to establish a growing economy. This period was commonly marked by weak policing, ineffective border and customs enforcement, and recurring economic and political problems in countries such as Zimbabwe, Angola, Mozambique, and South Africa. Such a situation facilitated the growth of organized crime, which created a network of smuggling routes and criminal markets in the region (Gastrow 2003).

South Africa, a major source country for wildlife products for both the international and domestic markets, faced a unique challenge. Although it did not experience the colonial period of the twentieth century, the internal struggle to end the apartheid system resulted in opportunities for organized crime. As law enforcement resources were diverted to deal with political instability, syndicates began to exploit the lack of attention to more conventional crimes, including poaching and trafficking in wildlife (Gastrow 2001). Interestingly, police often relied on smugglers for intelligence about political offenders and at times ignored wildlife traffickers or even colluded with them on wildlife violations. The apartheid system also restricted movement of the indigenous black population within the country. With the end of the system in 1994, controls on travel were relaxed. This period also coincided with a surge in immigration from other African countries of migrants in search of employment in this modern industrial nation. Thus, during this very turbulent period in Africa, the necessary elements were all present to foster increased organized crime, corruption, and smuggling of wildlife out of Africa (Gastrow 1999).

A major consequence of this development was the expansion of local organized crime groups into new overseas markets. For example, Chinese syndicates operating in the illegal abalone market could now sell and ship their product with greater ease to mainland China, where demand was high (Warchol and Harrington 2016). For wildlife traffickers, animal products could now be transshipped from source nations to consumer nations by individuals and criminal syndicates of varying size and structure. New markets emerged, with Vietnam's demand for rhinoceros horn being a recent example. Existing markets such as China expanded as that nation's transition to a market economy created prosperity for its expanding middle class. Furthermore, as the volume of global trade rapidly increased, the inspection of land, sea, and air cargo shipments became more difficult, especially in developing nations, where enforcement and regulations were lacking. Criminal syndicates recognized and capitalized on this situation. Traffickers, who banked on the fact that illegal cargo shipments would not be searched, also commonly secreted contraband in shipments of legitimate goods. These practices were supplemented with the corruption of government officials willing to turn a blind eye to contraband, the forging of manifests, or the falsifying of CITES permits (Warchol, Zupan, and Clack 2003; Director of

South African Police Service Endangered Species Protection Unit, personal communication, 2003).

Jay Albanese's (2011) analysis of organized crime noted how the expansion of the Internet and new money transfer systems have contributed to the growth of different types of transnational crime syndicates, including those trading in wildlife. The Internet facilitated communication between buyer and seller as websites emerged that catered to the consumers of exotic and rare species. Additionally, contemporary changes in money transfer systems, including the use of mobile phones to move funds from one party to another, are commonplace in parts of Africa. No longer do individuals need to physically provide the seller with currency. Albanese described these contemporary transnational networks as ranging from hierarchically structured criminal syndicates to small fluid groups using a flat structure. Some may be organized on ethnic lines, such as the Asian groups or the traditional Mafia, or they may be alliances between criminals with similar interests in a product. Furthermore, some criminal groups are temporary, lasting for only a limited period. It is no surprise that organized crime has entered this marketplace. Albanese (2003) noted that "organized crime is tenacious in its ability to change its form, targets, and operations in ways that respond directly to shifts in public demand, prosecution successes, and new criminal opportunities" (438). Modern organized crime often parallels legitimate business in its capacity to exploit new markets. Criminal syndicates can analyze supply and demand for a good or service and assess the viability of an illegal market to supply the product. Furthermore, they can change their methods quickly to take advantage of new opportunities (Irish and Qhobosheane 2003), frustrating law enforcement efforts to prevent their activities. The syndicates are well positioned to participate in the transnational part of the illegal wildlife trade. Wildlife products such as ivory and rhinoceros horn are illegally harvested for eventual international shipment to consumer markets by these modern transnational criminal networks.

Transnational crime syndicates provide illegal goods to an illegal consumer market. Transnational illegal markets are composed of a chain consisting of three essential components: the initial suppliers/sellers, middlemen, and end users/buyers (von Lampe 2015). Initial suppliers in the wildlife trade (poachers) are typically though not exclusively motivated by one of two reasons—sustenance or profit (Messer 2000). For-profit poachers may work alone or as part of a network supplying trafficking operations (Puffer 1982). The criminal networks may be loosely structured and temporary, consisting of a few participants with similar interests and motivations. However, some wildlife poaching operations are larger, more formal, and durable. They may traffic wildlife exclusively or as just one of many illegal commodities.

The trafficker—part of the second link in the supply chain—is a middleman who facilitates the movement of the product from the initial suppliers to the end users. Individuals in this part of the business also may be involved in bribing officials, supplying vehicles and firearms, temporarily storing illegal wildlife products, forging CITES permits, and securing shippers for moving contraband. As in the drug trade model, trafficking operations are composed of numerous actors who participate at various stages in the transportation and distribution process. They are responsible for transporting the product from the initial supplier across national borders and directly to the consumer or a retailer. As described in Chapter 3 in more detail, traffickers use a range of options to move wildlife. Depending on the amount and destination, it may be secreted on their person or in their luggage, sent via express mail, or sent on a container ship.

Finally, there is the consumer market for wildlife (the end users/buyers). The majority of wildlife products are sent in raw form to destination countries, where they may be processed into consumer products (WildAid 2004). For example, from the African source countries, raw poached ivory is smuggled into Asia to factories where it is carved into decorative items and then retailed to consumers. Wildlife products may be sold under the guise of being legitimate via the use of false documentation such as forged CITES permits or as contraband with no effort to disguise illegality. Consumers of these overseas products are motivated by a desire for prohibited, inexpensive, rare, or exotic items that can be used as a status symbol, specimen for a collection, culturally significant item, medicine, or traditional food.

Summary: Why It Matters

African elephants, rhinoceros, and lions, along with other species such as North American grizzlies and Asian tigers, have been referred to as *charismatic megafauna* (Mitchell 2006) that have always attracted the public's interest. They represent the wildness of a continent or country and foster tourism with its valuable economic benefits. These are the high-profile poster animals for wildlife conservation. The extensive development of the United States has dramatically reduced the numbers of the large mammals and confined many to national parks, refuges, and remote mountain ranges. However, in Africa and Asia, with the exception of a few nations, many of their large mammals are still present in traditional habitats and migratory ranges in the sub-Saharan part of Africa and in wilderness areas in parts of Asia. The unchecked poaching of elephants, rhinoceroses, and tigers can be viewed as the destruction of part of the natural heritage of Africa and Asia—their indigenous species and sense of having untamed and almost timeless lands.

Others have argued that, aside from the value of conserving wildlife for its own sake, rhinoceroses and elephants have a dollar value beyond the worth of their horns or ivory—that is, the economic benefits from tourism, including ecological and photographic safaris and regulated professional hunting. In an EIA report, it was estimated that if an elephant in Kenya was allowed to live out its entire natural life, it could generate as much as $1 million USD in tourism revenues, more than two hundred times the then market value of its ivory (Thornton 1997). Furthermore, conservation programs are often funded with tourism revenue, and if these species are neglected, the impact on the financial state of the respective game departments is obvious—less money for conservation and less protection of wildlife, leading to more extensive poaching and finally localized extinctions, as has occurred before. Even professional hunting companies in Africa that take a limited number of elephants each year generate considerable revenue, with some charging as much as $100,000 for a hunting safari.

One issue raised in the literature is the potential for political destabilization of a nation owing to the massive exploitation of its natural resources. Unlike diamond or gold reserves or old-growth timber, wildlife populations can recover from poaching relatively quickly given adequate protection. The exploitation of these animals alone may not completely imperil a nation's economy. However, beyond being a threat to countries' political stability, the extensive illegal hunting and trafficking in these species presents an obstacle to their struggling national and local economies. The loss of wildlife needed to attract tourists has a direct negative impact on local communities that depend on the species to generate revenue. Local communities in already impoverished nations slip further behind their more prosperous neighbors, as in the case of Mozambique and South Africa. The lack of tourist dollars also means less money for game departments charged with protecting the species. This, in turn, encourages more poaching until the species have been regionally decimated.

Finally, the cost of the illegal trade in natural resources must also include the impact of the criminal syndicates exploiting the resources and taking advantage of impoverished communities. Wildlife trafficking syndicates are embedded in the societies in some African nations. This is a critical problem, since these syndicates traffic not only in natural resources but also in other types of contraband. Their influence greatly contributes to the already pervasive problem of corruption in these nations, a problem that also inhibits their economic advancement. This view was summed up in the 1961 Arusha speech by Tanzania's first president, Julius Nyerere, when he stated: "The survival of our wildlife is a matter of grave concern to all of us in Africa. These wild creatures amid wild places they inhabit are not only important as a source of wonder and inspiration, but they are an integral part of our natural resources and of our future livelihood and well-being" (Nyerere 1961).

2

Wildlife Conservation Laws and Agreements

Protecting Wildlife

The need to regulate the trade in wildlife and protect this valuable national asset has long been recognized in many nations. One important objective of conservation laws and regulations is to set harvest limits to prevent the unsustainable loss of wildlife or to limit the trade in threatened or endangered species (Moyle 2005). Other provisions address habitat protection, species recovery efforts, import and export, and the sale of wildlife. This concern over the wildlife trade has resulted in a variety of national laws and international treaties and the emergence of various nongovernmental organizations (NGOs) that support wildlife protection, research the illegal trade, and lobby for new legislation. Conservation legislation may exist at just the national level or also involve state/provincial and municipal governments. Certain types of national legislation can limit the jurisdiction of the enforcement agencies to only domestic species, while others may include exotic or non-native wildlife. Furthermore, a nation may be a party to international agreements requiring that the provisions are incorporated into the signatory's national legislation and implemented by its conservation enforcement agencies. Overall, there exists a complex web of legislation across the globe to address different aspects of wildlife conservation, not to mention other environmental issues, such as pollution and land use. Rather than attempt to summarize wildlife law from many different nations dealing with the illegal trade, which would be a monumental task, this chapter provides an overview of selected major national legislation, including that directed at native and non-native species, major international treaties and agreements that specifically focus on the global trade in endangered and threatened species, and the involvement of some NGOs in the legislative process.

To examine the development and structure of national conservation legislation concerned with the legal and illegal trade in wildlife, this chapter discusses the origins and history of the laws of the use of wildlife, beginning with a brief summary of the origins of game laws followed by a review of the purpose and nature of selected major multinational agreements designed to regulate the trade in wildlife. These are the Convention on International Trade in Endangered Species of 1975 (CITES), the Convention on Biological Diversity of 1992 (CBD), and the Lusaka Agreement on Co-operative Enforcement Operations Directed at the Illegal Trade in Wild Fauna and Flora of 1996. Then the chapter examines significant national legislation focused on the trade in endangered and threatened species in consumer and source nations. This includes conservation legislation from three African nations that are key range states for threatened and protected wildlife and U.S. laws designed to conserve both native and foreign wildlife, to reduce the illegal trade, and to support the conservation of wildlife in Asia and Africa. The chapter concludes with an examination of several nongovernmental organizations that are dedicated to preventing the illegal trade in wildlife and are involved in supporting legislative efforts.

Criminalizing Poaching

Efforts to limit or end hunting rights among the citizenry by those in power has a very long history that is based on the realization of the economic and political value of wildlife. The illegal hunting or poaching of wild animals was first criminalized during the Middle Ages in England, when wild game became the property of wealthy landowners and the Crown. Among the early game legislation was the 1217 Charter of the Forest and the Game Law of 1485, which were created to deal with poachers. These laws restricted the taking of game to primarily landlords and nobility (Manning 1993). However, the establishment of these poaching laws resulted in conflict between the traditions and economic needs of the working classes, on one hand, and the interests of the wealthy and the state, on the other. As a result, people sometimes openly disregarded the new game laws and even treated poachers as local heroes to the point of protecting them from the authorities (Jones 1979). As discussed in more detail in Chapter 4, this was the case in East Africa and southern Africa, where the game reserves and laws were created during the nineteenth-century colonial period. In some instances, indigenous people were relocated from tribal lands, resulting in the loss of not only their land but also access to game. While this practice helped preserve numerous species, ranging from plains game to major predators, it also had several unintended consequences that exist to this day.

International Agreements

*United Nations Convention on International
Trade in Endangered Species*

The global wildlife trade of plant and animal species and their products is regulated in part under the 1975 Convention on International Trade in Endangered Species, which has 182 member nations, including the United States. This United Nations convention was developed in response to increasing threats to the survival of certain species, owing to growth in the international trade (CITES 2016a). Given that the wildlife trade is transnational, the instrument was developed to facilitate cooperation between exporting and importing nations. According to the convention, the member countries identify what species are at risk and then establish sustainable harvest quotas if any (Albanese 2011). CITES uses a three-tiered listing system of appendices. Appendix I lists the species that are banned from being traded for commercial purposes on the international market, such as tiger, gorilla, and Tibetan antelope. The international trade in species listed in Appendix I is completely banned, including trade in their parts. Some exceptions, however, are made for scientific research. Appendix II includes species that can be traded commercially, such as the gray wolf or hippo, but with regulation to ensure sustainability of use. This appendix lists species that might be threatened if their trade became unlimited. Appendix III lists species regulated only within a specific nation but still included because that nation needs assistance to prevent exploitation (WWF 2015a).

CITES operates in part by relying on an export permit system for Appendix I and II wildlife species, with the former being banned from commercial trade. The species listed on the first two appendices are the result of a vote of the member nations after review of proposals requesting addition to or deletion from the list. Species have been up-listed and down-listed over time to provide additional protection or allow their commercial sale. On Appendix III, a nation can add a species without the need for an affirmative vote from the other member nations (Orenstein 2013). The administration of CITES by its parties requires that each one create a management authority and a scientific authority. The management authority is charged with handling the CITES policy requirements and issuing the permits, while the scientific authority provides scientific advice to the former (Burgener, Snyman, and Hauck 2001).

CITES did not create an enforcement agency within the United Nations to police the wildlife trade. Rather, it requires that the member nations agree to regulate the trade with their own law enforcement agencies with regard to the listed species on the three appendices (Nurse 2015). Interestingly, non-governmental organizations also play a key role in monitoring the trade in wildlife. Some of these entities, in turn, promote legislation and assist law enforcement. Furthermore, the existence of the CITES agreement does not affect the nature of the supply or demand for the commodity. Rather, it affects the regulation and competition only in the product's market (Albanese 2011). Furthermore, the effectiveness of the CITES regulations is reliant on the individual nations' willingness and ability to properly enforce them.

United Nations Convention on Biological Diversity of 1992

The United Nations Convention on Biological Diversity (CBD) was a product of the Rio Earth Summit of 1992 and took effect in December of the following year. The impetus for the convention was a formal recognition of the importance of the earth's biodiversity and the corresponding threat to the survival of some species potentially facing extinction in part because of human activity. In Article I, the convention establishes three main objectives: (1) the conservation of biological diversity, (2) the sustainable use of its components, and (3) the fair and equitable sharing of the benefits arising out of the use of genetic resources (United Nations 2016). The convention calls for the parties to prepare a formal strategy for protecting their biodiversity and to integrate that strategy into the agencies that are involved in the conservation of these resources (Nurse 2015). Unlike CITES, the CBD does not focus specifically on poaching or trafficking in wildlife. Rather, concern over these problems is addressed in the individual articles and reports from member nations. For example, Article 6 calls for the parties to the convention to establish a system of protected areas to safeguard biodiversity and to develop legislation for the protection of the species. Article 10 addresses the sustainable use of biological resources, including consideration for cultural practices. The specific problem of poaching and the response to it may also be addressed in reports from individual countries to the CBD, as found in South Korea's 2014 document (Republic of Korea 2014).

Lusaka Agreement: A Regional Effort

In the early 1990s, the wildlife authorities of eight African nations conceived the idea of establishing a multinational law enforcement agency dedicated to preventing wildlife crimes. Their efforts resulted in the creation in 1994 of the Lusaka Agreement on Cooperative Enforcement Operations Directed at the Illegal Trade in Wild Fauna and Flora, which went into force two years later. The impetus for this agreement developed out of a realization of the need for better cooperation between national law enforcement agencies in East Africa and southern Africa that were charged with investigating the illegal trade in wildlife. The signatory nations to the agreement are Ethiopia, Kenya, Republic of Congo, Swaziland, South Africa, Tanzania, Uganda, and Zambia. Taking effect in 1996, the agreement was designed to promote cooperation between the signatory nations in investigations of the illegal trade in wildlife through the creation of a permanent task force—that is, the Lusaka Agreement Task Force (Lusaka Agreement Task Force 2016).

The Lusaka Agreement Task Force is a permanent, intergovernmental organization headquartered in Nairobi, Kenya. Its goal is to first reduce and then eventually eliminate the illegal trade in wildlife, both flora and fauna. This involves cooperation with law enforcement investigations, the sharing of information on the illegal trade, and capacity building by the member nations. The task force, which is staffed by law enforcement agents from the member countries, is dependent on the national bureaus created by these signatory nations as part of the agreement. These bureaus are required to cooperate in data collection on the illegal trade, investigations and enforcement efforts, and prosecution of offenders (Wildlife Direct 2010). The operations of the Task Force are administered by a governing council staffed by members of each state that is party to the agreement (Lusaka Agreement Task Force 2016). The Lusaka Task Force also works with international agencies, including INTERPOL, the U.S. Fish and Wildlife Service, and the India Wildlife Crime Control Bureau, on joint investigations on wildlife crimes. Since its inception, the task force has had several notable successes, including the multinational Operation Cobra III, which resulted in three hundred arrests and the seizure of over six hundred illegal wildlife shipments in May 2015 (WWF 2015c).

Selected African Legislation:
South Africa, Kenya, and Tanzania

The African nations with large wildlife populations take different approaches to their conservation and management depending on the wildlife's use as an economic asset and the nature of the threat from the illegal wildlife trade. Legislation may be quite restrictive, banning nearly all forms of hunting, or allow the precisely regulated use of the resource. Violations of the laws can result in a range of sanctions, including fines, forfeiture, and even life imprisonment. The wildlife conservation and management laws of South Africa, home to a highly profitable private hunting and wildlife tourism industry, are found at both the provincial and national levels. The national government's role is established in the National Environmental Management Biodiversity Act (NEMBA). This legislation requires that the minister of environmental affairs prepare lists of species that are in need of protection or are currently threatened. The law also criminalizes certain activities that involve a threatened or protected species. These so-called *restricted activities* include hunting, importing and exporting, possessing, growing and breeding, transporting and trading, and transferring the listed wildlife. The legislation further defines the allowable tools and techniques for legal hunting, such as firearm caliber for certain game species, hunting locations, and methods of pursuing and capturing game. It includes prohibitions on the use of automatic firearms, poisons, dogs, and snares along with the practice of spotlighting or using vehicles or aircraft for hunting. Elephant hunters, for example, are required to use a rifle with a minimum caliber of .375 and refrain from driving animals and using pitfalls for their capture.

The act is enforced by the Environmental Management Inspectorate, which maintains liaisons with officials from the national, provincial, and municipal governments. The Inspectorate has investigatory and enforcement powers, including inspection, arrest, and search and seizure. Interestingly, the enforcement provisions of the law allow warrantless searches of conveyances and containers and give agents arrest powers. However, unlike in some other nations, the enforcement agents within the Inspectorate do not have prosecutorial powers. The laws further establish the penalties for violations, which include fines and incarceration. Some fines can be up to three times the value of the animal for the killing of a protected species (Library of Congress 2015b).

In response to increasing problems with poaching and declines in some species, Kenya enacted the Wildlife Conservation and Management Act of 2013, its most current national legislation. It was an effort to create a comprehensive law to enhance the "protection, conservation and sustainable use and management of the country's wildlife resources" (WWF 2014a, 1). The act criminalizes the poaching, trafficking, and selling of protected wildlife. Furthermore, while all types of sport or recreational hunting along with bushmeat and subsistence hunting are prohibited in Kenya, the act allows some consumptive use of wildlife with a license. These activities include game farming and ranching, cropping, and culling. The act also provides for public input into wildlife management and the regulated use of wildlife by Kenyans. It addresses the problem of conflict animals by enhancing the compensation for those injured or killed by wildlife. This recent law also called for the creation of the Wildlife Crimes Prosecution Unit, consisting of thirty-five prosecutors with special training in wildlife law (Goitom 2014).

Hunting of protected species and hunting game animals without a license or in violation of the license's provisions is a criminal offense, and the recent legislation increased the severity of the sanctions. Appropriate locations for legal hunting are stated along with the allowable tools and techniques that can be employed to take game. The penalties for violations include a range of actions, such as the levying of fines; terms of incarceration, including life sentences for crimes involving endangered species; and forfeiture of both the instruments of and the proceeds from the violations of wildlife law. That is, vehicles used to transport illegally taken wildlife and revenue from their sale are subject to seizure and forfeiture by the state. The prime responsibility for enforcement resides with the Kenya Wildlife Service (KWS), though other government agencies have some level of involvement depending on the nature of the offense, such as a customs law violation. The KWS is a state agency charged with conserving and managing the nation's wildlife. In addition to enforcement, which includes intelligence and investigation activities, KWS staff above the rank of ranger hold the power to prosecute offenders under the supervision of the nation's attorney general (Library of Congress 2015a).

Tanzania's first wildlife laws date back to the colonial era of the late nineteenth century, when the nation was under German control; legislation defined the amount of wildlife that could be taken, hunting methods, and the trade in wildlife (Ministry of Natural Resources and Tourism 2016). Tanzania currently declares that its wildlife is public property whose protection is vested in the nation's president on behalf of the citizens. The nation's approach to wildlife conservation and management entails several laws: the Wildlife Conservation Act, the National Parks Act, and the Forest Resources Management and Conservation Act. The Wildlife Conservation Act (WCA) is the principal law that covers poaching and trafficking, and it also allows sustainable use of the resource. The WCA lists the different species by schedule, defines the allowable methods and locations for hunting, and addresses hunting trophies. The National Parks Act (NPA) addresses the issue of hunting within the national parks, stating the penalties for violations of the law. The Forest Resources Management and Conservation Act (FRMCA) is limited to forests on the island of Zanzibar; it concerns poaching and legal hunting within the forests along with the penalties for violations. The enforcement of provisions of these three legislative acts is split among three different entities. The WCA established the Wildlife Authority, which includes the specialized Wildlife Protection Unit. The NPA relies on the Trustees of the Tanzanian National Parks, and the FRMCA uses the Forest Authority for law enforcement. All three of these entities have powers of inspection, seizure, and arrest, and the NPA and FRMCA provide their investigators with prosecutorial power (Goitom 2013).

U.S. Legislation: International and Domestic

The U.S. government's efforts at international conservation are fairly extensive, dating back several decades. Not only is the United States a party to the CITES agreement, but it also enacted additional federal legislation in 1988 banning the importation of all ivory with the objective of ending the domestic market for this product. In the early 1990s, in an effort to further protect elephants from the ivory trade, the U.S. government, working through USAID, financed the development of Elephant Conservation Action Plans for thirty-four countries (Olindo 1997). The U.S. State Department has also facilitated conservation efforts, as illustrated by its support of an elephant reintroduction effort in Malawi in 2006. Finally, as described in more detail in Chapter 5, the Obama administration announced a new national strategy to combat wildlife trafficking in 2014 which includes a strong focus on preventing the illegal ivory trade.

Within the U.S. government's agencies, the Fish and Wildlife Service is often thought of as the principal federal organization responsible for managing and protecting domestic wildlife. The agency is charged with implementing U.S. government legislation designed to protect natural resources, including endangered species (USFWS n.d.). However, as a result of congressional legislation, the agency is also directly involved in international conservation efforts, including participation in numerous projects in East Africa and southern Africa. Examples of this are the African Elephant Conservation Act of 1988 and the Rhinoceros and Tiger Conservation Acts of 1994 and 1998. It is important to note that the USFWS does not involve itself in law enforcement in foreign nations. Rather, it provides financial assistance and expertise for selected overseas programs.

The African Elephant Conservation Act of 1988

U.S. law began to address the elephant and rhinoceros poaching crises that emerged in Africa with new conservation legislation. The African Elephant Conservation Act of 1988 was created to assist in the conservation of the species, which was suffering dramatic population declines under heavy poaching pressure. To accomplish this objective, the act included two main features, one financial and the other focused on the ivory trade. The first component developed an assistance program, the African Elephant Conservation Fund, for nations with wild elephant populations under threat from the illegal ivory trade. The fund was administered by the U.S. secretary of the interior and was intended to be a source of monies for conservation, research, and protection projects. The second part of the law focused on the ivory trade, establishing a moratorium on the importation of raw and finished/carved ivory products to the United States from an ivory-producing country. Exceptions were included for legally obtained hunting trophies, antique ivory products, and what became known as *pre-ban ivory* products. As a deterrent, the act listed both criminal and civil penalties for violations—incarceration of up to a year or a fine of not more than $5,000 USD. The act also placed limitations on the export of ivory from the United States. The law has been reauthorized to the year 2020. Currently, the U.S. Fish and Wildlife Service is working to enact a near-complete ban on the ivory trade that would prohibit the import of ivory for commercial purposes. However, there will be exceptions; pre-ban ivory would not be subject to the restrictions provided it meets CITES permit requirements.

The Rhinoceros and Tiger Conservation Acts of 1994 and 1998

The Rhinoceros and Tiger Conservation Acts were passed by the U.S. Congress in response to the rapid decline in both species and their listing on Appendix I of the CITES agreement (USFWS 2001). Before the acts, rhinoceros populations had dropped dramatically, to the point where rhino were extinct in fifteen African range states and were in steep declines in Asia. The remaining populations had been hunted and poached to dangerously low numbers, eventually leading to a major conservation effort to check the decline and restore the surviving species. This effort was mainly centered in South Africa and became a remarkable success: populations of the black rhino returned to about 5,000 animals, and the southern white rhino reached an estimated 20,000 animals, though current poaching trends are threatening to reverse this progress. Tiger populations, indigenous to regions of Asia and Russia, faced a similar threat, their numbers declining to about 3,400 animals, owing to excessive hunting and habitat loss. Tigers have long been hunted for their body parts for use in traditional medicines and for their pelts as decorative and cultural objects. They were also being lost because of conflicts with humans and commercial and residential development.

The Rhinoceros and Tiger Conservation Acts employed a two-prong approach to the conservation of both species. Included was the establishment of a fund managed by U.S. Fish and Wildlife to assist with the conservation of these species. According to the 2001–2003 summary report, the purpose of the fund is to "support rhinoceros and tiger conservation projects that strengthen law enforcement[,] . . . develop local support for conservation through environmental education, [and] strengthen habitat and nature reserve management" (USFWS 2004, 9). The fund was implemented in the site countries via grants that were, in turn, managed or supervised by the USFWS. In the 2001–2003 report, the USFWS reported on numerous rhino conservation projects in South Africa and Tanzania. These efforts included a wide range of projects that supported anti-poaching units, wildlife monitoring programs, increases in the amount of land in a rhinoceros reserve, expansion or improvements in water supplies on reserves, and rhinoceros reintroduction to selected areas. When these grants are provided, the USFWS project managers are responsible for oversight of the projects. The legislation also focused on the trade in rhino and tiger parts typically used in traditional Asian medicines. Specifically, it banned the trade (sales, import, or export) or any attempt thereof in rhino or tiger parts intended for use or consumption by humans. Part of the enforcement mechanism was the establishment of both criminal and civil penalties for violations of the act.

The Lacey Act of 1900

The oldest legislation in the United States designed to regulate the trade in wildlife, including foreign species, is the Lacey Act of 1900, which is still in effect today. The impetus for this legislation was a realization of the necessity to protect and preserve wild birds and game animals and to prevent poaching and trafficking in wildlife. At the time of its passage, illegal commercial hunting had become a threat to the survival of some species. At its core, the original act made it a crime to illegally harvest game in one state and transport it or intend to transport it to another for sale (EIA 2016b). The Lacey Act includes provisions to criminalize the acquisition, commerce, and transportation of prohibited wildlife. Essentially the Lacey Act made it criminal "to export, import, transport, sell, receive, acquire or purchase in interstate or foreign commerce in violation of US law, state law or tribal law or any foreign law that protects plants." The act covers "all fish and wildlife and their parts or products protected by the Convention on the International Trade in Endangered Species and those protected by State law" (USFWS n.d.). The act also provides for the Interior Department to assist in wildlife protection in parts of the United States where species have become rare or extinct.

The Lacey Act includes both civil and criminal penalties, including asset forfeiture for the illegal trade in wildlife, both flora and fauna. The act has been expanded with amendments over the decades to address additional issues, such as the importation of wildlife that is protected by U.S. or international law and the problem of invasive species that affect waterways and forests (USFWS n.d.). In 2008, the act was amended not only to include additional wildlife crimes but also to address the massive international illegal logging trade, which involves the United States as a consumer nation. This change to the act came about because of the lack of legislation prohibiting the importation and sale of illegally harvested wood in the United States (EIA 2016b). One high-profile case related to this amendment involved USFWS seizures of imported wood in 2009 and 2011 from Gibson Guitar Corporation. The company was accused by the federal government of illegally importing wood from endangered species in Madagascar and India for use in its guitars, a violation of the Lacey Act. However, rather than a prosecution, a criminal enforcement agreement was reached between Gibson and the U.S. government in which the charges were dropped and the company paid a fine. Both Gibson and the federal government acknowledged mistakes involving the purchase of the wood and the enforcement effort (Revkin 2012).

The Endangered Species Act

In 1973, perhaps the best-known domestic conservation legislation was passed by Congress and signed by President Richard Nixon—the Endangered Species Act (ESA). The impetus for this legislation was an awareness of the extinction of some domestic wildlife owing to a combination of development and lack of interest in their conservation. Furthermore, the decline in populations of other species was noted along with a realization of the significant value of these resources to the country. Finally, with the United States being a party to numerous international conservation treaties, it was time to take additional action to protect and preserve domestic wildlife (Endangered Species Act [hereafter ESA] 1973).

The Endangered Species Act is designed to foster the conservation of wildlife that is either threatened or endangered. Furthermore, it contains provisions for the conservation of the ecosystems of these listed species. Specifically, it is intended to "protect and recover imperiled species and the ecosystems upon which they depend" (USFWS 2015). The listing of species under the ESA as either endangered or threatened is a somewhat complex process. An endangered species is defined as "a species . . . in danger of extinction throughout all or a significant portion of its range. Threatened means a species is likely to become endangered within the foreseeable future" (ESA 1973). Once a species is listed, the result of a complex scientific analysis, enforcement of the ESA is based on the concept of a *taking* of a listed animal. This is defined as illegally taking a listed species without a permit from the USFWS. The definition of taking is rather broadly defined to include a range of actions and intents of the actors. Taking includes "to harass, harm, pursue, hunt, shoot, wound, kill, trap, capture or collect or attempt to engage in any such conduct" (USFWS 2015, 1). With regard to plant species, the concept of a taking is more limited to those found on federal land. However, the individual states can also enact legislation regarding the protection of these species. Like the other conservation acts previously described, the ESA provides for exceptions to the taking of listed species for scientific or conservation reasons with a federal permit. The ESA also provides for critical habitat protection, both by working with private landowners to conserve endangered species on their property and by protecting federal lands.

The ESA currently lists about 2,200 species that are classified as endangered or threatened. This number includes almost 650 foreign species that are found outside the United States, indicating the reach of the law. The administration of the ESA is the task of the U.S. Fish and Wildlife Service and the National Marine Fisheries Service, which is part of the U.S. Commerce Department. The purpose of the ESA is not to permanently list species as endangered and therefore off-limits. Rather, it is to promote the recovery of species so they can be de-listed from the ESA. This effort involves the development of recovery plans by the USFWS with the cooperation and assistance of other governmental and interested groups (USFWS 2015). Finally, the ESA is also tied to international conservation efforts by implementing U.S. participation in the CITES agreement.

Nongovernmental Conservation Organizations

In addition to countries, nongovernmental organizations are actively involved in conservation efforts. These entities may be engaged in monitoring the illegal trade, providing scientific expertise and training to government agencies, creating wildlife product demand reduction campaigns, investigating offenses, monitoring biodiversity, establishing conservation programs, or identifying weaknesses in legislation and policy and advocating for improvements (Nurse 2015). As a result, it is worthwhile to examine the role of selected organizations dedicated to conservation: the International Union for Conservation of Nature, the Wildlife Conservation Society, and the Environmental Investigation Agency.

The Role of the IUCN in Promoting Conservation Law

The International Union for Conservation of Nature (IUCN) was established in 1948 at an international conference in Fontainebleau, France, as an environmental network of civil society and government organizations; its first director was Julian Huxley. Its mission is to serve as a global, environmental parent organization broadly focused on conservation and sustainable development. The IUCN comprises over twelve hundred member organizations and more than eleven thousand scientists, allowing it to focus on its three main areas of science, action, and influence. While the IUCN's primary concern is conservation of the world's biodiversity, one approach to accomplish this goal is to advocate for and assist with the development of international conservation laws. This is done through the organization's environmental law program, which "assists decision makers with information, legal analysis, advisory services, legislative drafting, mentoring and capacity building at national, regional and global levels. The Program also provides the opportunity and the forum for governments, non-government organizations and others to network and to share information and discuss ideas" (International Union for Conservation of Nature [hereafter IUCN] 2015a, 1).

An example of the IUCN's work in the area of law is found in Vietnam, where the organization has a long history of helping the government promote conservation and protect its natural resources. Part of the IUCN's effort since the early 1990s has resulted in the passage of new laws and policies directed at protecting Vietnam's forests and biodiversity and fostering sustainable development. Furthermore, the IUCN reports that additional assistance is needed in Vietnam to help with the implementation of its environmental laws, an area identified as a weakness (IUCN 2013).

The Wildlife Conservation Society

The Wildlife Conservation Society (WCS), established in New York in 1895 as the New York Zoological Society, is well known for its work in developing numerous wildlife conservation programs in Africa. The WCS Africa program is described as "the largest and most effective field conservation program on the continent, active in 20 countries from Gabon to Kenya and Sudan to South Africa" (Wildlife Conservation Society [hereafter WCS] 2005, 4). The role of the WCS is to help governments and local communities with wildlife conservation issues. The organization provides training, scientific data, anti-poaching assistance, biodiversity monitoring, and conservation management techniques, including community-based models. The conservation activities of the WCS also involve attempting to influence conservation policy and "helping governments implement sound conservation laws and practices" (WCS 2005, 22). This is accomplished by providing expertise in conservation science and policy to local governments to influence laws, international agreements, and trade agreements (WCS 2016a).

The WCS supports the Monitoring the Illegal Killing of Elephants (MIKE) program, which collects data on poaching in Africa (WCS 2005). The MIKE program was developed as a requirement for the one-time CITES-approved sale of ivory by Namibia, South Africa, and Botswana in 2004. MIKE provides information on elephant movements and identifies areas that are subject to poaching. Using the data from the program, WCS works with local governments to take action if needed to protect the species. Beyond this, WCS's international conservation projects include training of local Africans in capacity building for conservation. An example of this is at Zambia's African

College for Community-Based Natural Resource Management in the Luangwa Valley. The objective of this program is to train local community leaders
to properly maintain the natural resources in the game management areas
that are adjacent to the Zambian national parks (WCS 2005). WCS also developed and implemented a program in Zambia called Community Markets
for Conservation (COMACO). This innovative program provides local participating farmers with both seeds for crops and food from the World Food
Program in order to reduce poaching. In addition, farmers are educated in
sustainable agricultural practices and provided with access to a market for
their crops. A requirement of the program is that farmers pledge to stop hunting on the reserves and turn in their firearms. This strategy helps reduce the
poaching pressure on game reserves (COMACO staffer in Lusaka, Zambia,
personal communication, 2005). In the same region of Zambia, the WCS supported a program called Administrative Management Design (AMADE). The
program was based on the idea that local communities could provide the best
protection for wildlife living on protected areas. WCS claims that AMADE
was a major success for participating local communities, which now had an
economic interest in protecting the populations and were benefiting financially (WCS 2005). More recently, in May 2016, the WCS was one of several
conservation agencies that supported new state legislation in Hawaii (Senate
Bill 2647), eventually signed into law, banning the sale of ivory, rhinoceros
horn, and other animal products. The WCS also contributed to successful
federal legislation that made the bison the national mammal of the United
States, a prominent designation for an animal that was hunted nearly to extinction in the nineteenth century.

The Environmental Investigation Agency

The Environmental Investigation Agency (EIA) is one of the better-known
and more innovative international conservation organizations in the world.
The EIA, founded in 1984 in the United Kingdom by Allen Thornton, Jen-
nifer Lonsdale, and Dave Currey, is a nongovernmental conservation agency
initially dedicated to protecting the African elephant and whale populations.
It has subsequently expanded its interests into a wide range of activities and
species. As discussed in more detail in subsequent chapters, the EIA is actively involved in undercover investigations, including identifying wildlife
trafficking operations. The intelligence gathered from these investigations is
provided to national policy makers to help shape new and more effective
conservation efforts. One current area of interest is the illegal trade in timber. The EIA is working with consumer nations to improve their domestic
policies regarding the importation of these products. The organization's

work contributed to the 2008 amendment to the Lacey Act of 1900 that prohibited the use of illegally harvested wood products in the United States (EIA 2016b).

Summary: Treaties, Laws, and NGOs

The purpose of this chapter has been to examine a selection of major international conventions and national laws designed to conserve biodiversity and address the illegal wildlife trade. Given the myriad of national laws and multinational agreements, the focus was directed at a limited but influential group representing different approaches to the problem of the wildlife trade. In the United States, concern over the exploitation of wildlife by illegal and commercial hunting resulted in the passage of the Lacey Act of 1900, the first federal wildlife law. This law is still in effect today, having been amended to expand its reach, resulting in the high-profile case involving Gibson Guitar Corporation. The Lacey Act was followed by additional legislation during the twentieth century, including the well-known Endangered Species Act of 1973 and, interestingly, three rather lesser known laws concerning non-native species in Africa and Asia under serious threat from poaching. The U.S. Fish and Wildlife Service plays an integral role in the enforcement of this legislation as a dedicated federal conservation law enforcement agency, among other things providing assistance to foreign law enforcement organizations. This national legislation serves as the foundation for wildlife conservation in the United States.

Global concern over the threat posed to wildlife resulted in the creation of major international conventions and regional agreements. With these efforts, sometimes just a few or in other cases nearly two hundred countries agreed to take action to protect their natural resources from exploitation and loss. The best known of these is the Convention on International Trade in Endangered Species, which concerns the legal and illegal trade in wildlife. The 182 parties to the CITES agreement have agreed to be bound by its provisions and to use their domestic agencies to adhere to its provisions. Similarly, the United Nations Convention on Biological Diversity includes 168 signatories that agree to act to protect the earth's biological resources. While these conventions illustrate an international concern for wildlife and ecosystems, their effectiveness is based on a nation's capacity and willingness to adhere to the provisions. At the regional level, concern over the illegal trade led a small group of African nations from different regions of the continent to establish the Lusaka Agreement. This agreement created a specialized enforcement task force that would share information, build capacity, and cooperate on investigations of the illegal trade, supplementing the nations' domestic wildlife conservation legislation.

An interesting aspect of controlling the illegal trade in wildlife is the role of nongovernmental organizations and their influence on laws. NGOs are involved in a wide array of conservation projects, from consumer demand reduction efforts, ranger training, investigations, and community conservation projects to providing data for policy makers and advocating for legislation. The International Union for Conservation of Nature represents a collection of over twelve hundred member groups with a shared focus on conservation. The Wildlife Conservation Society and the Environmental Investigation Agency are single entities that are concerned about conservation but employ differing approaches. While the WCS is heavily involved with developing conservation programs, the EIA uses investigative techniques to uncover various problems in the illegal trade in wildlife. All three organizations are actively involved in providing assistance for government policy formulation and have also influenced the passage of amendments to national conservation legislation.

3

The Offenders

The Actors in the Illegal Wildlife Trade

Some of the most interesting aspects of the illegal trade in wildlife are the individuals and organizations involved in the poaching and trafficking of animal and plant species. The offenders range from subsistence hunters who illegally hunt wildlife for food, medicines, or building materials to individuals who poach for specimens or trophies and finally to organized groups that take larger quantities of wildlife for profit. Unique among the last type is the involvement of military forces, both government and insurgency units, in exploiting wildlife populations in conflict zones for profit. Compounding this threat is recent evidence that some terrorist groups operating in Central Africa and East Africa have become involved in poaching to fund their operations.

There are shared characteristics and distinct differences among poachers. Nearly all poachers operate in an illegal marketplace and rely on some degree of stealth to trespass into protected areas and hunt their prey. However, depending on the species they seek, there is considerable variation in their techniques and organization and in willingness to use violence when confronted by the authorities. To better understand this key actor, this section first describes how poachers operate. The focus is on poachers of both high-profile (elephant, rhinoceros, and tiger) and common species to illustrate their methods and organization.

For many poachers who obtain wildlife for resale into the illegal marketplace, a second necessary actor emerges—the wildlife trafficker. The trafficker is a middleman in the illegal trade who is involved in the essential process of moving an illegally obtained product from the poacher, both within a country and across national borders, to the consumer markets. The movement of wildlife may involve a chain of several traffickers rather than just one person. The trafficker may move wildlife from the poacher in a rural area to a city for resale to consumers or to another smuggler who, in turn, takes it to a seaport or airport for overseas shipment. Once the wildlife is overseas, other traffickers may be involved in moving it from ports of entry to retailers or directly to consumers. The second part of the chapter examines the characteristics and operations of wildlife traffickers, including the smuggling techniques and routes employed to move their products from producers to consumers. Because of the massive scope of the global wildlife trade, the focus is mainly the trafficking of certain wildlife species out of several African and Asian countries to consumers in other regions. Finally, this chapter describes a major factor that facilitates wildlife poaching and trafficking: official corruption. The problem of official corruption has longed plagued many African nations rich in natural resources, including wildlife. The concept of official corruption refers to government officials who actively or passively participate in the illegal hunting and movement of wildlife. These include field rangers in protected areas, local police, customs authorities, diplomats, and higher-level government officials.

The Poacher: From Subsistence Hunter to Criminal Syndicate

The literature on transnational crime provides a model of the structure of illegal markets that can help describe the actors involved in the wildlife trade. Illegal markets utilize a supply chain consisting of three basic components: the initial suppliers, middlemen, and end users/consumers (von Lampe 2015). As applied to the illegal wildlife trade, these components are poachers, traffickers, and consumers. Poachers are typically motivated by one of two reasons—personal use or profit (Messer 2000; Schneider 2012). Personal use includes the consumption of wildlife for various uses: food; medicine; a household product, such as wood for making charcoal or animal skins for making clothing; a decorative item or a rare species for part of a collection; and the elimination of conflict animals, such as large herbivores that threaten crops or predators that attack livestock. Poachers within this category generally are not profit motivated. The other type of poacher is market-driven—that is, the poachers illegally obtain wildlife products for resale to generate revenue. This may include individuals, small informal networks, well-organized criminal syndicates, and military units. One defining difference between these two types is the amount of wildlife that is poached and trafficked. To better explain this model, the following section examines each of these types in more detail, using examples of the various kinds of poachers by the species they target and describing their motivations and poaching techniques.

Poaching for Food: Bushmeat and Marine Species

Bushmeat poaching is an extremely common type of illegal hunting in much of Africa because of widespread traditional practices of consuming wildlife as a source of protein. Though the term *bushmeat* is not commonly used in North America, this type of poaching includes Americans who illegally hunt game, or fish out of season to obtain protein—poachers of deer, elk, black bear, salmon, or abalone. The development of game reserves and conservation laws around the world had the effect of restricting access to some areas where wildlife were once commonly hunted. When the protected areas were created and some species declared off-limits either completely or for set time periods, the hunting did not necessarily end. A variety of motivating factors contribute to individuals continuing to illegally hunt in protected areas.

Poachers seldom have a problem in rationalizing their illegal behavior. In Africa, local residents living near protected areas may consider the wildlife a resource they have a traditional right to harvest. Others may view the protected areas as having little value for those living nearby. These areas could instead be used for agriculture or homes to accommodate growing populations. Furthermore, predators and large grazers on some reserves represent a threat to the lives and livelihoods of neighboring human settlements. When dangerous or large animals stray off protected areas into villages or farms and destroy crops, kill livestock, or attack humans, resentment at the existence of the game park can be considerable. Finally, high poverty rates may motivate individuals to engage in bushmeat poaching on nearby game parks either for individual subsistence or for resale. One attraction of bushmeat is that it is a valued commodity easily sold in local markets. Individuals in need of extra money to pay expenses may consider poaching a few animals that will quickly sell in their community (Pillinger 2003; Warchol and Johnson 2009).

The level of organization among bushmeat poachers ranges from individual subsistence hunters using traditional hunting methods to take one or two animals for personal consumption, to small groups of profit-driven actors taking a dozen animals for resale in local markets, to well-organized commercial firearms gangs moving tons of game meat out of protected areas to larger cities for resale (BCTF 2008). The last category may include military and insurgency units that exploit the breakdown in conservation enforcement to hunt in war-torn nations.

Bushmeat poachers use different techniques for different types and numbers of animals. These include silent methods that will not attract the attention of rangers or tourists in a game reserve. A simple and inexpensive method is the use of wire snares set along game trails or near water sources. Snares can be used to capture nearly any size of game, depending on the gauge of the wire and location of the snare. The wire for snares can be conveniently obtained by cutting it from the fences surrounding the game reserve. This hunting practice may involve gangs of ten or more poachers setting dozens of snares—a *snare line*—in a given area that can be a kilometer long. Poachers return a day or two later, sometimes with dogs, and run the snare line to check for their catch. Snares are indiscriminant killers, catching both desirable and undesirable species. Furthermore, not all set snares are necessarily checked by poachers, and some captured animals are not collected and left to decay. While poachers prefer the various antelope species and even hippo, owing to their value as a protein source, lions, zebra, and rhinoceros, among other animals, are also inadvertently caught in snares, only to be badly injured or die a slow death. Poachers also employ other traditional hunting methods, including the use of spears and homemade bows and arrows, to capture game. These methods are more labor intensive than snaring and generally provide less game but have the advantage of stealth (Warchol and Johnson 2009).

When bushmeat poachers use firearms, individuals and gangs can bring down large game or greater numbers of animals. Firearm types vary from relatively crude homemade, single-shot shotguns, to small and medium-caliber (.270 or 7 mm) bolt-action hunting rifles, to military firearms such as the 7.62-caliber select-fire AK 47 or South African FN-FAL R1 rifles. Firearms offer poachers both advantages and disadvantages. They provide for efficient killing of game at greater distances than using arrows or spears. Furthermore, poachers can take the animal immediately rather than have to return to check snares and risk apprehension by rangers. When field rangers discover an undisturbed snare line, they may establish an observation point in the area and wait for the poachers to return. The use of firearms avoids this situation. Firearms poachers may enter the protected area to track and shoot game or in some cases fire from outside the fence line if game is visible. However, firearms and ammunition are expensive in Africa, and the sound of multiple gunshots can alert ranger patrols or tourists to the presence of poachers in the park. Furthermore, being apprehended in a national park in South Africa with a firearm results in an enhanced violation even without direct evidence of poaching—that is, even without being in possession of animal carcasses. Removal of the game is straightforward with subsistence poachers carrying out one or two animals after field dressing them or with gangs moving larger numbers and even relying on all-terrain vehicles in the park to transfer the

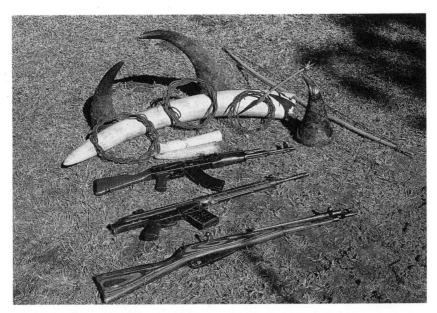

Poacher's tools confiscated by rangers in Kruger National Park, South Africa: military and bolt-action rifles; heavy-gauge wire snares; real rhino horns; a fake rhino horn (cow horn), used to deceive horn buyers; and a bow and arrow.

game to waiting trucks outside the fence line. Bushmeat may be butchered into smaller cuts prior to sale, sometimes even in the protected area, or sold as a complete carcass if buyers prefer larger amounts.

Like mammals, a large range of marine species are illegally harvested as a food source around the world. These include commonly found river, lake, and ocean fish for consumption and rare species that are sought after as delicacies rather than as a dietary staple. One example is abalone (*Haliotus* spp.), a shellfish found primarily in the waters of South Africa, Australia, the United States, Japan, and New Zealand (WWF 2015a). Abalone are easily located on the rocky seafloor in shallow, cold-water coastal areas. The meat is considered a delicacy (WWF 2007), and the shells are used to produce decorative objects. Raw abalone wholesales for about $40 per kilo and has retailed as high as $3,900 per kilo in some prime Asian markets (T. Chen 2012; WWF 2015a).

South Africa's major wild abalone fisheries, established in the 1940s, are located along about two-thirds of the country's coastline, including the Eastern and Western Capes. This area, sometimes referred to as the *abalone coast* (Redpath 2001), includes wild abalone fisheries within marine protected areas and commercial abalone farms. It is legal to harvest wild abalone as long as one obtains the necessary permits that specify fishing locations,

Abalone seizure in Table Mountain National Park. The illegally harvested abalone, which numbered nearly three hundred, were hidden in mesh bags just off the road in anticipation of pickup by a courier.

methods, and quantities (WWF 2007). However, the economic value of this desirable species incentivizes poachers to obtain large volumes of abalone. Wild abalone poaching, which began to significantly increase in the 1990s, has continued to expand to the point where it has become a serious threat to the future of the resource in South Africa (Plaganyi, Butterworth, and Burgener 2011). The steady increase in abalone poaching since the 1990s has been attributed to social, political, and economic changes in South Africa, such as the weakening of the South African currency (Rand) in relation to other currencies and a corresponding increase in barter systems; the end of the apartheid system, which changed the nation's governmental organizations, inadvertently creating inefficiencies; poor border controls (Steinberg 2005); and changes in fishing rights and permit allocations (Raemaekers and Britz 2009). Corresponding with these changes in South Africa was the expansion of the Chinese economy and increased demand for abalone in Taiwan, Japan, and Hong Kong (T. Chen 2012). These developments encouraged the Chinese criminal syndicates already operating in South Africa to target this resource as an additional revenue source (Hauck and Sweijd 1999). Chinese syndicates with connections to mainland China control the majority of the lucrative trade in abalone, including its shipment to end user markets in Asia (Redpath 2001; Steinberg 2005; Warchol and Harrington 2016).

The Chinese syndicates networked with local fishermen from poverty-stricken communities to obtain a portion of the abalone illegally exported to Asia (T. Chen 2012). Some of the poaching is done in marine protected areas just offshore of South Africa's national parks, including Cape Agulhas and Table Mountain. This type of poacher may enter the protected fishery from land rather than by boat. Once taken, the illegally harvested abalone is placed in diving bags and hidden in foliage in the park for later pickup by a co-conspirator with a vehicle. It is then transported to the local buyer for eventual export to an overseas market (Warchol and Harrington 2016). Other abalone poachers are South African criminal gangs that use modern diving gear and sometimes fully equipped fishing boats to increase their harvest and profit (Rogers 2010). In Cape Town's Table Mountain National Park, which includes a large wildlife abalone fishery, this threat is ever present. Some poaching gangs enter the park by car to access the fishery from the shoreline. Others work at night, entering the area by boat. Multiple divers using lights harvest abalone, placing their take on the boat for quick removal from the area. Confrontations with rangers have resulted in exchanges of gunfire on several occasions. These types of poaching gangs represent a serious threat, given the larger amount of abalone they poach and their willingness to use violence against rangers to defend it. Also involved in abalone poaching are sport divers who exceed their legal permitted catch. These individuals tend to harvest smaller amounts of the shellfish primarily for personal consumption and represent a far lesser threat to the survival of the species (Warchol and Harrington 2016).

Elephant Poachers

Of the various types of poachers, those that target the elephant and rhinoceros receive considerable attention from researchers, governments, and the media. Elephant poachers can be classified in several categories. The least dangerous type consists of those who kill the animals to protect their livelihoods or personal safety. Elephants that wander off reserves can consume entire crops planted by rural farmers or become a threat to the lives of residents of a village adjacent to protected areas. Rather than work with a game department, some local farmers, if they have the means, take matters into their own hands and eliminate the animal that threatens their livelihood. This may be done with firearms or poison. The number of these cases may never be accurately known to conservation officials.

The great majority of elephant poachers are profit-driven actors seeking ivory, at either a small-scale subsistence or large-scale commercial level. Regardless of who is involved, this poaching is strictly done by Africans. Many are impoverished farmers who have been recruited by middlemen from syndicates operating in local towns (Vira and Ewing 2014). As described in Chapter 1, the poaching of elephants is primarily done to obtain ivory, most of which will eventually be smuggled out of Africa to markets primarily though not exclusively in Asia (EIA 2002a). The tusks are carved into an array of items of cultural significance or purely for decoration. Individual poachers include opportunistic local villagers, unethical professional hunters, and corrupt game reserve rangers. Also involved and representing a far more serious threat to the species are criminal syndicates that fund mobile poaching groups, and military and insurgency/militia units that seek wildlife products to sell to fund their operations or simply for profit (Fay 2011). It is this latter group—militarized poaching operations—that is responsible for the greatest number of elephants killed for their ivory.

Subsistence elephant hunters kill elephants with the intent of selling the ivory to local craft or curio markets or providing it to buyers from criminal syndicates. Curio markets (gift shops) commonly found throughout East Africa and southern Africa offer an array of products for tourists, including ivory trinkets, sometimes for sale in plain view and at other times requiring a customer to ask the clerk. Tusks are bought by dealers, carved into an array of decorative consumer goods, such as bracelets, religious symbols, animals, or human figures, and offered for sale. The domestic ivory trade in the country may be legal, though it is illegal for tourists to ship the products home. Furthermore, in some markets there can be a commingling of legally obtained ivory with poached ivory. Even if the ivory is bought by a citizen of that nation, the legality of its origins may be in doubt. The type of poacher that supplies these markets may include residents of a village living near a protected area motivated by the potential for a large financial return from selling a good-sized ivory tusk. Yet, being the first link in the chain of the wildlife trade, poachers generally receive the lowest return for the wildlife products they obtain in comparison to the cost of the product on the retail market. Furthermore, these poachers are willing to assume considerable risk hunting potentially dangerous game and encountering armed ranger patrols. The current penalties in South Africa for elephant poaching—ten years in prison and a monetary fine three times the value of the animal—are substantial. Nevertheless, the amount the poacher would receive, perhaps $20 to $30 USD per kilo for a tusk, in the context of the local economy may still motivate an individual to take the risk and seek ivory.

My field research revealed that a poacher can enter a protected area with relative ease. Although some parks are fenced, the fencing is designed primarily to keep the wildlife in the reserve rather than prevent humans from trespassing. Fences can be bypassed by digging under them, climbing over them, or cutting the fence wires. While some reserves have installed electric

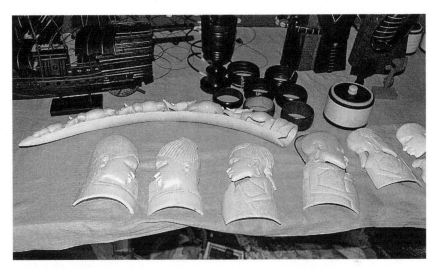

Carved ivory tusk and curios offered for sale to tourists near Pemba, Mozambique. The legality of their origins is unknown.

fencing, in some cases the authorities have turned off the current for humane reasons. In other cases, the electrified fence can be shorted out by poachers to gain access. Furthermore, some game reserves are not fenced in order to allow for migration of species of wildlife to traditional ranges outside the protected area or to an adjacent reserve.

Once in the reserve, poachers may be familiar with the location of elephants or be willing to track them. The operation may be conducted in one day or require the poachers to spend two or more days in the reserve. Given the size and remoteness of many protected areas, they may have limited concern about being found by ranger patrols. Once the poachers have found an elephant, they commonly use rifles to kill it, often relying on medium- or large-caliber hunting weapons such as a .303 British, .375 Holland and Holland, or .458 Winchester Magnum or, in other instances, military rifles. Rifles are expensive to purchase, but they may be borrowed, rented, or stolen. Though there is risk from multiple gunshot noise, depending on the location of rangers and the potential for an enhanced fine if one is caught with a firearm, it is the most efficient manner to take an elephant. In other instances, poachers may poison water holes or salt licks or use poisoned arrows and heavy-gauge wire snares as silent killers (Vira and Ewing 2014). After the animal is killed, the ivory is literally chopped out with axes or machetes. The tusks may be immediately taken out of the reserve or temporarily buried in the park to be obtained at a later date. The latter may be done if the poachers are concerned about encountering ranger patrols, desire to accumulate a larger cache, or prefer to conceal the ivory until a buyer can be found or is ready to collect the tusks. If trespassers are found on a game reserve, it is not a major crime as long as there is no evidence of poaching.

The third and most serious type of poaching is by organized gangs, military and insurgency groups, and, of late, terrorist organizations. The involvement of military and insurgency groups in elephant poaching is not a new phenomenon. It was prevalent during the extensive poaching of the 1970s and 1980s, when an estimated seven hundred tons of ivory annually, representing about 70,000 elephants, left Africa over a ten-year period corresponding with the bush wars in parts of southern Africa. The massive scale of the poaching during this time required well-armed and organized groups with the weaponry and transport needed to accomplish the task, rather than individual hunters (Vira and Ewing 2014). This situation has recurred, beginning in the early 2000s. These groups currently represent the gravest threat to elephant populations, owing to their ability to take dozens or even hundreds of animals during an operation, to evade detection, and to be willing to use violence against any rangers they may encounter.

In nations such as Somalia and Sudan, which are experiencing civil wars or where militia and terrorist groups have established operations, wildlife can be subject to exploitation as a source of food and money to purchase weapons and other needed goods. This can occur when the conflict zone includes conservation areas with game populations. In other instances, wildlife become vulnerable when the government's conservation agencies are weakened and opportunistic groups begin to target game out of greed rather than need. Past examples occurred during the first major wave of poaching beginning in the early 1970s in East Africa and southern Africa, where as many as 100,000 elephants were killed each year. This period of elephant poaching coincided with the liberation or bush wars involving South Africa, Namibia, and Angola; Mozambique; and Rhodesia. The South African military was implicated in extensive poaching operations, including ivory poaching in Namibia and Angola, which were sites of a long-term border war (Meredith 2003; Vira and Ewing 2014). A commission established by President Nelson Mandela in 1996 found that the South African military had sold ivory tusks and rhinoceros horn poached in Angola and killed large numbers of Cape buffalo for bushmeat (Koch 1996). A second example occurred during Mozambique's fifteen-year civil war, which ended in 1992. During the war its once large and flourishing wildlife populations were decimated by poaching operations by both combatant groups—RENAMO and FRELIMO—and by government forces. FRELIMO had the advantage of being based in Gorongosa National Park, which was inhabited by large numbers of elephants that were steadily reduced to fund the group's military operations with the sale of ivory. Even after peace, the poaching continued for a time, owing to the inability of the government to reestablish its conservation efforts in the park. It took about a decade for the park's wildlife to recover from the exploitation during the war (Barosso 2012).

This phenomenon of militarized poaching, some apparently state-supported, has recently reemerged, involving various groups that include insurgency forces and terrorist units operating in East Africa and Central Africa. These groups have realized the high value of ivory and seek to exploit it as one source of revenue. One elephant on average yields about twenty pounds of ivory, valued at about $13,000 retail. Garamba National Park in northeastern Democratic Republic of Congo has lost all its rhinoceros population and a substantial portion of its elephants. The poaching was attributed to the Ugandan designated terrorist group known as the Lord's Resistance Army (LRA), under the control of Joseph Kony. The LRA, intent on overthrowing the Ugandan government, established operations in 2006 in the 1,900-square-mile Garamba, which at one time was home to an estimated 40,000 elephants. The LRA began exploiting the resource for funding by killing hundreds of elephants each year (Associated Press [hereafter AP] 2015). Poachers operating in the Congo were believed to be using helicopters. The lack of human tracks leading to poaching sites along with the spotting of a military helicopter on an unauthorized low-altitude flight over Garamba offered proof of this strategy (Gettlemen 2012).

Poaching recurred in Mozambique in the 2000s, and the competing political groups and military forces were suspected of involvement. FRELIMO, the ruling party, was implicated in allowing the military to poach elephant to sell ivory, the proceeds of which were directed to the government officials. The charges were based in part on game rangers' claims of heavy-caliber firearms and helicopters being used in poaching—equipment that is restricted to military and police use only but is able to facilitate large-scale poaching. Elephant populations have again begun to decline, from about 20,000 in 2009 to an estimated 9,000 in 2013 (Huang and Valoi 2013). During this period, two major waves of poaching also occurred in Chad's Zakouma National Park by large groups of Sudanese and a smaller Chadian gang. A report concluded that Sudan had become an elephant poaching "super state" whose organized groups were exploiting the resources of its neighboring country (Neme 2015a). One group of poachers, with Sudan's Janjaweed militia, arrived on horseback with military firearms, while the other consisted of Chadians believed to be connected to government officials and Chinese workers at a local oil refinery (Orenstein 2013). Militarized poachers from Chad and Sudan's Janjaweed militia have also been implicated in ivory poaching in Cameroon and the Central African Republic (Neme 2015b).

The more recent involvement of terrorist groups in the wildlife trade has come to the attention of the U.S. government. The concern is that the nature and extent of the current large-scale poaching not only impacts wildlife populations but also hinders economic development, reduces national security, fosters corruption, and may even lead to regional instability when groups such as those from Sudan and Somalia operate with near impunity in exploiting natural resources. Poachers from war-torn Somalia, possibly representing al-Shabaab, have operated in northern Kenya. Even outside Africa, an al Qaeda affiliate group was involved in wildlife poaching in northwestern India to obtain revenue (International Fund for Animal Welfare [hereafter IFAW] 2013a).

In addition to the killing of large numbers of elephants, the return of militarized ivory poaching brings a high level of violence to the region. Large, well-armed groups possess a far greater threat to civilians, field rangers, and wildlife than individual poachers. The IUCN (2014) reported that worldwide, sixty-nine rangers were killed by poachers and militia in 2013 along with more than 20,000 elephants. While the 2013 poaching figure represented a decline over previous years, Wild Aid (2015b) reported that poachers killed more than 100,000 elephants between 2010 and 2012, with the smaller forest elephant species suffering the highest percentage of loss to its population. A record forty tons of illegal ivory were seized in 2011 (IFAW 2013a). As in the 1970s and 1980s, the modern-day ivory trade is a product of conflict and corruption. The end result is that the ivory trade in parts of Africa has again become militarized, owing to the involvement of these various military, insurgency, and terrorist groups linked to criminal syndicates and corrupt governments.

Rhinoceros Poachers

The African rhinoceros population once numbered at least in the hundreds of thousands, but extensive legal trophy hunting and poaching had decimated the species throughout the continent by the latter half of the twentieth century. An extensive and very successful recovery program instituted in South Africa in KwaZulu Natal, known as Operation Rhino, began in 1961, centered in two public game reserves in the province. South Africa's apartheid regime with its well-protected borders along with heavy security in the two game reserves helped prevent poachers from entering the country (Orenstein 2013). These efforts resulted in population increases of the southern white rhino and black rhino to about 20,000 and 5,000 animals, respectively (WWF 2016a). Rhino populations in other parts of Africa and Asia continued a steady decline, however, until later conservation efforts helped check the loss of the animals, though they are currently perilously low. It was estimated that Botswana, for example, lost its entire rhino population to poaching and hunting by the 1890s (Emslie and Brooks 1999). Reintroduc-

The author in front of a display of rhino skulls at Mkhaya Game Reserve, administered by Ted Reilly of Big Game Parks, in Swaziland. Many dozens of rhinos were killed during what became known as the rhino wars.

tion programs in the late 1960s involving animals from South Africa ultimately failed to succeed because of inadequate protective measures. Subsequent efforts to import and protect rhino have been more successful, and the country maintains a small population of the animals. The Kingdom of Swaziland experienced a period known as the rhino wars between 1988 and 1992. Poaching took one rhino every two weeks over a four-year period and up to three animals a day near the end of this scourge. Massive poaching nearly rendered the population extinct. New conservation efforts, enforcement, and the Game Act of 1992 helped reverse the situation (Reilly 2004). Tanzania demonstrated a measure of success in rhino conservation mainly owing to very intensive protective efforts in its game reserves. But animals that naturally wander off the protected areas face an uncertain future.

However, renewed heavy poaching in 2008 resulted in massive losses of rhinoceroses, primarily in South Africa but also in neighboring Namibia, Swaziland, and Zimbabwe. In 2004, officials at Kruger National Park began to notice a slight increase in rhino poaching within the park, a trend that would rapidly accelerate in the next few years. Investigations eventually led to the arrests of several Mozambican nationals. These events were the first indicators of a renewed wave of poaching that would continue for at least a decade. Between 2008 and 2015, at least 5,940 African rhino were lost to poachers, the majority taken in South Africa (Save the Rhino 2016a). This change was attributed to several factors, one being the CITES down-listing of the southern white to Appendix II, allowing limited hunting and a trade in live animal sales. Corresponding to this development was increased economic prosperity in both China and Vietnam, where demand grew for luxury goods and traditional medicines.

Unlike elephant poaching, in which large contingents of poachers may be operating together, the smaller rhino population requires fewer hunters. Contemporary rhinoceros poaching involves both individuals and small organized groups of hunters from Zimbabwe, Mozambique, and South Africa. Tom Milliken and Jo Shaw (2012) found that while rhino poaching is predominantly the domain of black Mozambicans and Zimbabweans, white Afrikaners seeking to profit from the illegal trade are also involved in this crime. The South Africans, some of whom are referred to as the Boer Mafia, are involved in recruiting and organizing poaching gangs, including former professional hunters, landowners, and corrupt game rangers seeking to profit from the demand for the highly valuable horn. These groups are networked with Vietnamese syndicates that initially were obtaining horn with quasi-legal pseudohunts and are now working with poachers. Rademeyer's (2012) in-depth investigation adds more detail to these different types of rhino poachers. One consisted of gangs of former or current soldiers based in Harare, Zimbabwe, and working for local syndicates. Operating in military fashion, they willingly engaged rangers in firefights if spotted, slaughtered rhino with automatic rifle fire, and then used axes to crudely chop out the horn. The second group was made up of experienced hunters working for South African syndicates with ties to Vietnamese networks. They efficiently killed rhino with well-placed shots using bolt-action rifles and almost surgically removed the horn. Both groups of experienced rhino poachers often collected intelligence from local communities about rhino whereabouts and surveilled game reserves and ranches to monitor staff activities and plan escape routes (Milliken and Shaw 2012).

Rhino poaching is not difficult or very dangerous. Rhino in Africa are located on game reserves, both public parks and private farms. Though this may imply that the animals are protected and secure, such is not always the case. As noted previously, accessing these locations is not overly challenging. Though some game parks are fenced, the fencing is typically designed to keep game from leaving rather than acting as a strong deterrent to trespassers. The sheer size of a game reserve combined with its terrain and vegetation make surveillance very challenging for rangers even with aircraft. Furthermore, contrary to some popular depictions of rhinoceros, the animals are not exceptionally aggressive toward humans, which provides the hunter with a distinct advantage. The process of hunting and killing a rhino was described by an investigative journalist as akin to "shooting a horse" (Rademeyer 2012). It can be assumed that rhino poachers face more danger from ranger patrols or large predatory animals in the game parks than from their intended prey. Rhinoceros also tend not to congregate in large herds like elephants or the African buffalo, which prevents poachers from killing them in greater numbers. More commonly, they are found alone or in small family groups of two or three animals, often including a calf lacking the desired horn. However, one horn is worth far more than an ivory tusk.

The location of nearly all rhino poaching in South Africa is Kruger National Park (KNP), which borders Mozambique to the east. In 2002, the Great Limpopo Transfrontier Park was established, straddling the borders of South Africa, Mozambique, and Zimbabwe to create a massive conservation area the size of the Netherlands (Peace Parks Foundation 2016). This development involved the removal of the fence on the eastern border of Kruger to facilitate wildlife migration. The unintended consequence was a route for Mozambican poachers to enter KNP, kill rhino, and return to the safety of Mozambique. South African National Parks (SANParks) rangers were not allowed to pursue fleeing poachers across the border into Mozambique. Further hindering enforcement, Mozambique lacked serious penalties for rhino poaching or possession of horn (Save the Rhino 2013). The situation began to improve when the two nations cooperated on anti-poaching efforts, leading to a reduction in incursions of poachers from Mozambique (Peace Parks Foundation 2016).

Contemporary rhinoceros poachers employ an array of techniques to kill their prey, including the use of firearms, both military and traditional bolt-action medium- to large-caliber hunting rifles (some with suppressors); powerful crossbows; heavy wire snares; and even poison added to water sources (Rademeyer 2012). The former method can ensure a quick kill of the animal, but the report of rifle fire may reveal the poachers' presence in the reserve. After entering the protected area, they establish camp near water sources or known locations or trails for rhino. Once the rhino is found, it is simply a matter of killing the animal, quickly removing the horn at its base, and fleeing the reserve as rapidly as possible. This type of poaching can be done faster than elephant poaching. Fewer rhino are taken at a given time, and removal of the horn is done more quickly than chopping out elephant tusks.

African and Asian Cat Poachers

The illegal hunting and killing of the various cat species in Africa is done by a range of actors and for a range of motivations. African cat poachers include livestock farmers and local residents dealing with conflict animals, as well as traditional medicine practitioners and game farm owners. Livestock farmers can be arrested for poaching when they disregard the legal requirements for dealing with problem animals—typically lion, leopard, and chee-tah—that threaten the lives and livelihoods of humans either by attacking people or by killing domestic animals. Farmers experiencing this problem may be required to call the local game department to report the conflict animal before taking action so it can be relocated rather than killed. In Namibia, with its large population of cheetahs, it can be legal for a rancher to kill these cats provided the rancher complies with government requirements of reporting the killing to local conservation officials and justifying the action (Magill 2003). Once he has reported the killing, the farmer may choose to keep the pelt or sell it domestically, but not on the international market. However, not all farmers and ranchers adhere to these requirements and may simply kill the suspect cats without making a report to officials. Evidence of this practice is found when ranchers have been caught by the police attempting to illegally sell cheetah pelts (Warchol, Zupan, and Clack 2003). The illegal killing of big cats also occurs in South Africa, where local villagers may consider them little more than dangerous pests. Rather than contact a game department for assistance, they take matters into their own hands. I found that a common method is the use of poison called Temik, which is nick-named "two-step," since that is as far as many animals will walk after ingesting it. The poison is commonly placed in a carcass used as bait for a stray big cat. At these poisoning sites, it is not uncommon to find an entire pride of dead lions and scavengers that also came to feed on the carcass.

In South Africa and Namibia, poachers seeking to profit are also active in killing African cats to supply these species to *muti traders*. These individuals provide traditional medicines using parts from the animals. During my visits to traditional medicine markets in South Africa, I saw pelts and bones from the big cat species (leopard and lion) on display for sale. Big cat poaching is also linked to dangerous game hunting, an economically significant industry in some East African and southern African countries. An entire industry of game farms and professional hunting guides has developed over the past decades to meet this demand. The incentive to provide a successful experience to the client can encourage some professional hunters to break the rules to obtain the sought-after animals. This gives a few unethical game farm owners a financial incentive to stock their farms with the illegally obtained desirable species when legally procured ones are either not available or too expensive to buy from animal brokers. On other rare occasions it may also encourage professional hunters to lure cat species out of national parks where they cannot be legally hunted into adjacent private game reserves or concessions. This was the accusation against the professional hunter in the so-called Cecil the lion case in 2015 in Zimbabwe.

Among the various Asian big cats, the tiger is perhaps the best-known species threatened with extinction because of extensive poaching. Found

A TYPOLOGY OF POACHING

Target of Poacher	Motivation	Methods	Organization
Bushmeat	Individual subsistence hunters. Individuals and small profit-motivated groups intending to sell game locally. Large-scale commercial hunters pursuing both domestic and foreign sales.	Snare, bow and arrow, spear, shotgun, and rifle. Handmade, borrowed, rented, stolen, or owned firearms. Dogs used to track game. Manual movement of game, using wheelbarrows, all-terrain vehicles, and trucks.	Individual hunters, small groups of local hunters supplying the local market, and larger groups of organized hunters with the resources to process and ship game domestically and internationally.
Elephant Ivory	Individuals killing conflict animals. Opportunists seeking profit from ivory. Small organized poaching gangs with profit motivation. State military units with superiors profiting from sales. Insurgency military units with profit motive. Terrorist groups with profit motive.	Medium- to large-caliber hunting rifles. Poison added to water source. Military firearms, including automatic weapons and rocket-propelled grenades. Horses, trucks, and (in rare instances) helicopters used to track animals and transport ivory, which may be moved immediately or cached until a sufficient quantity is collected or the courier is available—operation may last days or weeks.	No network affiliation for conflict-animal hunters and opportunists. Small criminal networks with links to local middlemen who can courier ivory to domestic buyers (curio markets) and to ports for export to Asia. Well-organized poaching units with the ability to kill, process, and ship large volumes of ivory. Individuals with links to established organized crime networks in Africa and Asia, with overseas transport of large quantities commonly achieved via shipping containers.
Rhinoceros Horn	Individual opportunists. Domestic, profit-motivated professional poachers—individuals or small groups. Militarized poaching gangs with superiors who profit from horn sales.	Medium-caliber hunting or military rifle, snares, and poison. Domestic poaching gangs skilled in tracking and shooting wildlife, with horns quickly removed after kill and removed from park—tracking and killing operation lasting from one to three days.	Individual opportunists who initially lack horn buyers. Well-organized groups consisting of corrupt landowners, game farmers, skilled poachers, professional hunters, and wildlife veterinarians. Individuals with links to criminal networks that can sell and courier horns to overseas Asian markets. Militarized poachers working for state-sponsored criminal networks with ties to Asian syndicates.

(Continued on next page)

A TYPOLOGY OF POACHING (*Continued*)

Target of Poacher	*Motivation*	*Methods*	*Organization*
Big Cats—e.g., Tiger, Lion, Cheetah	Conflict-animal hunters—typically local farmers. Individual opportunists with profit motive. Mobile poaching gangs that travel from region to region to exploit game for profit.	Snares, poison, firearms, and jaw traps, with cat quickly processed in the field, including removal of skin, internal organs, and other valuable body parts.	No network affiliation for conflict-animal hunters. Individual opportunists with ties to buyers. Individuals with links to established criminal networks that can move tiger parts within and across national borders to Asian market destinations.
Reptiles	Individual reptile dealers, collectors, and local poachers employed by dealers and collectors—may be residents or visitors who are knowledgeable about the desired species.	Legal entrance into nature reserve and subsequent hunt for desired species using digging tools, bags, and small cartons. Easy concealment of reptiles because of small size. Packing in luggage for overseas markets, body-carrying, or shipping via express mail services to ensure timely delivery.	Individual collectors who may not be part of a criminal network, who poach to add specimens to their personal collections. Local dealers who poach to add to their inventory and who may be involved in a criminal network. Foreign poachers who are part of a larger network and who offer reptiles for sale after they are shipped out of the country.
Abalone	Individual sport divers and local subsistence fishermen lacking a profit motive, who use abalone for individual consumption. Well-organized, well-equipped poaching gangs with a profit motive, who enter the area with several divers in boats or in cars.	Low-skill diving with or without oxygen tanks in relatively shallow coastal waters, with small quantities of abalone harvested by individual poachers. Fishing boats, operated by organized gangs, outfitted with diving and fishing gear, with large quantities of abalone taken and gangs often armed and willing to fire on ranger boats if confronted. Divers and diving equipment brought in by smaller, land-based poaching gangs in several vehicles to avoid suspicion, with abalone sometimes bagged and hidden in park foliage in anticipation of pickup by local couriers.	No network affiliation for individual sport divers and local fishermen. Poaching boat-gangs that rely on established criminal networks of equipment suppliers, couriers, buyers, and shippers of abalone—difficult to penetrate because of Asian organized crime involvement in South Africa. Land-based poachers with links to criminal syndicates of couriers and buyers of abalone—both local Africans and Asians.

mainly in India and Russia, with smaller populations in other Asian nations, the tiger is capable of surviving in a wide range of habitats. Tigers have long been subject to legal hunting and poaching pressures, first as a trophy animal and then illegally for skins and body parts for decorations and traditional Asian medicines (Davies 2005). Once legal in India, tiger hunting was prohibited in 1972, and the animal was listed as a CITES Appendix I species in subsequent years, prohibiting its commercial trade (EIA 2006). India, home to about half of the remaining wild tiger populations, provides examples of poachers and their operations that are useful for an understanding of the range of actors in this crime. As in southern Africa, some tigers are killed by local Indian farmers who have lost livestock to predation and have not received adequate or any compensation from forest departments (EIA 1998). The other and by far largest group are profit-driven tiger poachers who are recruited by middlemen or wildlife traders with the capacity to move products to market. These poachers are commonly well-organized gangs that move from location to location around India. Poachers cultivate local residents living near tiger reserves for knowledge of the area, likely tiger locations, and the operations of ranger units (EIA 2006).

Poachers often prefer to operate in reserves during full moon periods, allowing them to dispense with the need to carry lights, which make them more vulnerable to detection by rangers. Once in the reserve, they employ a number of relatively inexpensive techniques to capture and kill the tigers. These include heavy steel-jaw traps (Guynup 2014) produced by local blacksmiths and set near game trails. Poachers also use poisoned carcasses as bait, firearms in some instances, and even electrocution by pulling down local power lines if available and setting a live wire on a known game trail. Once caught, the animal, if alive, is quickly killed and processed for its skin and body parts. Poachers have been known to rely on local skin-tanning businesses in communities near reserves for processing the tiger pelts. The EIA found that a tiger poacher can earn as much as $1,500 USD for obtaining one skin, which can eventually sell for about ten times that amount in the consumer markets of China (EIA 2006).

Reptile Poachers

The poaching of reptiles (lizards, tortoises, and snakes), which accounts for a large volume of the wildlife species in the illegal trade, involves a range of unique actors with distinct differences from other types of wildlife poachers. South Africa offers many examples of how reptile poachers operate, illustrating their motivations and techniques. In South Africa this aspect of the illegal wildlife trade involves foreign nationals and local rural residents, collectors, and pet shop owners seeking to meet demand for African reptiles both internationally and domestically (Herbig and Warchol 2011). One type of buyer identified in the South African research was foreign tourists, commonly from central and western Europe, traveling to South Africa in search of selected species intended to become part of a collection or to be sold on the European Union's exotic pet market. These buyers sometimes pose as tourists on holiday, visiting nature specific nature reserves known to be inhabited by desired wildlife. Once on location, they may solicit local residents familiar with the nature reserve and its wildlife with a cash offer (generally the equivalent of a few U.S. dollars) to poach protected species of lizard or snake. After the price has been settled, the buyers wait a few days and then return to collect the poached reptiles. The locals procuring these protected animals are neither professional criminals nor full-time poachers. Rather, they are opportunists profiting from foreigners' desire for wildlife (Warchol, Zupan, and Clack 2003). The large size of many nature reserves, their extensive foliage and difficult terrain, and the limited numbers of park rangers work to the advantage of poachers seeking to avoid detection. SANParks investigations have revealed a second unique type of reptile poacher—well-educated offenders, sometimes academics or scientists. They have been apprehended in possession of the illegal wildlife along with reptile identification guidebooks, digging tools, and containers intended to package and ship the live animals overseas (Herbig and Warchol 2011). While some poachers are foreign visitors, a third type of reptile poacher is the South African citizen seeking to add to his collection or to sell a rare species to domestic buyers or even pet shop owners needing to add to their inventory. Finally, some reptile poaching is done for the traditional African medicine trade in South Africa. Certain reptile species are taken for use as ingredients in a range of medicines for either physical or social problems. These species can often be seen on display at traditional markets in South Africa (Warchol, Zupan, and Clack 2003).

Middlemen: The Wildlife Trafficker

The chain of participants in the illegal wildlife trade was previously described as including poachers, middlemen, and consumers. Yet not all wildlife crimes that constitute the illegal trade involve all three participants in the chain. The poacher can be trafficker and consumer of illegally obtained wildlife in cases in which an individual illegally harvests flora or fauna for his or her own consumption. At other times the poacher will supply the wildlife directly to the consumer without the need for a middleman. In other instances, once the valuable wildlife destined for a consumer market has been obtained, another actor in the illegal chain—a middleman—is required in the process.

Middlemen include those involved in recruiting poachers, providing their firearms, collecting the contraband, and trafficking the wildlife domestically and internationally. It is this last type of participant that is the focus of this section. The wildlife trafficker is a keystone of the illegal wildlife trade, relying on a range of techniques and routes to move the valuable contraband to consumer markets. The United Nations Office on Drugs and Crime (hereafter UNODC) (2016, 83) describes the task as "storing, handling, transporting, processing, packaging, exporting, marketing, security and retailing. Various participants may handle 'official' expenditures (such as purchasing permits and paying fines), and 'unofficial' expenditures (bribes)." Traffickers follow established smuggling routes to move wildlife within and over national borders to end users. These are sometimes the same routes used to move other contraband, such as narcotics, stolen cars, counterfeit products, and weapons. Wildlife trafficking may also involve one or more smugglers, depending on the size of the network and final destination. Traffickers operate differently on the basis of the type and volume of the species they are moving to consumers. They employ an array of techniques to secrete or disguise their contraband, including forged or false permits, commingling illegal with legal species to confuse inspectors, and efforts to compromise the inspection process with bribery when moving wildlife across national borders. Furthermore, they often use legitimate transportation businesses, such as express mail companies, sea and air cargo shippers, and ground transportation services, to move illegal products. Interestingly, traffickers will change their routes in response to law enforcement efforts, cost, or improvement in transportation infrastructure (UNODC 2016). This section examines different types of traffickers and their techniques employed to smuggle ivory, rhinoceros horn, reptiles, birds, and tiger parts. The goal is to illustrate several of the common practices employed by those moving these products from poacher to consumer.

Ivory Trafficking in Southern Africa and East Africa

Ivory smuggling techniques vary on the basis of the amount and type of the product. Small-scale ivory traffickers moving individual tusks or carvings can transport their products across some African borders in rather uncomplicated manners because of superficial or nonexistent inspections or they can employ simple methods to avoid customs officials. For example, in some locations in southern Africa traffickers can approach an international border, walk their contraband a few hundred meters away from the monitored crossing point to a remote spot along the frontier, and transfer it to a waiting confederate on the other side. The lack of fences and/or constant patrols allows this practice to occur. I found evidence of this method during interviews with South African Revenue Service (SARS) anti-smuggling officers at the Beitbridge border crossing from South Africa into northern Zimbabwe. Although the Limpopo River separates the two nations at this spot and most vehicle traffic is restricted to paved roads, there are numerous illegal crossing points within walking distance from the post. SARS officers stated that smugglers traveling on foot would ford the river at shallow points and then cross the sparsely populated and lightly patrolled border by cutting the fence or going through frontier areas that were not fenced. An alternative method was for Zimbabwean smugglers to transfer their contraband to South African couriers at the border. The couriers would then simply join the foot traffic or board buses or waiting cars to their final destination in South Africa. The transferring of contraband to South African couriers reduced the likelihood that they would be searched by SARS officers in their own country. More direct smuggling methods can involve the secreting of small tusks or bags of ivory carvings destined for the curio markets in vehicles, including in spare tires, or in luggage or on one's person with the hope of avoiding search (SARS officers, personal communication, 2005).

Moving larger amounts of illegal wildlife products across this border required different shipping methods than those employed by small-scale subsistence or craft smugglers. One method was to secrete contraband in cargo containers moved by truck. Because of the large volume of traffic and the lack of an X-ray scanner for containers on the South African side, searches were not commonplace. The SARS officers reported that four hundred or more containers can move across the border each day into South Africa. It would be rare for even three containers to be searched, since it can take three to four hours to unpack and repack cargo. A full inspection of a cargo container would require credible information that it had contraband. Rather, the anti-smuggling officers limited searches to those individuals suspected of smuggling owing to their appearance or responses to questions (SARS officers, personal communication, 2005).

Small amounts of ivory and other wildlife products are also smuggled via air, though this practice currently involves more risk in the age of global terrorism with enhanced screening of passengers and luggage. Officials at Johannesburg's O. R. Tambo International Airport regularly confiscate small amounts of wildlife products from departing passengers, including ivory, which is generally in the form of finished decorative products (O. R. Tambo customs officers, personal communication, March 2005). Given the high demand for ivory in China, Japan, Taiwan, Singapore, and South Korea, airport officials target passengers on flights destined for Asia. The majority of those found with ivory have no criminal background. They typically purchase the items at curio shops with the intent to take them back to their home country

Ivory *hankos* confiscated by authorities at South Africa's O. R. Tambo International Airport. The *hankos*, which were painted black to avoid detection, were most likely destined for Japan, where demand for them is high.

for personal use or resale. While they are amateur smugglers, it is apparent they know it is illegal to export ivory, as illustrated by the manner in which the items are disguised in their luggage. Ivory *hankos* destined for Japan are sometimes painted black to resemble batteries on an airport X-ray scanner or placed in cigarette packs, tea containers, or toothpaste tubes. Fines of about 10,000 Rand, or $1,000 USD, are levied for larger amounts, and the offender's name is placed in a database. Airport officials also intercept whole and ground rhinoceros horn from departing passengers (O. R. Tambo customs officers, personal communication, 2005). Furthermore, foreign diplomats and embassy employees, including those from Vietnam and North Korea, have long been implicated in wildlife trafficking (Warchol, Zupan, and Clack 2003), including in several recent instances (Rademeyer 2012, 2015).

The situation is different for traffickers who need to move larger amounts of raw ivory to the consumer markets of Asia. This scale of trafficking consists of two distinct phases, the first of which is the gathering and consolidation of the ivory. Groups of poachers, once they have obtained the raw ivory, can either move the tusks out of the game reserve to a secondary location or hide them in the park, typically by burying, until the traffickers are ready to accept the product. Oftentimes many small caches of ivory are gathered until a sufficient amount is available to warrant shipment overseas. It is during this first phase that discovery of the ivory and apprehension of the traffickers are more likely. The second phase of large-scale ivory trafficking is typically done by packing large quantities in twenty- or forty-foot cargo containers that are moved by truck to seaports such as Durban or Port Elizabeth, South Africa;

Mombasa, Kenya; or Dar es Salaam, Tanzania (Vira and Ewing 2014). Asian businesses in Africa that participate in the illegal trade offer good cover for shipping contraband. The use of shipping containers offers several advantages: the ivory tusks can be mixed with other legal products destined for Asia, ranging from timber to finished consumer goods, or they can be hidden in secret compartments (Ives 2015). Containers are constantly moving to and from Asia and Africa, and the sheer volume of them in transit prohibits their individual inspection. The opening of a container to conduct a search is generally based on strong intelligence that it has contraband. Even if opened, a full cargo container is very labor intensive to search, taking many hours, since it is generally completely packed with cargo. At the point where the ivory is containerized, it is under the control of an Asian ivory syndicate. As an example, between 2009 and 2014, about nineteen tons of ivory was seized in the Kenyan port of Mombasa, hidden among the hundreds of shipping containers destined for foreign markets. Mombasa is believed to be the most active illegal ivory export center in the world (McConnell 2015).

The East African nation of Tanzania has long experienced extensive ivory poaching and trafficking, with its elephant population declining from an estimated 109,051 in 2009 to 43,330 in 2014 (Lowry 2016). As in many other African nations, a link was uncovered between elephant poaching and Chinese organized crime groups that operate within legitimate businesses that have investments in Tanzania. In 2015, Tanzanian authorities arrested a sixty-six-year-old Chinese businesswoman, Yang Feng Glan, on suspicion of smuggling $3 million USD worth of ivory between 2000 and 2014 (Tilsley 2015). Following the pattern in other African nations, the Tanzanian government had awarded Chinese companies several road building projects in the country. Chinese contractors often brought in some of their own laborers from the PRC. In some instances, elephant poaching operations were initiated by those involved in the construction projects. The scenario described to me was that Chinese workers would approach local Tanzanians, inquiring about the availability of ivory and offering to purchase it. Given the poor economic situation in Tanzania, it was not difficult to find willing poachers. The Chinese typically supplied the weapons and ammunition, even renting them from local police or military units (Tanzanian National Parks staff, personal communication, May 2005). Ivory was then collected, containerized, and shipped out of the country to Asia for processing into finished goods that were sold on the consumer market. My 2005 research in Tanzania also revealed that illegally harvested ivory was not only exported to Asian markets but also supplied to an internal craft market in the capital of Dar es Salaam. In the early 2000s, there was an active domestic trade in ivory in Dar es Salaam, and ivory was readily found in the city curio markets.

My research in this region helped identify trafficking routes, one of which involved ivory poached in the northern part of Mozambique and smuggled into Dar es Salaam via the port city of Kilwa. This ivory was illegally harvested by local poachers supplying Chinese buyers associated with legitimate logging operations in northern Mozambique. Once collected, the ivory was secreted in shipping containers fully loaded with legally cut timber and shipped to the port at Dar es Salaam for export to Asia. A second trafficking route involved ivory poached in Zambia and moved by car and truck on remote back roads into Tanzania. After the contraband crossed the border, the final destination was again the harbor at Dar es Salaam. Customs enforcement efforts at this harbor were described to me as "poor or at times nonexistent." Ships' cargos were not always fully inspected, nor were customs agents always on staff to meet arriving vessels (wildlife NGO researcher, personal communication, May 2005).

The Singapore Seizure

In the early 2000s, a major seizure of ivory occurred in Asia that involved a well-organized ivory poaching and trafficking network in Zambia, Malawi, Mozambique, and South Africa; this case further helps illustrate how these operations function. A June 2002 seizure of 6.2 metric tons of ivory in Singapore served notice that the ivory trade was not only active but also increasing in southern Africa, evidencing the second major wave of elephant poaching (Orenstein 2013). The 2002 report by the EIA on this event provides valuable details on the participants and methods used to move large quantities of ivory from source countries in southern Africa to consumer markets in Asia (EIA 2002a).

The Singapore seizure resulted from an inspection of a cargo container that arrived by ship from Durban, South Africa. Relying on an informant's tip, Singaporean officials searched the container and discovered 532 elephant tusks and more than forty thousand *hankos* (destined for Japan) with a total weight of 6.2 metric tons. This amount of ivory, representing the killing of more than 600 African elephants, primarily originated from Zambia. The EIA's investigation later determined that this was not a one-off smuggling case. Rather, there were nineteen suspected ivory shipments from the same Chinese syndicate, fifteen sent to Singapore and the remaining four to China. Singapore was used as a transshipment point for ivory destined for Japan, then the world's largest market for this product. The sheer size of this shipment and the fact that it was grouped into just one consignment rather than being broken down into smaller amounts illustrated the confidence of the smugglers in their ability to avoid detection after eight years of successful trafficking in ivory. This case detailed the extent of the ivory trade, who is involved, and the potential for renewed devastation of elephant populations, particularly in Zambia and Mozambique (EIA 2002a).

The poaching was initiated by Chinese business owners in southern Africa. This particular syndicate moved from Singapore to Malawi, where it initially established a timber operation with some local Malawians. Some members of the syndicate relocated to the Zambian border city of Chipata to organize the poaching and smuggling operations in South Luangwa National Park. Interviews with Zambia Wildlife Authority (ZAWA) officials revealed that Chinese traffickers bought whatever ivory was currently available in the area and then requested larger amounts, often stating specific quantities and weights. Experienced local poachers were hired and supplied by the syndicate with firearms and ammunition. The syndicate would commonly buy or rent the firearms from local police or military posts. One poaching method was to shoot migrating elephants rather than take the risk of entering the protected reserves. The arrest and subsequent interrogation of one skilled poacher—Benson Nkunika—revealed not only the existence of the syndicate but also the involvement of corrupt ZAWA staff and the warden of a national park. The killing of elephants in close proximity to the ZAWA base at the park supported Nkunika's claim that ZAWA was involved. Official corruption among wildlife officials was not a new development. The Zambian government has previously acknowledged incidents of official involvement in elephant and rhino poaching among the police and military (EIA 2015b).

The poaching operation involved several small groups of four to five local hunters working in and around the parks to supply ivory to Zambian middlemen who, in turn, bribed local officials for protection. The middlemen would then supply the ivory to the Chinese buyers. The use of local Zambian middlemen for this task helped insulate the Chinese traffickers. Local Chinese businesses were sometimes used as collection points for ivory or as meeting places to organize the poaching. Chipata, in eastern Zambia near the Malawian border, became the base for the trafficking group and the first collection point for ivory. From Chipata, traffickers moved the ivory on rural secondary roads across the Zambian border to Malawi's business capital, Lilongwe. The 2002 EIA report and my interviews in 2005 with two ZAWA investigators in Lusaka revealed that a family-run ivory factory called Allena Curios existed in Lilongwe (ZAWA investigators in Lusaka, personal communication, 2005). This locale was eventually raided by the police, yielding an extensive amount of detailed records and receipts implicating numerous poachers operating in the park (including ZAWA game scouts), Allena Curios, and buyers from Asia in this illegal ivory operation. The next step for traffickers was to move the ivory from Lilongwe to Singapore. The ivory was containerized, labeled as stone sculptures, and shipped via a freight company in Lilongwe. The container then moved through Malawi to the Mozambican port of Beira and then to Durban, South Africa, before departing for Singapore (EIA 2002a). Once in Singapore, the ivory would have been shipped to its final destinations in Japan and China. My research in northern Mozambique found that it was common practice for poached ivory tusks to be secreted in cargo containers belonging to Chinese timber operations. The likelihood of these containers being searched was low, nearly guaranteeing that the contraband would reach its final market.

Rhinoceros Horn Trafficking

The shipment of highly valuable rhinoceros horn primarily involves Vietnamese criminal syndicates working with South Africans and Mozambicans to facilitate smuggling within and eventually out of Africa to the consumer markets of Asia. Milliken and Shaw's (2012) detailed analysis found that in South Africa, after the poacher obtains the rhino horn, Vietnamese syndicates rely on a network of middlemen (usually South Africans in different roles) to move the product through the transportation chain to the final destination. Once obtained, the horn is quickly transported by poachers, who may change vehicles to avoid detection, to a collection point generally in the vicinity of O. R. Tambo Airport. A network of middlemen couriers and dealers becomes involved in transporting and procuring multiple horns, assessing their quality, providing payment to poachers, and arranging for shipment out of Africa. They may rely on corruption and subversion to bypass government agents at transit points and can have connections with Vietnamese embassy staff willing to smuggle horn. Middlemen are also involved in transporting, packing, preparing fraudulent shipping documents, and bribing security staff at airports or seaports if necessary.

Compared with ivory, the smaller size of rhinoceros horn, the practice of shipping them individually or in relatively small numbers, and access to corrupt diplomats significantly ease the task of the middlemen in moving these items out of Africa. The NGO Save the Rhino (2016b) reported seizure data showing that most rhino horn being smuggled out of Africa to Asia is hidden in passenger luggage or on the passenger's person or it is shipped using express mail services. In 2014, two Vietnamese nationals were found with eighteen rhino horns in their luggage during a layover at Johannesburg's O. R. Tambo Airport (AP 2014). In 2015, a search of a North Korean's car with diplomatic plates in Maputo, Mozambique, resulted in the seizure of 4.5 kilograms of rhino horn (Rademeyer 2015). In the same year, four Chinese nationals were arrested for and subsequently convicted of smuggling eleven rhino horns into Tanzania from Malawi with the items hidden in their vehicle (Reuters 2015). Furthermore, since rhino horn is sought after primarily as a medicine in China and Vietnam, it can be shipped in various forms (rather than as intact horn), depending on its final use as a traditional Asian medicine (TAM). During my research on this issue, I found that some smugglers ship small containers of processed rhino horn ground into a fine powder. The powder is placed into an innocent-looking container and added to luggage before the smuggler boards an international flight with the hope that customs inspectors will overlook the item. Rhinoceros horn has also been cut into smaller slices while still maintaining its value. When the slices are eventually sold for use as medicines, they may be ground or sold as is in their destination market. Finally, intact rhinoceros horn can also be hidden in cargo shipments destined for consumer markets in Asia. This method may rely on falsified documents to hide the identity of a cargo shipment, bribery to obtain legitimate export permits, or inadequate inspection by customs officials. A search of a taxidermy shipment at South Africa's O. R. Tambo Airport revealed 10.5 kilograms of illegal rhino horn (Church 2015).

Mozambique's and Zambia's Roles in Wildlife Trafficking

As previously noted, Mozambique plays a central role in the illegal rhino horn trade in southern Africa. It also provides examples of other types of wildlife smuggling. My research in this region revealed that it is both a source of illegal ivory and rhino horn and a transshipment point through its land border crossings and ports, which facilitate overseas shipments to consumer markets in Asia. The country is also a recipient of bushmeat illegally harvested from several nearby public game reserves for its domestic market. Kruger National Park, Ndumo Game Reserve, Tembe Elephant Park, and Mkuze Game Reserve are all located in provinces adjacent to Mozambique. Ndumo Game Reserve, which borders Mozambique to the north, has been under heavy pressure from commercial poaching operations. Ndumo is separated from Mozambique by the Usutu River. When the water level is low, Mozambican poachers cross the shallows into South Africa to hunt in the reserve. Fleeing with the wildlife was uncomplicated; poachers simply return by fording the river to Mozambique. South Africa's lack of an extradition treaty further hampers efforts at enforcement.

The other technique exploited by wildlife traffickers was to move contraband from South Africa into Mozambique at its border station just east of the city of Nelspruit. Once they crossed the border into Mozambique, they had only about an hour's drive to Maputo and its large harbor. The border control situation was hardly any better at the South African/Mozambican frontier than at the South African/Zimbabwean post described previously in this chapter. When I interviewed South African border control officers at this post, they acknowledged the activities of smuggling networks moving contraband both ways over the frontier. The border fence was once electrified, but the current was turned off for humanitarian reasons to prevent injuries to illegal crossers, primarily migrants. When inspecting the fence line, I saw holes under the fence used by smugglers no more than fifty meters from the legal crossing point. Border guards made only a superficial effort to fill the holes by piling up rocks. Smugglers could crawl under the fencing to enter Mozambique or hand off contraband to waiting confederates. Seizures of ivory or rhino horn were described as mainly the result of luck or the recognition by officials of an individual as a known smuggler (South African border and customs officials, personal communication, March 2005).

The smuggling trail of illegal wildlife within Mozambique is multifaceted with at least three distinct components. One is the movement of ivory and rhinoceros horn from South Africa—namely from Kruger National Park and the game farms and reserves in Mpumalanga Province. The second is the smuggling of wildlife products from Tanzania into Mozambique for final shipment from its harbors at Pemba, Beira, or Maputo. Third is the internal poaching of elephant in the northern part of the country and its subsequent export. Related to all three were the direct connection of the ivory trade to a few legal Chinese-owned businesses and the influence of Chinese wildlife syndicates. Criminal elements have exploited these operations, hiding ivory in containerized legal shipments of timber and other consumer goods destined for China.

My research into this aspect of the trade revealed that in addition to the sea routes, ivory and rhinoceros horn were brought into and out of Mozambique by Tanzanians and even Somalis overland through the northern border. Wildlife products were also trafficked through Zimbabwe or Swaziland into Mozambique before leaving the country. Although Swaziland's wildlife populations were small, the country acted as a conduit for ivory and rhino horn from other parts of southern Africa, including South Africa, Zambia, and Mozambique. The problem was compounded by the large Taiwanese population in the country, some members of which have been repeatedly implicated in the trade (South African SARS officers, personal communication, March 2005).

A similar pattern was also found in Zambia, which had well-established overland and air trafficking routes for ivory into Swaziland and South Africa. Owing to the lack of personnel and/or equipment to search vehicles and the use of remote farm roads, traffickers need not be all that creative, though some methods are unusual. The EIA (2002a) reported that one ivory carver smuggled his curios inside spare truck tires that were slit open. Others placed ivory in bags and hid them in the bottom of water tanks. Some traffickers simply label the boxes as containing innocuous items such as toys or gifts and hope they will not be searched at borders.

Reptile and Bird Trafficking

As noted in Chapter 1, large volumes of live wildlife and their parts are legally shipped domestically and internationally every year. The sheer scope of the trade and the diversity of the species present significant challenges for government wildlife inspectors. When legal wildlife products are sent from source countries to consumer nations, customs documents and sometimes CITES permits are required to ensure the legitimacy of the shipment. Participants in illegal live reptile and bird trade, mainly the domain of smaller networks and individuals rather than large criminal syndicates, employ various techniques to avoid detection. Reptile and bird traffickers have the advantage of moving a physically smaller product compared with those who deal in ivory or bushmeat. Reptiles and birds destined for overseas pet or even exotic food markets need to be shipped alive, requiring timely delivery methods. A proven technique involves packing the animals in cartons, mislabeling the contents, and shipping via express mail services that, with luck, will not be searched by customs officials. This allows the wildlife to reach their destination quickly and alive. Another technique is to label the shipments as reptiles or birds but intentionally misidentify the species as one that is legal to export—a look-alike species—or to forge the export paperwork, which may include CITES permits (Warchol, Zupan, and Clack 2003). Other times, smaller numbers of protected species may be hidden in larger shipments of species that are legal to move. These methods have met with success in the past, as customs agents may have difficulty identifying the species or detecting forged permits. Some South African authorities have estimated that as many as 50 percent of CITES permits are fraudulent (South African Police Service Endangered Species Protection Unit [SAPS ESPU] director, personal communication, 2003).

Another common method is for traffickers traveling by air to conceal the animals either in their luggage or on their person. This more daring method may involve the traffickers secreting the reptiles on their body in specially designed undergarments with numerous pockets. Reptile and bird smugglers have been apprehended wearing custom-made cloth belts containing a series of sewn-in pouches, each containing a live animal. Other methods include reptiles being placed in pillowcases, cartons, or jars, or in hollowed-out objects, and then hidden inside luggage (Christy 2008; USFWS 2012; U.S. Department of Justice 2015a, 2015b).

Tiger Trafficking in Asia

Once a poacher kills a tiger, the animal can be processed in the field in about three hours. Poachers remove the pelt, bones, and any other valuable parts. The next requirement is to covertly move this extremely valuable species to the consumers. Traffickers may utilize women, who are considered less likely to be searched, to begin the movement of the contraband to the market (Guynup 2014). Tiger parts may be quickly sent to a domestic market for retail sale or shipped across several international borders to a final consumer nation. For example, the UNODC (2016) stated that tigers poached on the island of Sumatra may be trafficked north to Malaysia, Myanmar, Thailand, and finally to China. As with ivory and rhino horn, tiger trafficking may involve an array of individuals in a network that manages storage, packing, shipping, bribery, and marketing.

While the majority of wild tiger parts are destined for China for use as traditional medicines, there is also a market for the skins as luxury and culturally significant items (ceremonial clothing) in other parts of Asia. According to research by the EIA (2006), tiger products taken from India often are transshipped using ancient trading routes through Nepal in numerous small consignments or mixed in with legal cargo shipments. A small portion of the tiger skins remain in Nepal to meet local demand, while the remainder, along with body parts, continues onward to China. Smugglers can ship individual tiger pelts simply and relatively safely by hiding the skins in their personal luggage. Compounding the problem, the EIA found a serious lack of enforcement at border stations as well as cooperation by corrupt officials. Further contributing to the trade are cases in which a trafficker is apprehended but a follow-up investigation is not conducted to determine if this arrest represents an ongoing operation or criminal network of tiger smugglers. This is partly because wildlife offenses are considered lower priority than violent or other property crimes. Even in cases in which charges are filed, it may take many years before the case is brought to court. The end result is that smugglers have little to fear when moving these highly valuable wildlife products to buyers.

Summary: Corruption as the Necessary Facilitator

As noted earlier, a major contributor to the illegal trade in wildlife is corruption in the source, transit, and consumer nations. Although the term has different definitions, corruption occurs when a government official accepts something of value for granting a service of some kind to the provider. Corruption is commonly though not exclusively associated with organized crime. Corrupt practices include bribery of officials to get them to act in a specific manner, nepotism in hiring, or the illegal use of public resources for personal benefit. Gideon Nkala's (2003) analysis concluded that official corruption affects nearly every society to varying extents; however, it has permeated and become entrenched in some African nations. This has influenced the behavior of government officials at many levels, ranging from police officers to game rangers to high-level ministers. I encountered petty corruption on numerous occasions among low-level bureaucrats during research projects in East Africa and southern Africa. Local police, game rangers, park staff, and border officials solicited bribes and pocketed payment for entry visas or goods.

Corruption in Africa has been attributed to several possible causes. One argument is that certain behaviors that are considered corrupt by Western standards are not viewed that way in Africa. Rather, various manners of exchange of goods are based on long-standing customs or social practices in Africa. As Western practices have become institutionalized in Africa, they have come into conflict with old habits that are used to justify granting favors for money. Corruption has also been defined as a contemporary problem that developed in response to the loss of old values during the colonial and subsequent liberation periods. These events had a dramatic influence on African society, disrupting traditional ways, and resulted in new adaptations to the political and economic instability that followed. Corruption can also be viewed an age-old problem affecting all societies to some extent.

The illegal wildlife trade relies on corrupt officials to facilitate poaching and smuggling. This involves government officials at all levels who are actively involved in the illegal trade or who refuse to prevent conservation offenses in exchange for bribes. Research by the EIA (2015b) concluded that corruption and the illegal wildlife trade are so severe that they inhibit a nation's ability to attain sustainable development goals related to preserving its ecosystems. The EIA noted that corruption includes the use of false CITES permits, providing illegal wildlife products as gifts to government officials, bribery of border enforcement officials, theft of wildlife products from government stockpiles, and government agents tipping off offenders about their future enforcement actions.

During the first period of rife elephant poaching in Africa, in the early 1970s in East Africa, Martin Meredith (2003) described instances of corruption. He found that members of Kenya's game department were complicit in the ivory trade, along with government officials. Kenya, a model of relative postcolonial success and stability in East Africa, has long experienced rife corruption, including payment of petty bribes to civil servants, government job patronage based on tribal affiliation, and large-scale theft and fraud

(Wrong 2009). The EIA's research in neighboring Tanzania revealed that some members of that country's game department were directly complicit in poaching and trafficking in ivory and in selling ammunition to offenders. A Tanzanian minister of Parliament was also found to have been involved in moving ivory out of the country (Thornton 1997). Other research focusing on southern Africa illustrated how corruption was affecting wildlife conservation. Simon Pillinger's (2003) study found that border officials in Swaziland were very susceptible to bribery because of their extremely low salaries. Swaziland, whose rhinoceros populations were severely impacted by poaching, serves as a transshipment point for moving wildlife out of the region to overseas markets. Orenstein (2013) described the bold theft of three tons of ivory tusks from a Zambia Wildlife Authority storage vault in 2012. Two Zambian game scouts were arrested for the offense, which involved a Chinese ivory buyer.

Jenni Irish and Kevin Qhobosheane (2003) claimed that corruption has permeated nearly all levels of society in South Africa, including both public- and private-sector employees. For example, these groups commonly produce illegal identity documents—passports, work permits, and residency documents—for Chinese crime syndicates that are involved in their use and sale. These authors also found that the South African Police Service has been affected by corruption; officers committed crimes that even included providing names of witnesses to offenders and allowing the false registration of vehicles. Corruption in South Africa is especially problematic given its large wildlife populations combined with porous borders, high-quality transportation infrastructure, well-organized criminal gangs, and markets for illegal goods. On numerous occasions, I was told by interviewees of instances in which local police in South Africa would rent their firearms to poachers for temporary use. Rademeyer (2012) argued that in South Africa, conservation officials are prone to establish close relationships with professional hunters, whose businesses contribute to the national economy, fostering favoritism. Many examples of South African game rangers' participation in the illegal wildlife trade have been found, involving everything from taking petty bribes to allowing subsistence bushmeat hunters to enter a protected area to shooting rhinoceros or other large animals and trafficking in the products (Warchol and Johnson 2009). My research into the illegal avian trade in South Africa revealed another form of corruption by officials. Legal shipments of birds into South Africa are required to be quarantined for thirty days before being collected by their new owners. During this period, some birds will die and will be disposed of by the quarantine officers. However, some corrupt quarantine officers will overreport the number of deaths and sell live birds for their own profit (Warchol, Zupan, and Clack 2003).

The EIA (2015b) has uncovered cases of corrupt border officials in both Africa and Asia working together to facilitate the movement of illegal wildlife products in return for bribes. Syndicates simply view this as a necessary cost of conducting their very lucrative business. The presence of this problem is something that is not denied among the governments, and its extensiveness represents a significant challenge for anti-corruption units. Yet it needs to be factored in when solutions are developed to stem the illegal trade in wildlife.

4

Explaining Wildlife Crime

Causes of the Illegal Trade in Wildlife

One may speculate about the causes of crime and deviant behavior, questioning why someone commits an illegal act, especially when that act seems to defy explanation or logic. With regard to wildlife crime, one wonders why individuals would kill or remove an endangered or threatened species from its habitat, further reducing the population and imperiling its prospects for survival. These crimes might be attributed to greed or poverty, or might just be done for the thrill of killing an animal or committing an illegal act. While all of these factors can and often do influence the illegal trade in wildlife, there is not one simple explanation for this offense. Rather, the illegal trade in wildlife is driven by a myriad of influences that are the product of historical developments, opportunities, and consumer trends. In the previous chapter, we examined the different types of offenders and their operations in the illegal wildlife trade. Using examples primarily, though not exclusively, from Africa, this chapter focuses on *why crimes are committed against wildlife*. The discussion includes a description of political and historical developments that altered access to land once used for resource harvesting, the findings of contemporary descriptive research, and the results of theory-based approaches to explaining offender behavior—that is, the application of contemporary criminological explanations to the phenomenon of wildlife crime.

To better understand the influences on the causes of poaching and the illegal trade in Africa, we begin by examining the establishment of wildlife conservation laws and game parks. During the most recent European colonial period in Africa, starting in the late nineteenth century—what became known as the Scramble for Africa—the Germans and British established the first formal game laws and protected areas in their East African and southern African colonies. These developments had an immediate impact on local communities, which had a long tradition of relying on wild game as a food source and the regions as homelands. With the advent of new poaching laws, the economic, social, and cultural values of the native populations often conflicted with those of the Europeans who enacted this legislation (Steinhart 1989).

With the end of the colonial period in the twenty years after World War II, some of the newly independent African nations addressed the issues of land and wildlife. Returning land to its former residents and providing access to the game were key political issues for the rural citizens in many nations during this transition to self-governance. While land access and redistribution became a popular political promise for some future leaders, the realization of the value of land and game as a source of revenue and for granting favors sometimes won out over the demands of the citizenry. One end-result was a view that game reserves offer few if any benefits for rural residents. To this day, issues of access to land that has been designated a protected area are commonplace (Warchol and Harrington 2016). Though these political developments are not the primary driver of poaching and the illegal trade, they have contributed to the expansion of these wildlife offenses in Africa.

The next section of this chapter reviews a selection of research findings based on descriptive studies within the framework of some of the main types of wildlife crimes in different geographic regions. Descriptive social science research, while not focused on testing formal theoretical explanations, still helps identify and detail the structure of the illegal wildlife trade and the characteristics of those that facilitate the trade. This research reveals that opportunistic individuals, informal and formal criminal networks, and sometimes corrupt officials are involved in poaching and smuggling. What influences these actors to commit wildlife offenses includes but is not limited to the need for food, medicines, or fuel; resentment over restricted access to protected areas and their wildlife; and a desire to exploit soft targets for money. Descriptive studies also reveal that the illegal trade is facilitated by government corruption, ineffective guardianship of the resources, and high levels of consumer demand for wildlife. The findings from this kind of descriptive rather than explanatory research can often act as a basis for theoretical analyses of a social problem, which, in turn, serve as a foundation for developing solutions to the problem.

The final section of this chapter examines contemporary research that has applied criminological theory to various aspects of the illegal wildlife trade. The application of criminological theory to wildlife offenses is a relatively new practice within the discipline. Theory testing is used to identify the correlates and, one hopes, the eventual causes of an event. Criminologists interested in the study of green or environmental crimes have broken new ground by using theory to explain offender behavior. This research, in turn, can help guide the development of policies to prevent or control wildlife crime. Given that the application of criminological theory to the study of wildlife crimes is relatively recent, a somewhat limited range of approaches is available in the literature. These include the use of neutralization, rational choice, and routine activities theory (Eliason 2003a; Herbig and Warchol 2011; Lemieux 2014) to examine offender behavior. Yet this sort of approach has resulted in fully implemented programs that use situational crime prevention techniques to prevent poaching (Fei et al. 2016). As more interest develops in this area, additional theoretical approaches can be considered and applied to the phenomenon.

The Scramble for Africa:
Colonialization and Conservation

As a foundation for understanding some of the underlying causes of the illegal wildlife trade, it is useful to examine when and why the game laws and reserves were created and their subsequent impact on local populations that lived on the land and/or relied on wildlife as a food source. The focus here is during the most recent colonial era in East Africa and southern Africa, home to large populations of wildlife that periodically faced serious threats from poaching. Africa experienced several periods of colonization, dating back as far as 570 BC and involving Europeans, Arabs, and Malays seeking new territories and their valuable natural resources. The first game laws and conservation areas in sub-Saharan Africa were established during the last period of European colonialization of Africa, which began in the 1880s and ended during the two decades following World War II (Guest 2004).

While many European nations, including France, Portugal, and perhaps most notoriously Belgium, had colonies in Africa during the final period of colonization, the early concerns about wildlife and land were primarily attributed to two nations—Germany with its control of East Africa, and Great Britain with its colonization of much of southern Africa, both areas with very large game populations and rich agricultural land. Interestingly, their idea for protecting game and wilderness areas was influenced in part by developments in the United States that resulted in the establishment of Yellowstone National Park in 1872 (Gißibl 2006). A realization that these resources should be managed would eventually lead to early conservation efforts in Africa. Before this colonial period, hunting had been a necessity

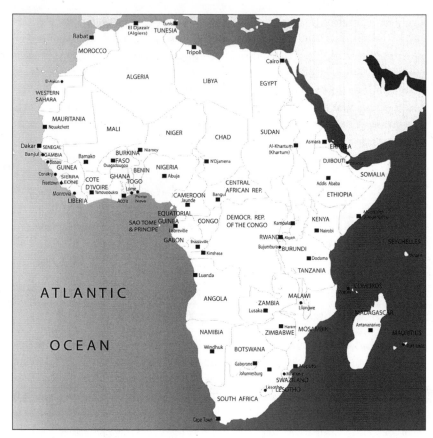

Map of the African continent. (© Fotosearch.com [www.fotosearch.com].)

for millennia (Donovan 2013), with game, if it was controlled at all, falling under the nominal authority of village or tribal chiefs. Not too much is known about the existence of game conservation practices during this period of African history. What can be garnered from the historical record reveals that wildlife was viewed as an important resource. It was regularly used as a food source in hunter-gatherer communities, but not to the extent of threatening the extinction of species. This was due in part to small human populations, primitive methods of hunting that did not necessarily result in the taking of large numbers of game animals, and a willingness of entire villages to relocate to new areas when local resources began to be depleted. This commonsense practice allowed wildlife populations to recover. It is also argued that precolonial African societies over time developed a basic understanding of their local ecosystems. This included knowledge of animal reproduction rates, sustainable rates of taking game animals, and appropriate methods of hunting (Murombedzi 2003).

Clark Gibson (1999) concluded that during the precolonial and colonial era in the former British colony of Northern Rhodesia (Zambia), wildlife was part of both the diet and the local economy as a valuable commodity. Yet this may have not been the case everywhere on the continent. Jonathan Adams and Thomas McShane (1992) noted that anthropological research done in Zaire found that indigenous people acted like Westerners with regard to their use of the land and its resources. The environment was necessary for survival, and little effort was made to limit the impact on the environment until it became obvious that the resource was in jeopardy. Nevertheless, we may conclude that these communities developed a strong connection between human populations and local ecosystems that were sources of critical resources. This resulted in knowledge of and concern for wildlife and land, though it did not necessarily lead to any formal conservation laws. An interesting aspect of the later part of the precolonial period was the flourishing trade in ivory, which was in great demand as a commodity for a global market. Ivory was *the* most important commodity produced in Africa. The control of ivory and elephant hunting was the domain of African chiefs, giving them influence, money, and control (Gißibl 2006). These early precolonial practices vested local control and management of wildlife and land with tribal leaders. This system provided for protection of the resources and sustainable use by villagers, which, in turn, benefited the local chiefs. James Murombedzi (2003) notes that this approach was contrary to the European model, which relied on bureaucratic and scientific management of the resource with prohibitions on its use codified in law.

The most recent European colonial period, beginning in the 1880s, would eventually include concern for conservation, though for somewhat different reasons than what one may think of today. The focus during much of this period was on the taming of the wilderness to facilitate commercial and agricultural development (Adams 2003) rather than concern over species decline. Before World War II, the abundant populations of wildlife in Africa were not commonly viewed as critically important to preserve in conservation areas. Rather, wildlife was more typically thought of as something to be hunted for sport, a threat to settlers, or competition to livestock due to disease or predation (Gißibl 2006). The idea of protecting some game species would eventually develop over time. This period was later marked by a realization that wildlife can be an important asset for a nation to expand or sustain its economy. This was especially important in some nations when other components of their economy were in decline, whether natural resources for export or consumer products (Gibson 1999).

The practice of sport hunting, which began in Europe, later developed in the game-rich East African colonies. Taking advantage of the seemingly inexhaustible and economically valuable supply of wildlife, including elephants for their in-demand ivory, both trophy and commercial hunting thrived in the region (MacKenzie 1988). This period corresponded with the development of large-scale agriculture and livestock farming, which required the clearing of land and extermination of species considered destructive to crops, livestock, and people. These mainly included large grazers and browsers such as elephant and rhinoceros and numerous big cat species such as lion, leopard, and cheetah. Both of these developments began to impact wildlife populations (Donovan 2013). This situation occurred even earlier in the Cape Colony in southern Africa, where farmers were allowed to kill game on cultivated land. As a result, wildlife populations began to quickly diminish in these colonies (Adams and McShane 1992). Such factors would contribute to the passage of the first game laws and game departments in East Africa and southern Africa—that is, legislation allowing the shooting of certain species that threatened farming and livestock, new administrative agencies to oversee its application, and eventually laws to protect certain species from overhunting.

The German colonial administrators would lead in establishing the first protected reserve in East Africa, in 1896. Bernhard Gißibl (2006) notes that it was based in part on the American idea of preserving wilderness combined with the German concept of the hunting estate controlled by a governor who, in turn, controlled access. The German policy also included the issuing of hunting licenses and enactment of laws that made distinctions between animals to be protected and those deemed vermin. The same practice would be adopted by the British in their colonies in southern Africa. This policy offered the benefits of protecting a renewable resource that generated revenue via hunting licenses. It also brought in the idea of hunting seasons and closed seasons that allowed wildlife populations to recover.

The next development that would have long-term impact on the use of the resource was a view that wildlife, especially big game animals, should be the domain of the wealthy elites for trophy hunting. This perspective would result in additional legislation, which included the development of a licensing system for hunters (MacKenzie 1988) in German East Africa in the late 1890s. While these laws sought to preserve wildlife for current and future generations, they also restricted access to wildlife for indigenous African populations. Hunting changed from a common practice for providing food to an elite form of recreation. Interestingly, these new laws were often of limited duration and scope and could at times be suspended if some wildlife were deemed to be a threat to livestock or agriculture—what was termed *vermin* animals (Gißibl 2006). The British colonial administrators followed suit with the help of an advocacy group called the Society for the Preservation of Fauna and Flora (SPFA). Similar highly detailed restrictions allowed Europeans to hunt game animals; however, Africans were prohibited from doing the same. Yet these new laws did not adequately control hunting by either the colonists or the indigenous Africans. Their complexity made them difficult to enforce, and there was a lack of personnel to monitor hunting in the vast wilderness areas (Adams and McShane 1992).

Over time, the German and British colonists began to notice the declines in not only elephants but also other plains species and big game. The same need to support agricultural development and protect sport hunting that contributed to the game laws would also result in the development of conservation areas in the colonies of East Africa and southern Africa (MacKenzie 1988). The creation of the game parks was initiated in German East Africa, and the British colonies of southern Africa later followed suit. A major impetus for the reserves was to protect a financial resource, including the elephant with its valuable ivory (Gißibl 2006). Additional regulations controlled access to the reserves, established hunting seasons, and addressed the use of firearms. The expansion of game reserves in East Africa and southern Africa, which would continue for decades, was the result of work of notable individuals such as James Stevenson-Hamilton, whose efforts resulted in the establishment of Kruger National Park in South Africa. In the southern colonies, legislation in 1929 in Southern Rhodesia (Zimbabwe) resulted in the creation of four game parks, though with opposition from local farmers, who feared the spread of disease from wildlife to livestock. John MacKenzie (1988) notes that these early game parks were designed mainly for the preservation of wildlife with little or no human access, by either Europeans or Africans. The idea of tourism would develop after World War II when additional public and later private game reserves were developed for *safaris* or recreational trips.

The creation of the game parks often required the problematic practice of relocating indigenous populations off their land, now designated a reserve. This corresponded with an inability of local communities to utilize wildlife, something they had previously done for centuries. Africans were now limited in their ability to continue their subsistence hunting lifestyle (Caruthers 1995). In the local people, these policies fostered both resentment of the parks' existence and more importantly a view that wildlife was no longer a valuable asset. Rather, it was just a liability because of the threat it posed to livestock and farming and therefore not worth protecting. Furthermore, tribal chiefs who once derived power from control of local wildlife and land had now lost that benefit (Gibson 1999). These developments would later contribute to the issue of land claims, common in post-apartheid South Africa, where indigenous peoples have asserted legal claims on parts of game reserves, both public and private, and demands for hunting rights on these lands. Over time there would be a realization of the need to link conservation to an economic benefit for local communities living adjacent to protected areas. This understanding was overlooked in early game policy. The

The entrance gate at Mkhaya Game Reserve in Swaziland.

concept of allowing sustainable wildlife utilization and economic benefits from protected areas would become a contemporary solution to poaching.

The Postcolonial Period

The two decades following the conclusion of World War II in 1945 included the end of the colonial period for many sub-Saharan African nations. Postcolonial Africa would experience dramatic political, social, and economic changes. Peaceful liberation movements and civil wars resulted in independent nations free from British, Belgian, and Portuguese control. This period also affected wildlife conservation policy in interesting and unexpected ways. Following the end of the colonial period, new political leaders emerged in the newly independent nations. One of many issues was land use and access to wildlife, mainly for rural residents. Politicians, notably in Zambia, Zimbabwe, and Kenya, made the popular promise that they would change the game laws and restore traditional hunting rights in areas that had been deemed protected reserves. Gibson's (1999) detailed analysis, however, revealed that after taking office, the new leaders of these nations soon broke their promises, maintaining the existing hunting restrictions and the game parks. In some instances, the game laws were further strengthened to prohibit hunting. The rationale for this policy was purely practical. Like the British and German colonial governments, the new administrations were quick to realize the political and economic benefits of game laws and game parks. Gibson concluded that the new leadership chose to ignore the electorate's widespread demand for hunting and land reform in favor of the status quo, given its ability to generate revenue from sport hunting and act as a source of political power. The control of wildlife, once vested in village chiefs in the precolonial period, was now firmly vested in the government. This meant that it could be used for revenue generation via high-priced trophy hunting licenses and for the doling out of favors or punishment. Hunting rights could be selectively granted to friends or restricted to punish enemies. Furthermore, the government could develop a patronage employment system with jobs in the game departments and reserves.

Perhaps not too surprisingly, there would be little political cost for the governments that chose to pursue this policy of continuing to restrict access to wildlife. Contrary to the view of many in the West, by the second half of the twentieth century, most Africans had little contact with wildlife. It is mainly in rural areas that people in the past relied on hunting for food and also had to cope with the problems of crop damage and dangerous predators. However, the rural dwellers' lack of political influence meant that wildlife became a valuable asset to the new governments. With the restrictions on hunting and the expansion of the game parks, the rural residents would continue to bear the costs of conservation. During this period in parts of Africa, conservation was not primarily directed at saving wildlife for its intrinsic value. Rather, political and economic reasons were driving the policies (Gibson 1999). It would take until the latter part of the twentieth century, with innovative programs like CAMPFIRE and COMACO in Zimbabwe and Zambia, which allowed access to resources in protected areas, for rural residents to again value these lands and their wildlife.

Contributions from Descriptive Research

One approach to research, especially for phenomena that have yet to be studied in great depth, is to first employ descriptive methods. This type of research does not seek to test a theory in an effort identify the correlates and potentially the causes of the phenomenon. Rather, the point of this approach is to begin to contribute to knowledge by describing the subject matter of interest while still using formal social scientific methods. The general goal is to define and describe the structure and nature of the events in question (Bachman and Schutt 2014). Descriptive research on the illegal wildlife trade also helps identify the factors that may be related to the phenomenon, including poaching and smuggling wildlife. While the descriptive criminological research on the illegal wildlife trade is still somewhat limited in quantity, additional information can be gleaned from studies conducted by nongovernmental organizations. The results of both early and contemporary descriptive research on the illegal wildlife trade, whether from academic sources or conservation agencies, serve as a foundation for future explanatory research. The focus of this section is on selected research that helps describe the individuals who illegally hunt and smuggle wildlife. The motivations of these individuals include poaching for food or a subsistence income, economic gain from the sale of high-value wildlife products destined for international markets, extra-legal control of problem or conflict wildlife, medicinal uses, thrills, and trophy hunting. Given the massive scope of the illegal wildlife trade, the review of this research is not intended to be comprehensive but rather highlights findings that describe and compare different aspects of this phenomenon in Africa, Asia, and the United States.

Hunting and Fishing for Subsistence and Profit

Illegal hunting to obtain protein for personal consumption and profit—on both a small and a large scale—is a very common form of poaching in Africa (Robinson and Bennett 2004). This aspect of the illegal trade, commonly known as bushmeat hunting, involves primarily taking mammals, though some marine species and insects are also harvested for food. While Africans have used wild game as a food source for millennia, illegal commercial hunting on protected areas is a more recent phenomenon that began attracting the attention of conservationists in the 1980s. Research revealed that this practice started several decades ago in western Africa and Central Africa in both protected areas and open forests and eventually spread to the public and private game reserves in South Africa, which are a major part of its ecotourism and trophy hunting industries (Pillinger 2003). Factors contributing to the trade were identified as human population increases, poverty, and a desire for profits (TRAFFIC 2002a).

Descriptive research on the illegal bushmeat trade in southern Africa has identified the offenders and their motivations and methods. An analysis of this trade in South Africa, where game is illegally harvested from protected areas, found that it involves an array of offenders, ranging from subsistence hunters who take very limited numbers of animals for personal consumption or sale in the local community to meet daily expenses to larger-scale commercial operations that illegally harvest dozens to hundreds of animals (Warchol, Zupan, and Clack 2003). Informal markets that offer bushmeat to local residents are commonplace in parts of South Africa and Mozambique. Often illegally harvested from nearby game reserves, bushmeat is readily found for sale. It serves a dual purpose as an affordable source of protein for low-income residents and an easy source of revenue for poachers. It is not unusual for subsistence poachers to become for-profit poachers who sell their catch in the community (Warchol and Johnson 2009).

The research on the trade in South Africa identified several factors that contributed to the poaching, including economic need, demand for access to protected areas for hunting and fishing, and ineffective management of game reserves (Pillinger 2003). In one instance in KwaZulu Natal Province, villagers living adjacent to a public game reserve had been demanding hunting rights on the protected area; they tore down a large section of the park's fence to both gain access and make a statement about their presumed rights to the land. Poaching trends were identified in the research, indicating that game was illegally taken before major holidays and before the beginning of the school year. Demand for protein for celebrations and the need to pay for children's school fees were correlated with the timing of poaching incidents. Private game farms were not immune to the problem of bushmeat poaching. Game farms, some of which were small wildlife breeding or ranching operations near Kruger National Park that lacked anti-poaching patrols, were often targeted by subsistence and small-scale commercial bushmeat poachers. The lack of security was simply a cost-saving technique based on the view that the wildlife losses were sustainable (Warchol and Johnson 2009).

Another example of profit-motivated poaching involves abalone, a highly desired shellfish found in protected coastal areas in South Africa's Eastern and Western Capes (WWF 2007). Confirming the conclusions about the impact of the creation of game laws and parks discussed previously, research on the abalone trade in Cape Agulhas National Park revealed that historical use of a resource influenced the illegal harvesting of the species. The park, which includes a marine protected area containing an abalone fishery, was established in 1998. Previously, the fishery had long been used by local communities as a resource for abalone for personal consumption and low-volume sale. Research found that changes in fishing rights and permit allocations contributed to abalone poaching (Raemaekers and Britz 2009); such changes were still viewed as discriminatory even with the end of apartheid in 1994 (Marshall 2002). Prohibited from fishing with the establishment of the park, some local residents rejected the restrictions and continued to access the fishery even though their activities now constituted a criminal offense (Warchol and Harrington 2016). While some abalone is illegally harvested for personal consumption, the majority of the trade is market driven (T. Chen 2012; WWF 2007).

While tiger poaching and the consumer market for African rhino horn and ivory receives considerable attention in the discussion of the wildlife trade in parts of Asia, the region also experiences high levels of illegal hunting for food products, for either personal consumption or local resale (Davies 2005). Unfortunately, little formal research has addressed the problem of subsistence poaching in this region. World Wildlife Fund (2015b), in a report on the greater Mekong region, concluded that wildlife use is extensive, with an estimated 3,700 to 4,500 metric tons being traded and consumed just in Vietnam. What is known is that wild harvested food, including fish, mammals, reptiles, and edible plants, has long been consumed both as a staple of the rural resident's diet and as a delicacy (TRAFFIC n.d.). Furthermore, wildlife products are used for fuel, food, building materials, and salable commodities in many rural communities in Southeast Asia. Research supported by the IUCN determined that many large animals are now at risk in Southeast Asia, owing to the illegal trade and habitat loss (European Association of Zoos and Aquaria 2011).

The problems of illegal hunting and fishing are not limited to Africa or Asia. While poaching for food, profit, and trophies is commonplace within the United States, this offense has received only limited attention from researchers. Yet the existing research provides unique information about American poachers' motivations. Stephen Eliason's (2008) typology of poachers in the western United States examined their behavior and motivations, adding needed detail to the description of offenders and offenses. Some of the motivations found were not commonly mentioned in studies of poachers in Africa or Asia. Among the offenders were trophy poachers, compulsive offenders, and backdoor poachers who hunt on their own land. Studies have also attributed poaching to the need for food (Muth and Bowe 1998) or to resistance to game laws (Eliason 2008). Finally, the thrill of committing a crime and avoiding apprehension has also been identified as a motivation for poaching in the United States (Forsyth and Marckese 1993).

High-Value Species Poaching

While poaching occurs for various reasons, contemporary analyses indicate that market demand for high-value wildlife products is the major driver of this offense (Schneider 2012). Though myriad species are illegally harvested for resale in international markets, a major focus of descriptive research has been on the illicit trade in elephant ivory, tiger parts, and rhinoceros horn. These species are illegally killed for specific parts that are used as both decorative items and traditional medicines. Although these animals make up a very small volume of the total amount of wildlife illegally harvested and trafficked annually, they offer a much greater incentive for those willing to take the risk of hunting and smuggling their products (Lemieux 2014; Warchol, Zupan, and Clack 2003) than snaring plains game for local bushmeat sales. The descriptive research on poaching and trafficking of these species provides additional insight into those motivated by the potential for high profits from products primarily destined for the consumer markets in Asia (Davies 2005; Orenstein 2013). An in-depth investigation of the illegal rhinoceros horn trade by Rademeyer (2012, 2015) resulted in a rich description of the criminal syndicates involved in this crime, including South African

Map of Southeast Asia. (© Fotosearch.com [www.fotosearch.com].)

and Vietnamese nationals, and the participation of diplomats in smuggling operations. Similarly, Orenstein (2013) provided a detailed analysis of the poaching, trafficking, and end users of illegally obtained ivory. Varun Vira and Thomas Ewing's (2014) and Milliken and Shaw's (2012) research into the ivory trade adds to the state of knowledge with a thorough portrayal of the operations of poachers and traffickers in Africa.

The international trade in illegal wildlife includes many other species beyond the well-known mammals. Antony Leberatto (2016) examined the extensive illegal commercial trade in Peru's live wildlife, some of which is destined for overseas markets. Other studies have documented a massive trade in marine species, including shark fin, abalone, and caviar, which involves formal criminal enterprises that often work with local poachers to obtain the desired goods (Hauck and Sweijd 1999; Redpath 2001). These types of wildlife products are smuggled to both local and international consumer markets (van Uhm and Siegel 2016). Studies by nongovernmental organizations also reveal how the poaching of one species affects others that are not being directly targeted. For instance, illegal timber harvesting in parts of Southeast Asia, which causes habitat destruction, represents a significant threat to not only the flora but also the fauna in the region, including the remaining tiger and elephant populations (WWF 2016b).

Conflict Animals

As discussed earlier, an issue common to rural parts of Africa and Asia, in both the developed and developing nations, is conflict animals. These are generally defined as wildlife species that represent a threat to agriculture or human life. They commonly include large grazers such as elephant, buffalo, and hippo and predators such as the large cat species of tiger, lion, leopard, and cheetah. With the creation of the game reserves, it was found that rural residents living near these areas often had to bear the burden of the negative aspects of conservation, which include wildlife leaving the parks and entering local farms and villages. Generally, under conservation law, residents losing crops or threatened by predators are required to contact local game departments. Yet in some cases they take action unilaterally, either driving the wildlife out or killing it. Research conducted in Namibia found that livestock ranchers occasionally face problems with large cats preying on their animals. Ranchers are required by law to report conflict animals to the authorities so they can be caught and relocated, if possible, rather than killed. If such an animal is killed, it needs to be reported and documented by the national government, though this is not always what happens. Viewing these species as little more than dangerous pests, farmers illegally kill and dispose of them. In some rare instances, farmers may take the risk and attempt to sell a valuable cheetah pelt for a profit (Warchol, Zupan, and Clack 2003). At other times the farmer may bait these animals with a poisoned carcass to kill them (Aguilar 2015).

Medicinal Use

The use of traditional medicines produced from wildlife is quite common in Asia and Africa, where there is a strong belief in their effectiveness to cure both physical ailments and social problems and where there is limited access to modern medicines and medical practitioners. Wildlife species, both plants and animals, including some endangered species, are used to create traditional medicines (Lee 1999; TRAFFIC 2002b, 2002c). Two of the more high-profile and most lucrative species commonly poached for the medicine trade are the Asian tiger and the African rhinoceros. Tigers have long been targeted by poachers seeking their body parts for use in traditional Asian medicines. The African rhinoceros is sought for its horn, which is believed to have medicinal properties; increased demand for it in China and, of late, Vietnam has contributed to accelerated poaching in South Africa (Orenstein 2013). An analysis by TRAFFIC (2002b) found that other, less well known plant and animal species, both common and endangered, are also illegally harvested for use as ingredients in traditional African medicines thought to cure both physical and social problems. These species include leopards, vultures, vervet monkeys, the devil's claw plant, a large variety of tree bark, and cycad palms, used by traditional healers in both rural areas and large urban centers, where residents have strong beliefs in traditional remedies and/or lack access to or the ability to pay for modern treatments.

Collecting for Personal Use and Sales

Another aspect of the illegal trade that has been the subject of somewhat limited descriptive research is the poaching of wildlife for personal collections and the live pet trade. This activity involves a range of actors, including trophy hunters, scientists, and individual collectors in search of rare species (Eliason 2011b; Warchol and Kapla 2012). A very small percentage of wildlife in the illegal trade is illegally taken by trophy hunters seeking prime examples of animals or rare species for their collections. This type of poaching is quite risky in Africa, where tourist hunters are required to work with local professional hunters on their safaris. The latter risk losing their license and livelihood for engaging in illegal acts to obtain game species for their clients, such as was claimed in the 2015 case of Cecil the lion. Interestingly, Eliason's (2011a) research indicates that illegal trophy hunting may be somewhat more common in the western United States, often occurring on private land. Lacking a warrant or probable cause, state game wardens are prohibited from accessing private land, making it quite difficult to determine what species has been taken and when poaching occurred.

The second type of collector is the scientist in search of rare specimens. Research revealed that scientists as poachers are likely motivated by the professional desire to add difficult-to-obtain wildlife species, both live and dead, to their personal collections. A study conducted in South Africa showed evidence of their involvement (Warchol and Kapla 2012). Conservation officers reported that foreign scientists were implicated in illegally harvesting rare plants and small reptile species from a nature reserve in the Western Cape. The investigation also found that this had been occurring for many years as the same individuals returned to the reserve in search of additional specimens.

The final type of collector includes individual hobbyists and exotic pet dealers. This group is more commonly associated with the large-scale reptile and bird trades found in South America, Africa, and Asia (Schneider 2012; TRAFFIC 2015a). The small size of many reptile and bird species facilitates their shipment out of source nations to destination countries, where they are sold in the exotic pet trade. Research indicated that poachers commonly used express mail companies to ship animals or secreted them in their luggage or on their person. A strong market for African reptiles exists in western Europe, notably Germany and the Czech Republic, where demand is high (Warchol,

Zupan, and Clack 2003). Individual poachers seeking to add to their personal collections have been apprehended along with traffickers supplying animals to dealers for resale. Leberatto (2016) described the flourishing organized illegal trade in birds and reptiles from Peru, and a 2015 report by TRAFFIC described the massive illegal and unsustainable domestic trade in live songbirds in Indonesia fueled by consumer demand for the species as pets.

Contributions from Criminology

The earliest explanations of criminality attributed aberrant behavior to the influences of supernatural forces on humans. As these views were dismissed over time, an interest in a scientific approach to studying crime led to the emergence of the field of criminology, which focuses on crime, criminals, and criminal behavior (Hagan 2017), relying on formal explanations or theories based on scientific approaches to allow us to be more precise in explaining a phenomenon of interest. Criminologists are interested in identifying the factors that lead to criminal behavior. The initial step is to discover the correlates of crime—that is, those factors linked or related to the phenomenon of interest (Walsh and Ellis 2007). The next objective is to attempt to determine the actual causes of crime, a more difficult challenge than identifying the correlates. This is the role of criminological theory. Social scientific theories allow criminologists to apply formal research methods to the study of criminal behavior. These include the collection and analysis of valid and reliable data. A social scientist studying wildlife crimes, for example, may observe relationships in the analyzed data that are stated in the theory, such as a positive correlation between poverty rates and incidents of subsistence bushmeat poaching. If these are consistently present, they support the theory. If not, they serve to falsify the theory.

The increasing amount of empirical research on the illegal trade grounded in criminological theory is one of the more positive developments in this area. An emerging subfield of criminology known as *green or conservation criminology*, which focuses on crimes affecting the environment, including humanity and animals (Beirne and South 2013), serves as a foundation for theory-based research on these natural resource offenses. The application of theory to explain the causes of one type of green crime—the illegal trade in wildlife—has steadily increased, not only contributing to the literature but also facilitating policy makers' ability to develop solutions to the problem. This final section examines a group of theories of crime that have been applied to better understand various offenses making up the illegal trade in wildlife in the United States and Africa, including poaching and trafficking of wildlife.

Neutralization and Focal Concerns Theories

One explanation eventually applied to poaching developed out of the study of delinquency. Gresham Sykes and David Matza (1957) theorized that individual members of delinquent subcultures are also part of a larger and more conventional culture of law-abiding citizens (Hagan 2017). The researchers concluded that offenders are well aware of the norms and values of the larger conventional society and also know that their behavior is wrong. Offenders employ what are known as *neutralization techniques* to allow themselves to overcome any resistance or feelings of responsibility for their criminal actions (Sykes and Matza 1957). These techniques of neutralization include denying responsibility for their actions, denying injury to the victim, justifying harm to the victim, condemning those who condemn the offenders, and appealing to the higher loyalties of their subculture. Craig Forsyth (1993a) and Stephen Eliason and Richard Dodder (1999) applied the theory to better understand deer poaching in the United States. They concluded that poachers employ the techniques of neutralization to deny their role as criminals, thereby reducing guilt among offenders and mitigating their responsibility. The theory was subsequently used in a study of Canadian poachers that revealed how illegal hunting became part of the community's social structure (McMullan and Perrier 1997, 2002). By employing these neutralization techniques, poachers are able to accept their own actions as justifiable.

In a somewhat similar approach applied to the study of delinquency in Boston, anthropologist Walter Miller argued that people in the lower social classes tend to have a different set of what he termed *focal concerns*. These were defined as "features or aspects of a subculture that required constant attention and care" (Williams and McShane 2010, 100). Focal concerns represent the values that encourage members of lower-class subcultures to engage in delinquency. These include trouble, toughness, smartness, excitement, fate, and autonomy, with trouble being a main feature of the lower-class life (Hagan 2017). These values represent the guiding principles for what Miller termed the *hard-core lower class* (Walsh and Ellis 2007). Craig Forsyth and Thomas Marckese (1993) applied Miller's focal concerns theory to their study of poachers in Louisiana. Miller contended that crime and delinquency is a function of lower-class culture, which maintains its own unique value system in response to economically disadvantaged neighborhoods (Miller 1958). Applied to American poachers, the theory supported long-standing subcultural norms and views about the conflict between game wardens and hunters (Forsyth and Marckese 1993).

General Deterrence and Rational Choice Theories

The concept of general deterrence is based on the view that offenders are rational actors who weigh the costs and benefits of their personal actions, including crimes. Therefore, it follows that the state can design sentencing practices that will deter potential offenders from committing crimes. Punishing an offender serves as a lesson for the rest of the members of society should they also choose to violate the law. Eleanor Milner-Gulland and Nigel Williams (1992) applied general deterrence theory to rhinoceros poaching in Africa. They found that poaching operations were based on rational decisions by offenders who examined the behavioral patterns of the desired wildlife and the game ranger charged to protect the animals.

A related approach to explaining crime is also based on the idea that offenders act rationally by calculating risk and reward. This perspective led to the development of rational choice theories, which advanced the simple general and specific deterrence models set forth by Cesare Beccaria (1963). These theories also dismiss the idea of the irrational or senseless criminal act. Furthermore, they propose that offenders do not always make the right choice when considering how to act, and their calculations and strategies vary on the basis of the different types of offenses (Bernard, Snipes, and Gerould 2010). For example, someone poaching bushmeat in a private game reserve will operate quite differently from an abalone poacher working for a criminal syndicate. The solutions to crime, according to rational choice adherents, is to make crimes riskier to commit, require greater effort, and result in fewer benefits to the offender. The idea of situational crime prevention developed as the policy implication from rational choice theory. It focuses not just on the offender but on the physical and social environment where the crimes occur (Clarke 1997). Prevention techniques should therefore be tailored to fit each crime. A criticism of this approach is that it merely results in crime displacement: that is, wildlife poachers will simply target another game reserve when faced with crime prevention efforts. However, the research has disputed this claim, arguing that although displacement occurs, it is neither complete nor serious (Bernard, Snipes, and Gerould 2010).

Situational crime prevention has fostered considerable interest among researchers working to reduce and prevent poaching. Corné Eloff and Andrew Lemieux (2014) explored the problem of rhinoceros poaching in South Africa's Kruger National Park in the context of opportunity theory. The authors contended that offenders who act rationally in their decision to hunt illegally might be deterred if access to the park was made significantly more difficult, rendering it a less desirable location for hunting. Relying on a similar theoretical approach, Lemieux et al.'s (2014) research on poaching in Uganda concluded that variation in the intensity and efficiency of ranger patrols in a national park influenced the activity of poachers. Stephen Pires, Jacqueline Schneider, and Mauricio Herrera (2016) analyzed parrot poaching in Bolivia in the context of situational crime prevention theory, examining how the organization of offenders and the illegal markets for avian species help foster the crime. Advancing the research in this framework, Schneider (2012) used a market reduction approach, concluding that a solution to the illegal trade can be found by focusing on the opportunities that place wildlife at risk of exploitation.

Routine Activities and Opportunity Theory

Related to rational choice theory is the routine activities approach (Cohen and Felson 1979), which asserts that crime is opportunistic and dynamic in nature. Routine activities are defined as "the day to day activities that characterize a particular community. In disorganized communities, the routine activities are such that they practically invite crime" (Walsh and Ellis 2007, 66). The theory is based on three key components: motivated offenders, suitable targets, and the lack of capable guardians for those targets. According to the theory, for crime to occur, there must be a convergence of the three components. *Motivated offenders* are the opportunistic criminals commonly present in socially disorganized communities. *Suitable target* refers to the value or desirability of the target, including access, visibility, and physical size. *Capable guardianship* refers to the amount of protection afforded the target by a person such as a law enforcement officer or physical deterrent such as a fence or security system. Crime rates will vary on the basis of changes in capable guardianship and suitable targets (Felson 2006; Felson and Cohen 1980).

The theory is based in part on the rational choice model (Cornish and Clarke 1987), one of whose core assumptions is that individuals make rational decisions to commit crimes (Walsh and Ellis 2007). They weigh the benefits and liabilities associated with crime before deciding to commit the act. The routine activities approach, however, views the offender as only one component of the crime. It also considers two other key factors—guardianship and targets—that contribute to the crime equation. The approach is premised on crime occurring in a social system (Winslow and Zhang 2008), where criminals feed on and depend on the patterns of everyday life. It further considers the structural conditions that may explain the distribution of crime in society. Finally, it is not concerned with the personal backgrounds of criminals. Rather, it considers the crime's situational characteristics, the involvement of particular persons or objects, and the target's degree of attractiveness in the context of levels of guardianship (Cohen and Felson 1979). Its focus on the three key elements of the criminal event has led to its extensive application to explain a variety of offenses, including residential burglary (Wright and Decker 1994), domestic violence (Mannon 1998), and urban homicide (Messner and Tardiff 2006). Additional research has expanded the theory to focus on offenders, not just the nature of victimization (Gilbertson 2006; Meith and Meier 1994).

Routine activities theory has been applied to bushmeat poaching in the game reserves in South Africa (Herbig and Warchol 2011). This research revealed distinct variations among poaching events in public and private game reserves. While motivated offenders and suitable targets were readily present at each, variations in poaching were a function of the effectiveness of ranger units and the willingness of reserve managers to maintain proper staffing levels among rangers and monitor their work. Eliason (2011b) used the approach in a study of illegal trophy hunting in the western United States, concluding that the convergence of the three components of the theory resulted in opportunities for extensive poaching of trophy animals. Similarly, William Moreto and Andrew Lemieux (2015) relied on the routine activities perspective to explain poaching in East Africa, advancing the theory to include poaching hardware as proxy offenders. Finally, a study of abalone poaching in South Africa through the lens of routine activities theory found that the effectiveness of ranger units and ease of access to the protected game reserves strongly influenced poaching rates (Warchol and Harrington 2016).

Other contemporary analyses of wildlife crime have adapted the CRAVED (concealable, removable, available, valuable, enjoyable, and disposable) model of theft, which is based on rational choice and routine activities. CRAVED was used to explain the theft preferences that made certain goods more desirable to thieves. These goods had the attributes of being concealable, removable, available, valuable, enjoyable, and disposable. The research revealed that avian poaching is mainly due to the accessibility and abundance of the desired species. Pires and Clarke (2011, 2012) found that avian poachers, who are commonly low-income local residents, preferred to poach the readily available and accessible species even though they provided less profit compared to rare and more valuable species sold in open markets. This form of opportunity poaching occurred more frequently when the birds, the hunter, and the market converged in a manner that allowed an efficient and inexpensive process for capture and sale. Similar observations were noted in a study by Gohar Petrossian and Ronald Clarke (2013) in nations with an illegal commercial fish trade. Their findings suggested that such trade was likely to occur in countries that were in close proximity to the resource and offered the opportunity to market the illicit harvest in ports with commercial fish processing plants.

Conflict Criminology

A final theoretical approach is conflict criminology, which came to prominence during the 1960s and mid-1970s—a period of considerable political and social unrest in both the United States and Europe. This time was also marked by interest in disenfranchised classes or groups in society, often defined by their behavior, some of it criminalized. The origins of the conflict theories of crime are generally traced to Marx, whose views were refined and advanced by numerous scholars before and during the emergence of conflict criminology. As the name implies, conflict theories reject the idea that society's laws are formed by a consensus among the different groups in society. Rather, the theories hold that societies are better characterized by conflict, which, in turn, influences the creation of laws. Specifically, societies consist of different groups with different priorities competing to advance their interests. These groups vary in terms of wealth, political influence, and size. They compete in society to advance their own interests, realizing that they need the power of government to attain their goals. The more powerful the group, the more likely it will be to assert its influence on the law for its own benefits, but often at a cost to the other competing groups. Therefore, according to the conflict perspective, the law reflects what is important to the powerful and influential groups in society. Another way to think of it is that the powerful in society are able to use the law to ensure that their values are legal and to criminalize the actions of others. This is done in the legislative process, where groups struggle for control of state power to protect their interests (Bernard, Snipes, and Gerould 2010) and are able to define crimes via their exercise of political power (Williams and McShane 2010). Another focus of conflict theories is on economic conditions attributed to capitalism. These radical theories contend that capitalism results in the development of socioeconomic classes and a resulting income inequality, which is identified as a cause of crime. In order to survive, the economically disenfranchised resort to alternative means to acquire that which is needed for their survival. In our area of interest, the impoverished in rural Africa kill game as a source of food—an act defined as criminal by the ruling class.

The conflict theories may hold promise for identifying the correlates and causes of some types of wildlife crimes. When examining the creation of the game laws, game departments, and national parks, one can see the influence of politically and economically powerful groups, as far back as medieval England and the colonial era in East Africa and southern Africa. The restrictions on hunting game animals illustrate the conflict between the indigenous Africans and the colonists and later, during the independence period, the conflict between rural residents and the ruling classes in Africa.

Summary: Why It Is Done

The global illegal trade in wildlife is driven by a wide range of complex, contributing factors. The purpose of this chapter was not to present a comprehensive and conclusive explanation of why this crime occurs. Rather, it was to examine several major factors that have contributed to the crime. The establishment of the protected areas and corresponding game laws in Africa during the colonial period of the nineteenth and early twentieth centuries had both intended and unintended negative consequences that are still being addressed today with community conservation programs. These early efforts at protecting wildlife and their habitat were not made for the sake of preserving game for their intrinsic value. Rather, they were made to protect an economic asset valuable to the German and British colonists in East Africa and southern Africa. In some instances, they required the relocating of indigenous Africans off their lands while also preventing them from accessing the game they once commonly utilized as a food source. The negative impact of these developments was not necessarily mitigated with the end of the colonial period. Some of the new African leaders, realizing wildlife's political value, decided to go beyond keeping the game laws in place, strengthening them to further restrict local use of the wildlife resource. This contributed to current views about the value of game reserves by local communities.

The descriptive research by criminologists and nongovernmental conservation organizations on the illegal trade adds to a better understanding of wildlife crime, including the offenders and victims. This type of research is designed to describe the phenomenon of interest rather than attempt to precisely identify its correlates or causes. For instance, the descriptive research provides details about the species that are targeted, the different types of poachers and their motivations, the techniques used to traffic wildlife, the impact of this crime on ecosystems, and the consumer markets for wildlife. While such research is not intended to formally explain why this crime is occurring, it serves as a necessary foundation for subsequent theory-based analyses. This steadily expanding body of scholarship falls under the relatively new area of *green criminology*. Over the last fifteen years, several theoretical approaches have been applied to the illegal wildlife trade to better understand its causes and develop solutions to control and prevent the problem. Somewhat older theories originally used to explain delinquency, property, and violent crime in mainstream criminology have been applied to the study of poachers in the United States. More recently, rational choice, routine activities, and opportunity theories have been used to analyze poaching in Africa and South America. This research has helped reveal where poaching is likely to occur. An interest has also developed in applying situational crime prevention to improve enforcement efforts. The contemporary research in this area offers considerable promise in developing techniques to improve ranger effectiveness in both preventing poaching and apprehending offenders.

5

Consumers of
Protected Wildlife

The End Users of Wildlife

If a species of flora or fauna can be used as food, a pet, medicine, decoration, clothing, or building materials, it will have a value and likely be consumed. Whether sourced in Africa, Asia, or the Americas, wildlife is sold in domestic markets and exported overseas to meet demand from international buyers. While legal wildlife products are regularly used around the world, the supply can be finite if not properly managed to ensure sustainable use. This requires biodiversity monitoring and smart regulation to balance consumer demand with protection of the resource from overharvesting. The illegal component of the wildlife trade must also be controlled via enforcement efforts directed at the participants and protection of the exploited species.

The previous chapters examined the structure of the illegal wildlife trade, treaties and legislation, explanations of its possible causes, and the nature of illegal markets, primarily in Africa though with reference to other geographic regions for comparison. Operating within the markets are the poacher and the middleman, two of the three key actors necessary for an illegal market to function. The final participant in the illegal trade is the *end user*, or consumer of wildlife products. Since the majority of the illegal wildlife trade is profit driven, most species are illegally harvested by poachers for eventual sale in consumer markets in their source nations or for export to overseas end users. A smaller portion is taken for subsistence reasons: for food, for medicine, for fuel, or to eliminate a conflict animal.

The smuggling of illegal wildlife into the consumer markets around the world has been facilitated by the adoption of the same innovations used in legal commerce. Internet sales currently play a crucial role in the global trade in wildlife, along with modern electronic banking systems that facilitate buying and shipping products across national borders. No longer is it necessary for consumers and sellers to meet in discreet locations to make these illegal transactions. The use of the Internet has allowed buyers, or end users, in domestic and foreign markets to order and pay for products online, without any face-to-face contact, and to simply await receipt of the purchase (UNODC 2016).

The main subject of this chapter is the end users and the consumer markets for illegally harvested and trafficked wildlife. Although illegally obtained wildlife is harvested and used in virtually every nation, the focus here is limited to three geographic regions that include major consumer nations of wildlife products, whether smuggled from abroad or domestically sourced. Various aspects of the consumer markets for wildlife products in Asia, southern Africa, and the European Union are described in this chapter to illustrate the structure of these markets. While it would be helpful to provide specific economic values for each of these markets to enhance the descriptions, it is difficult to put a *precise* figure on the amount of illegally sourced wildlife trafficked to consumers in a given nation. Data just from wildlife seizures by law enforcement serve as one, albeit imprecise, measure. Wildlife seizures in a given nation will vary with the ability and interest of law enforcement in focusing on this crime. They are further influenced by the skill of smugglers, retailers, and consumers to conceal the products from detection by the authorities. The available data from governments, TRAFFIC, and other NGOs provide some additional assistance in assessing how much wildlife is shipped to the consumer markets in regions of Asia, Africa, and the European Union.

As a result of high demand for legal and illegal wildlife, China and Japan have become major consumer nations of products imported from Africa. More recently, Vietnam has emerged as a significant consumer of illegal rhinoceros horn. One focus of the chapter is the markets for traditional medicines, rhino horn, and ivory products in these three nations. Other East Asian nations play multiple roles in the wildlife trade, including as source, transshipment, and consumer nations. Malaysia, Singapore, and Thailand have all been listed as transshipment nations for illegally obtained wildlife products destined for China (UNODC 2016). While Africa is often thought of as the supplier of the ivory and rhinoceros horn to the consumer nations in Asia, it also has a thriving domestic market for its locally sourced wildlife products. These include a wide range of species illegally harvested for their value as traditional African medicines, dietary protein, and decorations. The chapter next examines the demand for traditional medicines and bushmeat in southern Africa to illustrate two different domestic consumer markets. Finally, the European Union is a major destination for wildlife products, both legal and illegal (TRAFFIC 2014a). The chapter describes how this region of the world provides a dynamic market for a wide range of wildlife products consumed for food or added to specimen collections. The focus is on the illegal importation of African bushmeat products into the European Union and the market for exotic pets poached from the wild.

The Asian Market: From Traditional Medicines to Decorative Objects

A portion of illegally obtained wildlife products harvested in Africa are destined for the overseas markets of Asia, China being the largest consumer in the region by volume and the leading consumer of illegal ivory (Davies 2005; Shepherd, Compton, and Warne 2007; WildAid 2015b). Japan and, more recently, Vietnam are also prime markets for poached African wildlife, including ivory and rhino horn (Ishihara et al. 2010; Orenstein 2013; Van Song 2003). The demand for wildlife in China involves a wide array of species for used for building materials, decorative and luxury items, pets, medicines, and exotic foods. These include but are not limited to illegally harvested timber, ivory, rhinoceros horn, songbirds, reptiles, tigers, and various marine species (IFAW 2016). The impact of consumer demand in China, and to a lesser extent Japan and Vietnam, for illegally harvested wildlife and their products cannot be understated. Japan has a smaller though well-established strong market for ivory, while Vietnam, due to economic growth, is an emerging market with strong demand for wildlife, including rhinoceros horns for medicinal use and as a luxury good. These three nations alone contribute significantly to the illegal trade because of the large volume of wildlife consumed, which includes the high-profile species of tiger, rhinoceros, and elephant. Without the illegal markets in these nations, the illicit trade in wildlife would not necessarily disappear but would certainly be significantly diminished. As a result, demand reduction efforts in these countries, especially China, would have a great impact on certain species, including the African elephant and rhinoceros. While the wildlife trade in Asia and Southeast Asia is extensive in scope, involving many countries and a tremendous variety of species, the focus in this section is necessarily limited to the illegal markets in these three nations, which have strong demand for elephant ivory, rhinoceros horn, and wildlife used in traditional Asian medicines (TAMs), including tiger parts (Mills 1999).

Consumer demand for wildlife products in China involves both plant and animal species indigenous to Africa and various regions in Asia. A portion of the demand is a function of long-held acceptance of traditional medicines, the desire for exotic game meat from mammals and from reptiles such as the African pangolin and Asian freshwater turtles, and the desire for foods that are considered healthy to consume (TRAFFIC 2016b). The largest consumption of wildlife products is believed to be centered in the southeastern provinces of China. Law enforcement data on wildlife seizures destined for China noted tons of reptiles, plants, timber, and mammals, primarily shipped by overland routes from Southeast Asian nations, where border enforcement is weak (Shepherd, Compton, and Warne 2007). United Nations analyses concluded that both free trade policies resulting from globalization and poor border enforcement facilitated the increase in wildlife trafficking and consumption in Southeast Asia. Cambodia, Laos, and Myanmar have become sources of wildlife, and Vietnam and Thailand serve as transshipment centers for products eventually destined for China. Vietnam, for example, serves as both a consumer country and transit source for illegally obtained wildlife from Africa and other parts of Asia. The transshipped wildlife is commonly destined for the high-demand markets in China. Traffickers often mix wildlife products with legal goods and rely on lax border enforcement to ship their products to market (Davies 2005). Further contributing to the illegal trade are improvements in transportation infrastructure in the region. New and improved airports, seaports, and roads allow more wildlife to be smuggled with little risk of detection by authorities because of weak enforcement efforts (Shepherd, Compton, and Warne 2007). Once at their destination in Southeast Asia, illegally obtained wildlife products are often sold in the open in local markets that also sell legal consumer goods with little concern for enforcement efforts (UNODC 2016). The rampant and often uncontrolled exploitation of wildlife for consumer demand along with habitat loss owing to development were identified as the main causes of species decline in the region.

Traditional Medicines

A portion of the illegal wildlife trade involves obtaining plant and animal products for use as ingredients in traditional Asian medicines (Davies 2005). According to World Wildlife Fund (WWF), traditional medicines are used for health care by an estimated 80 percent of the world's population. Residents of rural and low-income communities may lack access to or the ability to pay for modern medicine and also may have a strong cultural belief in the healing powers of natural remedies (Lee 1999; Schneider 2012). Traditional Asian medicines (TAMs) do not exclusively require endangered or threatened species and there is a legal trade in these products, but some TAMs require parts from protected species as ingredients for specific cures, contributing to poaching in other parts of the world. Unique to the Asian market is the use of several endangered species—bears, rhinoceros, tigers, and lions—for their body parts to produce medicines that supposedly cure a variety of physical and psychological ailments (Mills 1999). Products from bears, including bile, are used as treatments for cancers, burns, sinus problems, and pain (TRAFFIC 1995). While tigers are poached for their pelts, a wide variety of the tiger's other body parts are believed to have curative powers for a range of human psychological and physical illnesses and conditions (Schneider 2012). Rhinoceros horn, whether from the African or Asian species, is thought to have medicinal properties that can cure various maladies (Davies 2005).

Some of the animals most used to create TAMs are bears. There are eight remaining bear species in the world, five of which are found in Asia. The animal is viewed as a near complete drugstore by Chinese traditional medicine practitioners, making live and dead bears quite valuable. Bear parts, including gall bladder, bile, fat, brain, and spinal cord, have been used as cures for over a thousand years in China (Davies 2005). Even some Chinese medical books recommend using bear bile for its medicinal value. These products are used in not only China but also Japan, South Korea, Taiwan, and Macau. The widespread traditional regional beliefs along with habitat loss owing to development, legal hunting, and killing of conflict animals have strongly impacted the Asian species. The Malayan sun bear, for example, which is listed as a CITES I species, is threatened for the previously mentioned reasons in addition to poaching. Interestingly, these bears are poached not only for use in medicines. Their paws are served as a delicacy in restaurants, and their claws and teeth are marketed as decorative or luxury items (Shepherd and Shepherd 2010). While four of the five bear species indigenous to Asia are protected by CITES from being commercially traded, a legal industry of bear farms to mass-produce bile for TAMs has existed in China for more than twenty years (TRAFFIC 1995). Even given this development, illegally harvested parts from brown and black bears are still smuggled into the region from Russia and North America (Davies 2005).

Rhinoceros horn has a long history of use in China as a traditional medicine, dating back as far as two thousand years, though its early use was likely limited because of lack of availability. Contrary to popular belief, it is unlikely that rhino horn was viewed as an aphrodisiac. The horn was initially thought to have supernatural properties, and later medicinal ones, when mixed with other traditional remedies (Orenstein 2013). Rademeyer (2012) found that the Chinese resurgence in the use of traditional medicines in the 1970s was a product of its Maoist Cultural Revolution. The renewed interest in these remedies contributed to significant increases in demand for rhinoceros horns from Africa and other Asian nations. In 1988, Chinese stockpiles of horn were estimated at nearly ten tons of product. The horn is typically ground into a fine powder and mixed with other natural ingredients to be dispensed by traditional healers in Asia. Asian communities in the West have also been known to offer this product to their consumers for a variety of maladies.

While some rhino horn is still smuggled into China, after the country joined CITES, its efforts to register the stockpile and ban the domestic commercial trade in the product have been fairly successful. However, a new market emerged in the early 2000s in Vietnam. Economic prosperity and an expanding wealthy class, combined with a new belief that rhinoceros horn can cure cancer and other less serious illnesses, led to steadily increasing demand for rhinoceros horn. Desire for rhino horn was also due to demand for status symbols among the newly rich. Some horns are displayed as a show of wealth, while others are ground into powder and added to drinks at social occasions, including as a supposed cure for hangovers (Ellis 2013).

As described in Chapter 1, a century of habitat loss, trophy hunting, poaching, and retaliatory killing has resulted in massive population declines of the Asian tiger. According to the International Union for the Conservation of Nature, wild tiger populations have declined by 97 percent since 1900, and about 3,400 animals remain in the wild today (Goodrich et al. 2015). While habitat loss played a role in the decline of the species, in recent decades in India, home to the majority of the world's remaining tigers, tiger losses are attributed mainly to demand for their body parts for traditional medicines and decorative objects. Research by Davies (2005) found that nearly every part of the tiger has an economic value, from the bones to the whiskers, for which the principal consumer market is in China. Tiger claws have sold for $150 USD, and bones, which are used to produce an anti-inflammatory medicine, for as much as $400 USD per kilo in Asia in the late 1990s. A drug manufacturer in Japan produced a tiger penis pill that sold for $27,000 USD per bottle. Tiger parts are not exclusively used in China. Markets for their products also exist in Malaysia and Vietnam (Goodrich et al. 2015), putting additional pressure on the species.

While the tiger population has stabilized of late, owing to conservation efforts, their numbers are precariously low in the wild. As tiger populations declined, making the animals more difficult to find, a new legal trade developed that used the bones of lions as a substitute, with the animals primarily coming from South Africa. Captive or bred lions were being legally killed and their bones exported to Southeast Asia. The available data on this trade are sketchy, but research by Rademeyer (2012) found that hundreds of kilograms of lion bones, along with complete skeletons and dozens of bodies, were exported to Laos in 2009 and 2010.

Although the use of traditional medicines in Asia is unlikely to disappear even with the expansion of modern medicine, it remains important to focus on wildlife conservation efforts related to species used for medicines. This approach can both reduce the pressure on selected species and prevent overregulation or restrictions on TAMs. Lee (1999) notes that in some Asian cultures, wildlife is viewed as a resource to benefit humanity. As a result, some may reject the concept of conservation of species in favor of protecting human health and lives, and they may view efforts at conservation as both foreign and culturally imperialistic. Furthermore, efforts to conserve wildlife used in TAMs can certainly be viewed as a threat to the livelihoods of practitioners in Asia (TRAFFIC 2002b, 2002c). Health care practices are integrated with Asian cultural beliefs, making it very difficult to end the use of TAMs, although some positive changes have occurred with advancements in pharmaceuticals that provide the same results as natural remedies made from endangered wildlife.

Ivory

The use of ivory in mainland China and Hong Kong has a very long cultural history, dating back thousands of years, which has included the development of established carving operations and retail ivory markets (Jackson 2003). Since the late 1990s, there has been much higher consumer demand for precisely carved ivory objects, largely because of increased prosperity and the expansion of the middle class. The cities of Beijing and Guangzhou are historical centers of ivory carving and sale. The raw ivory is taken to carving factories, where skilled artisans, using the equivalent of precision dental tools, produce a wide range of decorative luxury goods. The goods are then supplied to retail stores to sell to consumers (EIA 2000). Over time, China has become the world's largest consumer of ivory. Hong Kong, which has the largest retail ivory market in the world, is a prime destination for visitors from the mainland who seek to purchase the finished products (Denyer 2015). The Chinese ivory market consists of both a legal and illegal component. In accordance with the 1989 international ivory trade ban, Chinese carvers should be using only pre-ban ivory, which is legal to sell on its domestic market. In 2008, China also received permission via CITES to legally buy ivory from a one-time approved sale of ivory from four southern African nations. The problem was that the existing reserves of legal ivory were being restocked with illegal ivory smuggled from traffickers in Africa. The final product was labeled pre-ban or legal to deceive buyers and the authorities. An investigation in Hong Kong revealed that a combination of governmental licensing flaws, corrupt businesses, and customers avoiding permits and smuggling ivory into mainland China contributed to this ivory laundering system (WWF 2015c). The evidence of commingling of legal and illegal ivory for purposes of laundering was that stockpiles of pre-ban ivory had barely

Bags of carved ivory *hankos* and other assorted ivory curios confiscated at the border crossing in Beitbridge, South Africa. The contraband was smuggled into South Africa from Zimbabwe for sale at curio markets.

declined over the last thirty-five years of sales (Denyer 2015). A similar situation was found on mainland China in the late 1990s. Soon after the 1989 ban, legal ivory stockpiles in Guangzhou were reported near exhaustion. Yet ivory, raw and finished, continued to be readily available well after it should have disappeared (EIA 2002a). Police and customs seizures revealed that China had developed into a major destination for smuggled ivory, but the very high consumer demand for ivory and the ability of the market to meet it did not correspond to the expected decline in legal or pre-ban ivory stockpiles (EIA 2000). What happened is that the retail trade in both mainland China and Hong Kong served as a cover for ivory smugglers.

The issue of illegal ivory sales in China may finally be resolved in favor of conservation with an effort that could end the legal trade. In 2015, Chinese president Xi Jinping promised to end the commercial trade in ivory, though no final dates were provided (Denyer 2015). Central to the plan is that China would need to destroy, sell, or (the least desirable option) store the ivory to prevent it from entering the marketplace. Resistance to the policy from ivory carvers and retailers might be overcome by a compensation plan in the form of a government buyback of existing stockpiles (Bale 2015), though a total ban on ivory in China is considered preferable for ending the poaching crisis in Africa. However, keeping the promise, the Chinese government announced a ban on commercial ivory, scheduled to take full effect by the end of 2017.

Before the expansion of China's economy, with its corresponding increased demand for natural resources, including wildlife, Japan was the major Asian destination for a wide range of legal and illegally obtained wildlife products. Japan has long been a consumer of natural resources as a way to maintain and expand its economy. This includes a large market for legally obtained wildlife, including timber products for commercial applications. Japan's need for wildlife is filled by source regions of the world known for their biodiversity, which includes species listed as threatened or endangered, such as the African elephant, reptiles, fish, and plants in demand for medicinal use. The steady growth in Japanese demand over the past several decades and the pressure it has placed on source nations have fostered increased poaching of some wildlife species. This, in turn, results in both risk to the species and more attention to the need for sound conservation and monitoring of the trade to reduce its illegal component (Ishihara et al. 2010).

Before the economic rise of China, Japan was the largest market for ivory in the world. The EIA's (2000) investigation determined that Japan's elephant ivory imports between 1979 and 1989 totaled 2,827 tons. Its analysis concluded that about half of this amount was of suspect origin. As described in Chapter 3, a major shipment of 6.2 metric tons of ivory, destined for Japan but seized in Singapore in June 2002, indicated a resurgence of elephant poaching because of increased demand in Asia. The Japanese consumer market also benefited from two CITES-approved legal ivory auctions from selected African elephant range states. These auctions allowed Japan to legally import nearly 100 tons of ivory from Africa for its large retail market, comprising more than seventy-five hundred ivory retailers (Ishihara et al. 2010). The Japanese consumer demand is principally oriented toward ornate carvings and *hankos*, which are small rectangular or cylindrical ivory blocks. On the base of the *hanko* is carved the owner's personal seal. During my research, *hankos* were regularly offered for sale in the markets of South Africa and seized by customs officials at Tambo International Airport in Johannesburg from Japanese tourists returning home.

Japan's consumer demand for ivory was ultimately considered responsible for the loss of more than 250,000 elephants since 1970 (Thornton 2015). One type of preferred hard ivory suitable for *hankos* and decorative objects comes only from forest elephants in Central Africa. The rampant increase in poaching in Africa—more than 100,000 elephants just between 2010 and 2012—has also included a dramatic reduction in forest elephants. It is estimated that between 2002 and 2013 the population of this species in Africa fell by about 65 percent (Thornton 2015).

Though Japan signed and ratified the CITES treaty in 1980, it has been accused of only weakly enforcing its laws pertaining to the international trade. EIA found that Japan took fourteen years to enact new legislation to

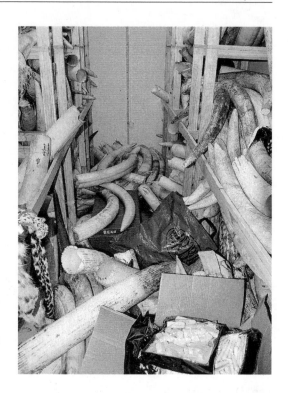

Confiscated tusks and bags of ivory curios confiscated at the Beitbridge, South Africa, border post.

comply with the requirements of CITES as outlined in the treaty. Even with new laws and a monitoring system, Japan remained a major destination for ivory, including imports via transshipment through China, Taiwan, Korea, and even Europe, as shown by numerous seizures in the 1980s and 1990s (EIA 2000). Japan has faced criticism for its long participation in the wildlife trade, specifically regarding rather lax enforcement efforts when it comes to ivory.

Investigations into the legal ivory held by Japan, stemming in part from its purchases from the two legal African sales, found discrepancies in the amount of ivory. EIA research showed that while legal ivory sales were strong after the first auction and should have diminished the country's stockpile, Japan's reported legal ivory holdings were not declining. This was attributed to the inclusion of illegally obtained ivory with the legal ivory and sold as lawfully obtained product (EIA 2000). Japan was also found to be consuming more ivory than its government claimed it held. More recently, Japan has taken steps to improve its enforcement, including its ability to monitor its legal ivory stocks and the registration of dealers. The monitoring system of the illegal trade in ivory products—Elephant Trade Information System (ETIS)—reported that while problems still existed in Japan, its ivory trade enforcement efforts were improving (Ishihara et al. 2010).

Africa's Domestic Market for Wildlife

While much of sub-Saharan Africa is a major source of wildlife products for nations in Europe, Asia, and North America, there is also a thriving domestic market for illegally obtained goods. Poaching of certain kinds of wildlife—bushmeat for protein, flora and fauna believed to have medicinal properties, and rare plants for decorations—is done to supply consumers in the domestic markets of Africa in both rural and urban areas. This section examines selected aspects of the illegal trade within Africa to illustrate different domestic markets. The focus is on the trade in wildlife for traditional African medicines, the rare plant trade, and bushmeat poaching.

African Traditional Medicines

As in China, there is a long-documented tradition among indigenous African health practitioners for using natural remedies made from thousands of plant and animal species (Warchol, Zupan, and Clack 2003). The use of traditional medicines in Africa is based on both cultural and practical reasons. A TRAFFIC study concluded that this "medical system is affordable, accessible, and culturally acceptable. In the past, colonial regimes legislated against the use of traditional medicine and prohibited or restricted the activities of traditional medicine practitioners, largely in an effort to extirpate traditional belief systems" (1999, 1–2). Some estimates state that at least 85 percent of Africans rely on traditional medicines as a primary or supplemental treatment (Kofi-Tsekpo 2003). While many Africans in rural areas may not have access to modern health care or the ability to afford treatment and pharmaceuticals, traditional medicine practitioners can be found readily in almost every village, where they provide a low-cost alternative to Western medicines. For example, in Mozambique there was just one conventional doctor practicing modern medicine for every fifty thousand people but one traditional medicine practitioner for every two hundred people (TRAFFIC 1998, 1999). In South Africa, this individual can be a trained or gifted healer—the *inyanga* and *sangoma*—or just a village elder familiar with treatments for common ailments. Mariana Hewson (1998) states that traditional healers hold an important position in societies in southern Africa. Their roles include that of doctor, priest, and psychiatrist. Significantly, traditional medicines are not just for physical ailments. They are also used for social and supernatural problems. An individual may go to the healer for help in finding work, obtaining a husband or wife, or getting revenge on an enemy. The healer will diagnose the condition and prescribe plant or animal parts or products that are to be worn, buried, or ingested. The term *muti* is used to describe these products in South Africa.

Traditional African market product display at Durban's Victoria Street Market. A wide variety of animal and plant products were offered for sale as ingredients in traditional African medicines. But those that were from endangered species were not confiscated by the authorities, since they feared that doing so would only encourage more poaching to replace them.

The traditional medicine trade is more commercialized in urban areas, where larger markets have become permanently established, such as the Victoria Street Market in Durban, South Africa. This urban market serves rural people who have relocated to the city in search of employment but still rely on traditional medicines for health care and also caters to steady demand by long-time city residents. I visited this traditional market on several occasions, noting the wide array of plant and animal products for sale and the row of healers' offices. The species offered as cures were both common and endangered, including cycads, tree barks, primates, leopard paws, vultures, and reptiles.

Analyses done in East Africa and southern Africa found that traditional medicine markets and practitioners commonly sell an array of wildlife products (TRAFFIC 2002b). The wildlife is harvested primarily to supply the domestic market, both rural and urban, for traditional medicines. Nearly all of this wildlife is taken from the wild, not purposely grown in private gardens or raised like livestock. It is legal to harvest many of these wildlife products. South Africa, for example, relies on a licensing system for commercial bark harvesting in its natural forests and also allows cultural and domestic use exemptions ("Sustainable management of bark harvesting for traditional medicine" 2011). A problematic finding, though, was the unsustainable rate of harvesting, done in part to meet demand in the larger urban markets. Not only endangered species but also once common and widespread wildlife species were being negatively affected. The concern over the impact of the wild harvesting of some products has long been felt in South Africa and Malawi, where some species have been scarce for many years (TRAFFIC 1998). Regional practices include overharvesting of common and endangered wild plants, poaching of endangered fauna, and incorrect bark stripping practices that eventually kill trees. TRAFFIC's (2002b, 2002c) long-term study identified over one hundred indigenous plant species and twenty-nine animal species being used for African traditional medicines as priority conservation targets, including pythons, birds, and baobab trees. The products are primarily taken from the wild rather than from nurseries. One solution implemented in South Africa was to develop nurseries to produce the desired plant species for the traditional medicine market. My research, however, revealed that traditional medicine collectors preferred wild-harvested products because of the belief that they were of a higher quality and therefore more effective in treating physical and social maladies. As the human population increases with corresponding agricultural and commercial development, habitat for wildlife, including those species used in medicines, declines, which, in turn, puts additional pressure on what remains (TRAFFIC 1998). The solutions to this problem are to be found in proper resource management, appropriate harvesting practices, and better monitoring of the commercial trade in these products.

The African Bushmeat Market

Hunting is a traditional practice, and game has been consumed as a food source for millennia, even with the expansion of modern agriculture and livestock production (Robinson and Bennett 2004). Bushmeat serves as a source of inexpensive protein in rural areas and as a traditional delicacy in urban markets. Some bushmeat is used for daily consumption, and at times it has a very practical application as a *famine food* used in extreme situations when agricultural production is greatly diminished because of drought (Broad, Mulliken, and Roe 2005). While the use of bushmeat was at one time sustainable, a series of developments over the past twenty years have made this practice problematic in some parts of Africa. Over time, the combination of human population growth, poverty, and the creation of conservation areas restricting access to game species has contributed to steady increases in bushmeat hunting. TRAFFIC (2002a) found that in rural Kenya approximately 80 percent of the households it surveyed relied on bushmeat. Similar patterns were found in other southern African nations, including Botswana, Zambia, Mozambique, and South Africa. The steady expansion of the mar-

Cuts of bushmeat for sale at KwaPuza informal market, which straddles the border between South Africa and Mozambique.

ket for bushmeat over the past decades has been viewed by some researchers as the most significant threat to biological diversity (Robinson, Redford, and Bennett 1999), increasing to the point where millions of tons are harvested annually for domestic consumption in rural villages and large cities ("Bushmeat trade threatens African wildlife" 2008).

Bushmeat poaching started in western Africa and Central Africa and slowly expanded to South Africa to meet domestic demand. It has become the most typical form of subsistence and for-profit poaching on the private and public game reserves (Pillinger 2003). Game meat harvested illegally from local protected areas can be found with relative ease in parts of southern Africa at local and informal markets (Warchol and Johnson 2009). While in KwaZulu Natal Province, I traveled to the far northern town of Jozini and found examples of small-scale rural bushmeat markets. Just outside the town was an informal market called KwaPuza, meaning "place of drink." The market literally straddled the fence on the South African/Mozambican border and operated about once per week. Large cuts of raw bushmeat—typically duiker and other small to midsized antelope—were readily found on display hanging from the barbed wire border fence. The source of the bushmeat was not revealed; however, this area is adjacent to several public game reserves containing popular species. While driving though Jozini, I saw more bushmeat on display hanging at roadside stands in local markets. These were larger antelopes that had been semi-processed and offered for sale to local residents.

Bushmeat is part of the local economy in some rural areas. Poachers target protected areas, often using snares to capture game, which is the type of meat many individuals prefer for daily consumption. Consumer demand for bushmeat also increases during the holidays and special occasions such as weddings. Interestingly, while many rural South Africans own and breed cattle, goats, or other types of livestock, these animals are often held as assets representing wealth, rather than as a ready source of food (Warchol and Johnson 2009). Wild game, on the other hand, is not a personal asset for rural residents. Rather, it may be viewed as belonging to everyone. It is also readily available, inexpensive compared to livestock that must be fed and cared for, and readily salable in local markets. The African bush-pig, an animal about the size of a medium dog, sold for 200 Rand, or about $2.00 USD, in Jozini. An entire hind quarter of a small antelope would sell for about 50 U.S. cents. In regions with high unemployment and poverty, bushmeat becomes a means of survival for many families. The bushmeat trade was also reported to be a means of employment of last resort. Individuals unable to find legitimate jobs may turn to the illegal hunting and selling of bushmeat to survive (Warchol and Johnson 2009).

The European Market for Wildlife

The European Union is a major destination for legal wildlife products sourced in developing countries, which gain economic benefits from this commercial trade. However, a portion of illegally obtained wildlife from Asia and Africa is also exported to the European Union's consumer markets. The illegal portion is multifaceted, involving large shipments of timber, fish, and mammals and their products (TRAFFIC 2008). It is difficult to place a definitive figure on the amount of illegal wildlife that is exported into the European Union for domestic consumption. Seizures of contraband provide one estimate of the illegal trade. For example, between 2005 and 2009, more than twelve thousand illegal wildlife products were seized in the European Union. This figure may be used for extrapolation, though with uncertain accuracy. Furthermore, shipments of legal products may be commingled with illegally obtained wildlife products, and CITES permit forgeries also help conceal contraband. The European Union is the second-largest market for timber and processed wood products, however, with more than 80 percent sourced from nations designated high-risk for corruption. This can cast doubt on the legality of these wildlife products. Estimates of illegal timber and fish shipments into the European Union were at EUR 3.8 billion and EUR 10 billion, respectively. The European Union is also estimated to have imported EUR 499 million of CITES-listed animals and animal products in 2011 (TRAFFIC 2014a). What can be concluded is the European Union imports a very large quantity of wildlife from the developing world, including large amounts from regions where the illegal trade is well established. Seizures of contraband occur regularly and may total in the tens of billions of euros when the high-volume global illegal trade in timber and fish products is factored in.

Part of the illegal wildlife trade in the European Union is controlled by criminal enterprises that are involved in supplying products to the lucrative markets in the United Kingdom and other western European countries. Syndicate involvement was believed to be a function of the high profits and relatively low risk of apprehension or serious sanctions for offending. In terms of the illegally sourced wildlife imported into the European Union, analysis determined that the trading block imported an estimated EUR 3.8 billion of illegally harvested timber. European Union CITES enforcement authorities have seized about twenty-five hundred shipments of illegal wildlife products annually since 2000. Traditional Asian medicines, ivory products, and bushmeat were commonplace among these seizures (Chaber et al. 2010; TRAFFIC 2014a). Previous research revealed that one popular aspect of the illegal trade is the demand for reptiles by collectors centered in the Czech Republic. This fairly modern development is a function of demand for exotic pets from Africa. Wildlife is ordered and shipped, often via express mail, to the final markets in western Europe (Warchol, Zupan, and Clack 2003).

France has a small domestic market for illegal ivory products, both raw and processed. About three tons of illegal ivory, mostly carvings with some complete tusks, were confiscated in France between 1987 and 2007, mainly from airline passengers returning from Africa. As in Kenya and the United States, French customs authorities publicly destroyed this stockpile, which amounted to more than fifteen thousand ivory tusks and carved objects. This was the first public destruction of ivory done by a European nation. The objective of the destruction was to draw more attention to the problem of trafficking and poaching among the public, including travelers to elephant range states, thereby reducing consumer demand for these products (TRAFFIC 2014d).

In the United Kingdom, shipments of illegal wildlife are routinely intercepted by customs officers at ports of entry, including airports. The wildlife, often found in cargo or luggage or on passengers, includes dead specimens of tigers and crocodiles, bushmeat, and live birds destined for collectors (Davies 2005). While interviewing customs officers at Heathrow International Airport, I found that shipments of semi-processed bushmeat from Africa have been regularly confiscated on inspection of passenger luggage (H.M. Customs officer, personal communication, May 2006). This product was shipped to meet demand for wild game meat in the African immigrant communities in and around London. Paralleling the situation in South Africa, a consumer market for African bushmeat developed in the United Kingdom that fluctuated with holidays or family celebrations. Because the bushmeat lacked any health inspection or permits, it was seized and destroyed by the authorities. Over time, as enforcement efforts have succeeded in confiscating more shipments of illegal wildlife products, traffickers have resorted to transshipping the items through other European nations before entering the United Kingdom.

The illegal importation of bushmeat is not confined to the United Kingdom; bushmeat is also regularly confiscated in other European Union nations with large African immigrant populations. An analysis estimated that two hundred seventy tons of bushmeat was shipped through Charles de Gaulle Airport in Paris in 2010 (TRAFFIC 2014a). The bushmeat trade presents two problems for European authorities, the first being health concerns. The game meat is semi-processed after capture—commonly dried or smoked in the field to preserve it during shipment. Once in transit, it is not subject to any inspection in either Africa or Europe. The second threat is to the survival of the threatened or endangered species that are hunted. Common meat species ranged from primates to rodents to antelopes and on rare occasion elephant. A fascinating analysis of illegal wildlife seizures at EU airports found that aside from wild game meat from mammals, fish were commonly seized from passengers returning from Africa. The average amount of game meat seized was twenty kilograms, and for fish it was nine kilograms (Chaber et al. 2010). The authors concluded that the combination of weak enforcement of poaching laws in Africa, low penalties for offenders in the European Union, strong consumer demand for the products, and high profits facilitated this illegal European wildlife market. They further noted that the bushmeat trade in Paris was run by dealers who supplied the product to order for customers who are primarily African immigrants. The game meat is a luxury item that sells at prices comparable to those for premium cuts of livestock.

The problem of the illegal trade has not gone unnoticed in the European Union by the legal authorities and major NGOs. The European Union's Environmental Commission has acknowledged the severity of the problem and the corresponding need to control and prevent it (TRAFFIC 2014b). World Wildlife Fund and TRAFFIC lobbied the EU member states to both strengthen and fully implement their legislation designed to deal with the illegal trade and its participants. They have also advocated for better border controls and cooperation between member states on this issue (TRAFFIC 2014c). In the summer of 2015, the government of the United Kingdom announced it would provide as much as five million pounds to help combat the illegal wildlife trade, recognizing that the trade not only harms selected species but also fosters corruption and organized crime and hinders the economic development of the source countries, many of which are developing nations (TRAFFIC 2015c). Interestingly, the eventual departure of the United Kingdom from the European Union may allow improved border controls that would reduce wildlife trafficking.

Summary: Global Demand

Given that the majority of the illicit trade is profit driven, it would be a fraction of its current state if there were no consumers of illegally obtained wildlife. This demand for wildlife and its products for a wide range of uses has fostered the development of a multi-billion-dollar illegal business. The objective of this chapter has been to examine the nature of the consumer markets for illegally obtained wildlife. Rather than attempt to provide a detailed analysis of the end user markets in all major wildlife consumer nations, the chapter focused on markets for different types of wildlife products in several major consumer regions—Asia, Africa, and the European Union.

While many regions of the African continent may commonly be thought of as major sources for wildlife, these areas are also home to dynamic internal markets for domestically available products. Africa's large domestic wildlife markets include bushmeat sales that range from small-scale local operations selling a few animals to large commercial enterprises moving shipments by the truckload from forests to urban areas, where consumer demand is strong. Protein consumption is quite high in many African nations, and wild game is considered by some to be for the taking regardless if it is from a protected area. A small portion of wild game meat is also shipped to Europe to meet consumer demand in African immigrant communities. This has been a source of concern in the European Union, not so much in terms of species depletion but in terms of disease transmission from wild game into human populations.

Common in both the African and Asian markets is demand for traditional medicines. Having very long cultural use, traditional remedies serve a valuable purpose in these nations, where modern medicines are often unavailable or prohibitively expensive. In other instances, traditional medicines are used when modern medical technology and pharmaceuticals cannot cure the physical illness or solve a social problem. While most traditional medicines are made from wildlife products that are not threatened or endangered, a portion comes from these protected flora and fauna, which places them at greater risk of extinction. This includes demand for rhinoceros horn in Vietnam, tiger and bear parts in China, and protected plants in South Africa, including the cycad. The use of endangered species, whose population numbers are already greatly diminished, as medicines that have dubious curative powers represents a significant threat to their survival.

The ivory markets of Asia, primarily in mainland China, Hong Kong, and Japan, have histories dating back thousands of years. Ivory use for cultural reasons and as a status symbol was sustainable for most of this period until the 1980s, when increased demand corresponded to dramatic increases in poaching. With the 1989 ban on commercial ivory sales, it was thought that poaching would naturally decline, and once stockpiles of legal or pre-ban ivory were exhausted, the trade would diminish. However, the commingling of illegal ivory with pre-ban ivory to meet growing consumer demand in China and Japan contributed to increased poaching and trafficking. A possible complete ban on the commercial ivory trade in China, under consideration in 2016, if it comes to fruition, may ultimately bring an end to most elephant poaching and save the species. Part of the multifaceted solution to the illegal trade is demand reduction for wildlife products among consumers. Efforts are being made in this direction by both governments and nongovernmental organizations through education, public relations, and legislation. This subject is addressed in more detail in Chapter 7.

6

Protecting Wildlife

Guarding the Wilderness

The value of wildlife, from both economic and intrinsic viewpoints, has long been recognized by governmental agencies and private organizations. To protect and preserve wildlife and ecosystems, game laws were enacted in the United States more than one hundred years ago, even earlier in East Africa and England. In addition to national legislation, in the latter half of the twentieth century international and regional agreements and treaties were signed by countries to protect the world's biodiversity and prevent the exploitation of wildlife by the illegal trade. To enforce the conservation laws, a variety of government agencies and departments were developed at the national level, and in the case of the United States, also the state level. In Africa and Asia, these included the numerous wildlife or game departments staffed with rangers responsible for patrolling national and provincial parks and game management areas. Some well-known examples of these organizations are the Kenya Wildlife Service (KWS), Zambia Wildlife Authority (ZAWA), South African National Parks (SANParks), and National Park Rangers of Thailand. Within some of the Asian and African game departments are elite anti- or counter-poaching units such as Thailand's King Tigers or SANParks Corporate Investigations Service. Unique in South Africa, owing to the private ownership of wildlife, was the emergence of private anti-poaching units to protect for-profit game farms and reserves that cater to photo safaris, wildlife breeding, and hunting. The United States also has an extensive array of public-sector wildlife protection agencies. The most common are the state game wardens or conservation officers who work to protect natural resources. These agencies all serve as the main defense against poaching and destruction of habitat on protected and in some circumstances private lands. Yet despite the need for these agencies to protect wildlife, especially with the surge in certain types of poaching in Africa, only a very limited amount of research describes their structure and operations. Compared to research on traditional policing, far fewer scholars have examined this aspect of law enforcement in the United States and abroad.

Wildlife conservation law enforcement is not limited to policing the protected areas to stop illegal hunting and habitat destruction. A large portion of illegally harvested wildlife is trafficked from source countries to consumer nations. As described in previous chapters, wildlife is smuggled in great quantities via air and sea freight and in smaller quantities by individual airline passengers on their persons or in their luggage (Christy 2008). To prevent this offense, there are dedicated government agencies charged with inspecting international passengers and the cargo entering and exiting a nation. In the United States, the inspectors with the U.S. Fish and Wildlife Service and U.S. Customs and Border Protection assume this critical role. Agencies charged with cargo inspection face a daunting job, given the enormous volume of trade in transit around the world. Agents must not only inspect legal shipments of wildlife but also detect contraband secreted in cargo. This can include mislabeled, disguised, or hidden protected species commingled with legal wildlife in the same shipment. Such inspection requires an ability to identify the myriad of species to determine what is legal or illegal. Furthermore, agents must assess the validity of the shipping manifests and authenticity of CITES permits accompanying the cargo. Finally, inspectors must focus on individual airline passengers who illegally carry both live wildlife and wildlife items that are destined for resale or personal use. Simply stated, it is an enormous task for inspectors within these agencies in the United States and abroad.

As with violent or property criminals, after a wildlife crime offender (poacher or trafficker) is apprehended, the matter is resolved in various ways. Depending on the seriousness of the offense, it may be an extra-judicial resolution, a warning, or a small monetary fine. For more serious crimes that carry incarceration or large fines and forfeitures as a penalty, arrested wildlife crime offenders may have their cases forwarded to the local court for prosecution. Although the laws exist and the conservation officers and customs inspectors are willing and able to enforce them, even in the more serious instances not all wildlife crime cases necessarily make it to the docket for trial or even a plea. This lack of follow-through can be a function of the priority given these offenses by a national government or a local magistrate (South African magistrate KwaZulu Natal, personal communication, 2004). It may also be influenced by legal expertise of the prosecutor and judge in conservation laws. While this is not a serious issue in the United States, it is a problem in many developing nations, where wildlife poaching and trafficking is a common offense yet an arrest for poaching may seldom make it to court (SANParks section ranger, personal communication, 2008).

The focus of this chapter is how governments protect their national wildlife resources. Three different components of the justice system have been designed to prevent the illegal exploitation of wildlife and deter and punish offenders. These are rangers, customs inspectors, and the judicial system. Since it would beyond the scope of a single chapter to present a comprehensive description of these various agencies throughout different regions of the world or even on one continent, the approach used here draws from selected examples in South Africa, the United States, and Asia to illustrate the different organizations and their operations and challenges.

The front lines of conservation are manned by the rangers working in the protected areas. These include both government rangers working in the public parks and private-sector rangers responsible for private game parks. While these units exist around the world, this description focuses first on Africa, where game ranger units have existed for well over a hundred years. This chapter examines the development and operations of field rangers in Africa for later comparison to their game warden and conservation officer counterparts in the United States. It helps illustrate some distinct differences and similarities in operations, threats, and jurisdiction. Based in part on my research in Africa, the chapter describes how these public and private entities recruit, train, and function; the organization of specialized elite ranger units; the challenges faced by rangers; and the contemporary issue of militarized conservation enforcement units. Next the focus turns to the role of customs officers and wildlife inspectors in the illegal trade. Then the chapter examines the process of moving wildlife crime cases into the courts to obtain prosecutions and convictions of offenders. The final topic is the concept of establishing dedicated environmental crime courts, or *green courts*, that adjudicate only wildlife crime cases, as a method to increase prosecutions.

African Field Rangers

Recruiting, Training, and Structure

Wildlife rangers serve as the first line of protection for game and human visitors on the reserves and, in some cases, adjacent to them. While popular media portrayals of the job may give the impression that it involves excitement and adventure, the reality is quite different. The work of a field ranger is difficult, often dangerous, and at times tedious; in its long days of hard outdoor labor, it may be more like agricultural work than wildlife conservation (Warchol and Kapla 2012). The literature on the operations of field rangers is rather limited, though by drawing on biographical accounts and academic research, we may obtain a better understanding of how they are recruited and trained and how they operate in the parks. Because of the availability of sources and my previous research, this section focuses primarily on the field rangers in southern Africa and East Africa. While different titles are used to describe these individuals, such as park ranger, game scout, game ranger, and anti-poaching ranger, the term *field ranger* is employed here as the general term to refer to those charged with protecting wildlife in both public and private protected areas in Africa.

One starting point for understanding the recruitment of field rangers is the autobiographical accounts of those working in the career. These accounts can reveal unique career paths such as the *poacher to gamekeeper transition,* not commonplace but certainly not unheard of in Africa and the United States. Richard Leakey, director of the Kenya Wildlife Service from 1989 to 1994 and from 1998 to 1999, wrote about his willingness to recruit and hire former poachers, owing to their specialized skills. His rationale for the practice was that these men were familiar with a park's terrain and poaching techniques yet also desired a steady income. After employing this practice, he concluded that a former poacher can become a very effective field ranger (Leakey and Morell 2001). This practice was also mentioned by Ian Nyschens (1997) in his autobiography, *Months of the Sun.* Nyschens, a former talented professional hunter and admitted occasional poacher, later transitioned to a career as a field ranger in Southern Rhodesia, now Zimbabwe. This employment practice is not necessarily restricted to African game departments. Academic research about game wardens in the United States found that some American conservation officers were former poachers (Carter 2006; Eliason 2003b).

An examination of South Africa, with its extensive network of public parks and private game reserves, offers details about the different routes one can take to become a field ranger. Notably, South Africa has not enacted a universal standard for those interested in this profession. Rather, the hiring standards vary by park and by its private or public status. Standards are individualized on the basis of the type of wildlife, severity of the poaching threat, maintenance needs, and function of the protected area—tourism, hunting, or game farming. Parks that face serious threats from armed poachers place more value on finding individuals with past military experience, bush and agricultural skills, and an ability to work in difficult conditions. However, parks facing less serious poaching problems prefer candidates with some academic training in wildlife conservation and biodiversity management (Warchol and Kapla 2012).

While becoming a field ranger does not necessarily require university credentials or a diploma, rangers must complete a basic Environmental

Management Inspector (EMI) course mandated by national legislation. Five levels of certification are available, ranging from one to five, with five being the lowest. A field ranger candidate could be nearly illiterate and able to complete the exam for the level-five certification. Beyond the EMI certification there are no uniform standards for reserves in the training of their field ranger staffs (Warchol and Kapla 2012). There are, however, public and private educational institutions that offer training to facilitate entry into this career. These include traditional four-year college degrees and diplomas from private training schools offering a variety of short-term programs. The former are more oriented toward students eventually seeking a management career in the parks, while the latter are primarily for career field rangers. The subject matter covered in these programs includes biodiversity monitoring, alien species removal, fire control, trapping, off-road driving, weapons training, and anti-poaching operations, including the law of arrest and basic court processes. On completion of their university degree, students are qualified to begin work in the South African parks systems (Warchol and Kapla 2012).

Other short-term programs provide in-service training for individuals currently working in game reserves and seeking career advancement. A variety of courses designed to match the needs of the different provinces' public wildlife reserves offer training in soft skills and hard skills. The former refer to specimen collection, species identification, communication skills, park maintenance, report writing, and conservation law while the latter focus on tracking, problem animal control, arrest procedures, establishing and maintaining surveillance points, and counter-poaching. The training consists of a mix of theoretical and applied, including both classroom and fieldwork. Other types of short-term, privately run programs are oriented strictly toward training anti-poaching officers. These specialized for-profit institutions offer high-intensity, shorter-duration training courses for prospective anti-poaching rangers desiring work on private game farms or tourist reserves. The curriculum is primarily designed to develop specific hard skills, such as firearms use, tracking, detecting and removing snares, surveillance, and apprehension of poachers. On completion of the training, graduates are contracted out by the schools to private game farms and reserves as anti-poaching officers. Additional courses offered in South Africa include law enforcement management and wildlife monitoring. The latter is oriented toward training rangers to record their observations about the wildlife they encounter while on patrol, and the former is for rangers who have the potential to become team leaders and instructors (Warchol and Kapla 2012). A similar program was carried out in Southeast Asia by the NGO WildAid, which offered short-duration courses for field rangers operating in the parks in this region (WildAid 2004). These courses included basic ranger training in a wide range of modules, such as patrolling, intelligence gathering, crime scene processing, surveillance, and the law. The training also included management techniques and preparing poaching cases for the courts (WildAid 2003).

Entry into the profession in a public park can involve a fairly rigorous selection and training program. Kruger National Park provides an example of this process for a park facing a serious poaching problem. KNP seeks individuals between eighteen and thirty-five, physically fit and with an agricultural background and tracking skills. Interestingly, a preference for candidates with a rural farming background has also been found in conservation agencies in the United States (Forsyth and Forsyth 2009). University degrees or diplomas are not required for the job. If a candidate meets the basic requirements to apply to KNP, he or she must successfully complete two phases of challenging paramilitary training over the next eight weeks. These training courses, which have very high attrition rates, entail difficult living conditions, food deprivation, long-distance forced marches, and physical and psychological stress (Warchol and Kapla 2012). Demographically, Kruger Park's ranger candidates mainly consist of black, male South Africans. There are some female and white recruits, but they have exhibited a higher dropout rate, owing to the difficulty of the training or a realization of the limited number of advancement opportunities once they enter their careers as field rangers.

While rangers often need a broad skill set, part of their training, as I observed in South Africa, is specific to their location and the known threats facing the reserve. While Kruger National Park, for example, emphasizes anti-poaching skills as a critical primary duty, the Table Mountain National Park at Cape Town and the smaller Jonkershoek Nature Reserve in the Western Cape place equal emphasis on an array of general duties in addition to preventing marine, reptile, or plant poaching. These include trail maintenance, visitor assistance, preventing thefts from parked vehicles, and biodiversity management.

Like American game wardens, African field rangers work within a somewhat less structured bureaucratic environment in the public parks than do urban police officers (Carter 2006). The typical organizational hierarchy at many reserves for the rangers consisted of section rangers at the top followed by noncommissioned officers (rangers holding the ranks of corporal and sergeant) and field rangers. Section rangers are supervisors responsible for a designated area of the reserve. To patrol this area, they have a dedicated contingent of field rangers, including NCOs, in their command. Also included in some locales are specialized investigative units, as found at Kruger, Table Mountain, and Jonkershoek. These units are charged with investigating crimes, developing informants, gathering intelligence, operating undercover, and working with the courts in the prosecution of offenders. Though

Morning parade of field rangers in Swaziland's Mkhaya Game Reserve, which is home to a small population of southern white and black rhinos.

not involved in daily patrols, investigative units are actively involved in developing the information generated from ranger patrols (Warchol and Kapla 2012). KNP's Corporate Investigations Service (CIS), for example, collects and analyzes poaching intelligence data to assist the park's twenty-two section rangers in their enforcement efforts (South African National Parks [hereafter SANParks] 2016). As in policing in the United States, research has shown that the investigative function can be very effective in preventing poaching and apprehending poachers and traffickers (Hess and Hess-Orthmann 2010).

Operations

While field rangers have numerous responsibilities, a central duty is a daily patrol to ensure that their section of the park is protected from poaching (Jachmann and Billiouw 1997). Patrol is both proactive to deter poachers and reactive to respond to wildlife crimes in the park (SANParks 2016). Kruger provides an example of the ranger operations in a large African park. Daily operations commence with a morning parade of rangers that includes a briefing of known or potential problems in the section. Intelligence from the previous day may include spotting human spoor (tracks) indicating trespassers, or rangers may report vulture sightings indicating a carcass, potentially from a poacher's kill (KNP section ranger, personal communication, 2005). Section rangers work with their NCOs to utilize intelligence from investigators inside and outside the park to plan the daily field ranger patrol. When a patrol route is designed, it is critical to avoid routine patterns, thus hindering poachers who attempt to observe rangers' activities. Observations made during the ranger patrol are also recorded, once on paper but more commonly now on handheld digital devices. These data are analyzed to assess the patrol's effectiveness and findings and then used as a basis for routing future patrols (Moreto et al. 2014). The field rangers in KNP, because of the threats presented by both poaching gangs and dangerous wildlife, carry firearms on patrol. Their armaments have evolved over time as a necessity to match the firepower of illegal hunters. Once armed with World War II vintage British Enfield bolt-action rifles, they now employ modern automatic military rifles.

Unlike American game wardens, who usually operate alone and use various types of conveyances, rangers in KNP more commonly patrol in groups of two or three on foot or via bicycle. Patrols can be daily operations (morning or afternoon) or multiday, in which case rangers carry supplies and shelters or access prepositioned ones. A common example is a three-man ranger patrol whose objective is to look for animal carcasses and human spoor, which nearly always indicate trespassers, either poachers or immigrants entering illegally from Mozambique. If the spoor appears to be recent and indicative of a problem, rangers report in and track. Contact with a human is seldom made during their tracking, though animal carcasses are regularly encountered. Rangers sometimes employ metal detectors on carcasses to confirm if the animal was shot or died of natural causes or predation. All carcass finds are required to be reported to the section rangers (KNP section ranger, personal communication, 2003). Lemieux et al. (2014) found that ranger patrols in a Ugandan national park are a function of a poacher's methods. Given the large size of protected areas, weather conditions, and terrain variations, what a patrolling ranger can observe is quite limited. As a result, intelligence-planned patrols based on known offender operations and tactics are essential for any chance of success.

If evidence of poaching is found on patrol, rangers plan and set up *observation points*, formerly known as *ambushes*—owing to the negative connotation of the latter term, *observation point* was substituted. These are commonly though not exclusively established near game trails and water sources. Rangers in many reserves, not just KNP, very often find snares, the most common tool of the bushmeat poacher. Though these are challenging to find, when one is discovered, rangers may close it and then return later to see if it has been reset, indicating active poachers in the area. The policy for field rangers is to pursue, confront, and arrest any poachers or unauthorized migrants. As with police practices in the United States, deadly force is allowed, but only for self-defense. A continuum of force policy was established with regard to the use of firearms. While on patrol—the lowest level—rangers carry their rifles unloaded. The highest level requires the ranger to have a magazine inserted in the rifle with a chambered cartridge (Warchol and Kapla 2012).

One question raised in contemporary research on ranger patrols is how much crime in the protected areas is not detected. Lemieux et al. (2014) found that ranger operations are guided by human intelligence based on increasingly sophisticated data collection and analysis to increase effectiveness in finding and deterring poachers. Nevertheless, an unknown amount of poaching will always go undetected. A KNP section ranger told me that poachers employ counter-intelligence operations in response to ranger patrolling. This may include having an inside source within the park to inform them of the day's patrol route or directly observing ranger operations from outside the park if conditions warrant (KNP section ranger, personal communication, 2003).

Ranger patrols in South Africa's Table Mountain National Park (TMNP) and Jonkershoek Nature Reserve (JNR) employ a somewhat different approach in response to the needs of their parks and the poaching threat. Rangers at these locales have a broader range of responsibilities in addition to counter-poaching. These include biodiversity monitoring, trail maintenance, fence repair, erosion control, and traditional law enforcement. TMNP, for example, is divided into just three sections, each of which has a section ranger, sergeant, and field rangers. This national park has long had a serious problem with armed abalone poachers fishing in their offshore marine protected areas in addition to thefts from vehicles and visitors. As a result, rangers perform both environmental and traditional law enforcement to protect wildlife, visitors, and their property. With their EMI credentials, rangers all have civil arrest powers similar to those of private security officers in the United States, which allow them to legally apprehend offenders (Warchol and Kapla 2012).

Field ranger operations in JNR also include a wide range of non–law enforcement maintenance duties along with anti-poaching. Jonkershoek Nature Reserve is an example of a park that faces a unique poaching threat that does not generally involve armed offenders. While this landlocked nature reserve does not have populations of dangerous game or large mammals, it is home to some endangered and highly sought-after insects, reptiles, and plants. The illegal trade in these species constitutes the greatest component of the entire illegal wildlife trade by volume (Warchol, Zupan, and Clack

2003). These species are poached by offenders who fit a distinctly different profile from those who target bushmeat, ivory, or rhinoceros horn. As described earlier, they are often found to be specimen collectors, nearly all of whom are foreigners, targeting the park for its diverse wildlife. The security force at JNR is composed of an eight-man field ranger force and a two-officer Biodiversity Crimes Unit (BCU). The field rangers at this site perform a mix of activities, including patrol, guiding of visitors, staff transport in the reserve, trail maintenance, and reactive anti-poaching if someone is spotted taking a plant or small reptile. The BCU is similar to Kruger Park's Corporate Investigations Service Unit. If poaching is suspected or known to be occurring, the BCU, ranger staff, and park workers observe visitors both casually and tactically and gather intelligence about known poachers in the area. For the latter, the investigators request information from police and local community members. As in the other parks, the BCU investigators establish observation points based on intelligence in order to apprehend poachers. The field rangers receive annual training to update their skills. The BCU also trains the local criminal court prosecutors to familiarize them with poaching law and cases (Warchol and Kapla 2012) in order to improve the likelihood of a prosecution.

The creation of specialized counter-poaching units is not limited to Africa. In response to ranger deaths and injuries, as well as species loss, the Department of National Parks in Thailand announced the creation of an elite counter-poaching and trafficking unit that is within the ranger force rather than a separate entity. Unlike the CIS in Kruger Park, the Thai unit, called the King Tigers, is made up of specially qualified field rangers who have trained in advanced operations to improve the overall capacity of the wildlife law enforcement component in the national parks department (Freeland 2013). This well-armed special response unit claimed its first success against timber poaching in 2013 in an effort called Operation Bloodwood. The objective is not to kill poachers but to apprehend them and gather intelligence about their operations and networks (Herman 2013). This information, in turn, can be used for successful prosecution of poaching syndicates.

Working Environment

Examinations of the few autobiographical accounts of field rangers in southern Africa illustrate some of the difficulties inherent in this job, problems that are a function of social and working conditions. Graham Root's (2005) account of his career with the Natal Parks Board in South Africa provides detail about the job requirements and the distinctions made between white and black rangers during the apartheid period. In the Natal Parks, black

South Africans were generally hired as game guards, a lower position than field rangers, who were predominantly white. The field ranger position held a higher rank with more complex responsibilities, including anti-poaching, investigations, game management, game capture and relocation, and problem animal control. While field rangers received higher salaries and had better accommodations within the park, including family housing if needed, the game guards were often stationed in basic picket stations or primitive camps throughout the park and served strictly as the title implies, just to protect game. Interestingly, even with this disparity in treatment and benefits, the level of dedication to wildlife conservation in both groups was high.

Richard Leakey's autobiographical account of his service as Kenya Wildlife Service director mentioned the problems of inadequate pay, low morale, poor equipment, and challenging working conditions for the rangers. These included very long patrols over difficult terrain and the inherent dangers posed by armed poachers and large or predatory wildlife. Describing the working conditions, Leakey stated that "rangers earned barely enough to feed and clothe their families . . . and you couldn't expect a man with a .303 Enfield to take on someone wielding a modern assault rifle" (Leakey and Morell 2001, 63). Leakey's solutions included the imposition of strict military discipline on the rangers to enhance their effectiveness and morale, the issuing of modern military firearms, and the use of new vehicles for patrolling and tactical operations (Warchol and Kapla 2012).

Academic research on the creation and operations of the protected areas in Africa provides additional detail about field rangers. Johan Toit, Kevin Rogers, and Harry Biggs's (2003) study of management practices in Kruger National Park offers insight into the early years of the reserve with some attention paid to the role and responsibilities of the field rangers. Jane Caruthers (2007) contributed to this history in a study about wildlife management practices in South Africa from 1930 to 1960, describing the development of a scientific and professional approach to running the parks. Her research also notes the early dichotomy of park staff in which white employees were designated game rangers and black employees were relegated to the lower position of native police. Caruthers's (2008) subsequent research further revealed the past discriminatory nature of game protection positions in Kruger National Park decades ago, noting that black rangers were paid less and treated poorly compared to their white counterparts. These employment practices of the apartheid period were eliminated by the new government.

Researchers have focused on the sociological aspects of wildlife conservation, including the impact of protected areas on the adjacent communities in terms of the critical issues of employment opportunities, economic growth, community involvement, and suspicion of resident rangers. Michael Wells (1996) and Anna Spenceley (2003) examined the effect of the South African

Fence line at Ndumo Game Reserve in KwaZulu Natal, South Africa. The purpose of the cleared area along both sides of the fence is to allow better surveillance to prevent trespassing.

game reserves on these local communities, including their role in poverty reduction. The staff at some game reserves includes biologists, veterinarians, and land management experts in addition to field rangers. Though this well-skilled staff can offer benefits to the adjacent agricultural communities, they are not necessarily permitted to work outside the park by management, sometimes fostering resentment among local residents in need of assistance. Emmanuel Asibey's (1972) research in Ghana examined this issue from an interesting approach, wondering if a reserve's wildlife should be used for food, and if so, at what level would be sustainable. Although this research was done decades ago, it is still relevant today in the context of modern community conservation programs. As human populations increase, there are corresponding pressures on game reserves, including demands for hunting and fishing rights. Qualitative research on bushmeat poaching found evidence of this in South Africa's KwaZulu Natal Province when local villagers tore down a section of the park's fence and demanded access to the wildlife at Ndumo Game Reserve (Warchol and Johnson 2009).

Gibson's (1999) study of poaching in Zambia included a thorough overview of game rangers' duties and hardships. The job entailed difficult and dangerous working conditions, and rangers often lacked basic equipment, such as boots, properly functioning firearms, and even ammunition. These shortages were attributed to inefficiencies in the central administration of their wildlife department. Compounding the situation was the social isolation they faced in local communities. Rangers generally live in local communities, supporting the economy and sometimes helping protect residents from dangerous wildlife that leave the reserve to raid crops or livestock. Yet the law enforcement responsibilities of a ranger "often overcame the positive features of the scout-villager interactions producing a frequently tense—sometimes overly hostile—relationship" (Gibson 1999, 25). This was attributed to the ranger's sworn duty to enforce poaching laws in rural areas where illegal bushmeat can represent a significant part of the local villagers' diet and income. Given that much illegal hunting was committed by local people living near the reserves, it was highly likely that the ranger would arrest one of his neighbors for illegal hunting (Warchol and Kapla 2012). Gibson (1999) noted some instances of Zambian rangers abusing their authority by conducting frequent searches of residences for illegal bushmeat, using physical force on poaching suspects, and occasionally keeping the carcass for their own consumption, resulting in increased animosity by local residents toward the rangers.

The difficult working conditions, equipment shortages, and social isolation facing African field rangers are well documented in the literature and raise questions about job satisfaction. While there is considerable research on job satisfaction in traditional urban policing, very few recent studies specifically address the issue among African field rangers. Research completed at Nigeria's Yankari Game Reserve found that ranger job dissatisfaction and low morale were the result of working in remote areas with dangerous wildlife, physically challenging terrain, limited opportunities for promotion and advanced training, and inadequate pay. The authors also concluded that this situation fostered corruption, including ranger complicity with poachers, as shown by instances of rangers allowing poachers to access the park, accepting bribes from poachers and livestock grazers, and informing them of the location of game animals (Ogunjinmi, Umunna, and Ogunjinmi 2008). Research in Nigeria on this issue found that ineffective park management practices and salaries contributed to lower than expected performance of the ranger staff (Meduna, Ogunjinmi, and Onadeko 2009). The possible connection between employee corruption and working conditions was described in a recent analysis of ranger misconduct in a Ugandan national park (Moreto, Brunson, and Braga 2015). Finally, the individual impact of workplace and personal stress from field rangers' working and living conditions has also been addressed in current research (Moreto 2015).

Threats

The threats to African field rangers commonly stem from the wildlife, poachers, the environment, and common criminals in the parks. Dangerous animals, including predators such as lion or leopard and large grazers such as elephant, buffalo, or hippo, represent a significant hazard for patrolling rangers in some parks, such as KNP. In other reserves lacking these species, the threat from wildlife may emanate from a snake or an insect bite. While parks such as Table Mountain or Cape Agulhas lack the dangerous game, their environments present risks for field rangers. The need to patrol the abalone habitat in the offshore marine protected areas presents the risk of boating accidents in the volatile South Atlantic weather, for example.

The more serious threat in the South African reserves with high-value wildlife—elephant, rhinoceros, and abalone—is the risk of violent confrontations with poachers. This threat was constant in Kruger and Table Mountain Parks because of their respective large populations of rhinoceros and abalone sought after by poaching gangs. In these national parks, all rhino and some abalone poachers were armed and often willing to resort to violence when encountered. The penalty for poachers if apprehended was severe—a cash fine plus three times the value of the poached wildlife and possible incarceration. These sanctions, when combined with the value of the wildlife on the illegal market, created a strong incentive to use force to prevent its confiscation by rangers (Warchol and Kapla 2012). In Table Mountain's marine protected areas, numerous instances of firefights between field rangers and poachers occurred, along with cases of poachers ramming ranger patrol boats to prevent apprehension. The risk of violence in these national parks justified the adoption of modern 7.62-caliber automatic military rifles for ranger forces (Warchol and Harrington 2016).

In comparison, Forsyth and Forsyth's (2009) research in Louisiana found that state game wardens dealt with an unexpectedly high level of danger and violence when patrolling waterways and coastal areas. Like U.S. parks and public lands, South African parks face the threat of violent criminals victimizing tourists (Tynon, Chavez, and Baur 2010). Common crimes in Table Mountain National Park were theft from vehicles and robberies of tourists. Attempts by rangers to apprehend a suspect would occasionally result in fights when the suspects resisted arrest. Park management realized that rangers needed to be able to contend with both wildlife and street crimes, which necessitated field ranger training in both anti-poaching techniques and basic law enforcement. Table Mountain National Park responded to this problem by training rangers in civil arrest procedures, the proper use of physical force to restrain suspects, and the basics of criminal law (Warchol and Kapla 2012).

Technology

Some African field ranger units have steadily adopted contemporary communications and surveillance technology, along with improved forensic capabilities, in response to increased threats from poaching and to enhance efficiency and worker productivity. While light and ultra-light aircraft have long been employed for observation, mobility, and deterrence in Kruger Park (SANParks 2016), the current trend in several southern African nations is to employ small UAVs, or drones, as part of the anti-poaching strategy. This aerial technology is used for surveillance and data collection, the latter intended to develop algorithms for ranger patrol routes. However, drones also have significant limitations, including high cost, the need for skilled operators, limited battery life that inhibits their ability to linger, and lower effectiveness when overflying forested terrain (Payne 2015). UAVs represent just one component of a multipart solution to enhanced counter-poaching. For instance, though it may identify poachers, the park must have the capability to move a field ranger force into the targeted area to interdict the offenders. In turn, the ranger force must have the training and equipment to match the threat posed by poachers, who are also adopting new weaponry and communications technology.

While radios and mobile phones are used by rangers, GPS tracking units have also been employed in South Africa for nearly two decades in an effort to collect scientific data and improve ranger efficiency and accountability. Cyber Tracker, a 1996 South African invention, is a handheld computer with a software program that allows rangers to monitor and record their daily patrol activities and encounters. The software is icon-driven, so rangers, even if illiterate, can simply select from various icons depicting different types of animals, plants, or geographic features to document their observations. The unit also serves as a GPS device, providing the supervisory ranger with a complete map of the patrol route taken by the rangers. As discussed in more detail in Chapter 7, the data from these devices can also be incorporated into predictive analysis models to design ranger patrols. Furthermore, Cyber Tracker also helps deter rangers from not completing their patrols or from shirking because of bad weather or difficult terrain (SANParks section ranger, personal communication, 2005). The use of this technology is widespread within the public parks of South Africa. Cyber Tracker was not designed initially as an anti-poaching tool, nor is it currently used in only that capacity. Rather, it was initially intended for environmental monitoring and research and is currently part of KNP's Strategic Adaptive Management program. Kruger Park can also employ sophisticated forensic investigative techniques if warranted. These include ballistics testing to link bullets to specific firearms and the use of DNA analysis to match carcasses with ivory or rhinoceros horns if these are confiscated. These tasks are carried out by KNPs Corporate Investigation Service, a well-organized and highly skilled criminal investigations unit in the park.

Private-Sector Anti-poaching Ranger Units

The legal right to private ownership of game in South Africa fostered the creation of thousands of private, for-profit wildlife reserves for photo safaris, hunting, and breeding. This contributed to employment opportunities for rangers, who left the public park service. It also fostered the development of private businesses that offer anti-poaching units and/or provide training for individuals seeking a career as a ranger. Adjacent to KNP are numerous private game reserves and game breeding operations. Their need for security units to protect wildlife were met in part by a private training academy in the area called ProTrack. This sophisticated operation provides short-duration, high-intensity anti-poaching courses for in-service guards employed by private game reserves and inexperienced individuals interested in this career. The curriculum was similar to the training provided by the public sector for government park rangers. Students received instruction in firearms use, tracking, methods used by poachers, surveillance, concealment, wilderness survival, and crime scene analysis. Once the training was completed, students worked under contract for the private game reserves and farms (ProTrack owner Vincent Varkas, personal communication, 2004). A second type of business was the anti-poaching operation. I interviewed the owner of one of these operations, which provided security for a high-end private game reserve in KwaZulu Natal Province. Unlike ProTrack, this organization did not provide training. Rather, it was staffed with eight fully trained anti-poaching rangers who worked under contract with private reserves to provide wildlife protection services. All individuals in this operation had previous experience in the South African military and/or public parks. Included in the business's offerings was threat analysis and investigations of poaching networks. The contracted services provided to customers by private-sector anti-poaching operations were not necessarily year-round. In some game breeding farms in this area, security forces did not operate on a daily basis. Some game farms contracted for security only during those times of year when bushmeat poaching—the most common type—was likely to occur, such as holiday periods and the beginning of the school year, when game was poached for resale to raise money. Overall, the rangers from both organizations projected a strong military image. The all-male force was a mix of white and black South Africans who carried select-fire rifles and wore full military-style battle dress uniforms.

Their overall appearance was indicative of a well-equipped, professional anti-poaching ranger unit. Interestingly, when asked about how these rangers apprehended bushmeat poachers, the owner of the anti-poaching unit mentioned the use of discretion and extra-judicial solutions. Young offenders were more likely to be sent home for discipline from their fathers and village chiefs. The owner felt this was a more effective deterrent than taking the poacher to the local police department, where any type of punishment may be unlikely (Didier Vern, owner of Umkontho Anti-Poaching Unit, personal communication, 2003). Such discretionary decisions on whether to prosecute on the basis of offender characteristics or motives for poaching were found in research on game warden discretion in the United States as well. Forsyth (1993b) found that officers were more likely to arrest offenders in lower social classes than those of higher status. Additionally, apprehended poachers who violated for reasons of survival tended to be overlooked by U.S. game wardens.

Not all field rangers employed by private reserves worked for private security companies. Some were rangers who had resigned or retired from the public parks and still desired employment in wildlife protection. I visited one such private game farm in the KNP area which employed a full-time year-round ranger force. The rangers in this unit, all of whom had public-sector experience, were somewhat older and far less militaristic in appearance. They carried only sidearms and dressed in ordinary work clothing rather than camouflage uniforms. Though less militaristic in appearance, the rangers were highly motivated and very willing to detect, pursue, and apprehend poachers in this for-profit reserve, which housed high-value wildlife, including black rhino. Having the power of civil arrest, rangers reported that they did not hesitate to pursue suspected poachers both on and off the property.

The American Approach to Conservation Law Enforcement: The Game Warden

At the state level in the United States, wildlife law enforcement is carried out by the various fish and game, conservation, or natural resource departments. The emergence of specialized police for state conservation areas began in the post–World War II era as increasing prosperity among Americans, combined with more time for recreation, an expanding road network, and increased private vehicle ownership, led to more travel. A popular destination for travelers were the public lands—national and state parks, forests, and shorelines (Falcone 2004). This trend eventually resulted in concern over how to protect these natural resources, given the increased usage by the vacationing public. One solution involved the establishment of departments of natural resources or conservation agencies charged with protecting the resource. These entities would include law enforcement agencies staffed by game wardens. By the 1990s, these agencies became more commonplace across the country, though they do not exist in every state. Furthermore, the numbers of game wardens in state conservation agencies are very low in comparison to police officers serving in departments in similarly sized metropolitan areas (Tobias 1998).

Like their African or Asian counterparts, American game wardens, also referred to as conservation officers, natural resource officers, or park rangers, have been the subject of very limited scholarly research—somewhat surprising given the uniqueness of the job. Interestingly, American game wardens have both distinct similarities to and differences from African field rangers. Game wardens often come from a rural background, having hunted and fished before entering their career (Lawson 2003). These attributes both facilitate their ability to work out-of-doors in wilderness areas and provide them with basic knowledge about proper hunting and fishing techniques. Game wardens are unique law enforcement officers requiring a wide range of knowledge, often exceeding that required for traditional urban policing. These individuals must not only be well versed in conservation law but also have enough of a background in biology to identify the various wildlife species in their jurisdiction. It also is common for game wardens to regularly encounter armed individuals during the course of their duties (Eliason 2011a). Unlike their African counterparts, American game wardens are more likely to work alone, though rangers in both parts of the world are not always able to rely on access to supporting officers in case of emergency. Finally, unlike the African field rangers, game wardens are typically able to operate a wide range of conveyances, ranging from all-terrain vehicles to boats, trucks, and even light aircraft (Michigan Department of Natural Resources Conservation Officer, personal communication, 2016). Field rangers patrolling in Africa or Asia are more likely to operate on foot or by bicycle. This is more a function of lack of funding for the equipment than lack of ability (KNP section ranger, personal communication, 2003).

State game wardens are primarily responsible for enforcement of state wildlife laws. Their legal authority varies by state, though the trend is toward game wardens having full police powers (Oliver and Meier 2006). Game wardens can often be state law enforcement officers whose duties include assisting city or county police when needed. This characteristic of being certified peace officers, providing them with the same law enforcement authority as U.S. police officers, makes the game wardens distinctly different from the typical field rangers in Africa or Asia. Game wardens are responsible for a wide range of activities, requiring extensive training and knowledge that exceeds that of their overseas ranger counterparts. These include basic law enforcement investigative techniques, familiarity with criminal and conservation law, search and rescue training, biodiversity monitoring, wildlife management, problem animal control, patrolling, and apprehension of suspects. While the training of African or Asian rangers focuses more on tactical aspects of the job and utilizes a military model, owing to the nature of the threat, U.S. game ranger training is more similar to police training in that it is lengthier and more comprehensive. Unlike their African or Asian counterparts, game wardens or conservation officers often have full police powers and are not restricted to just enforcing the state's conservation laws. Rather, their jurisdiction may include enforcement of state and federal laws (Falcone 2004).

Just as urban police face the threat of violence during the course of their daily patrols, game wardens regularly face risks to their safety. Game wardens are involved in rural, specialized policing that is inherently dangerous: threats come from people; the environment, including wildlife; and vehicles (Carter 2006; Eliason 2008). Since these officers commonly work alone in remote areas, they cannot always count on receiving help from assisting officers in times of need. Like their overseas counterparts, game wardens live and work in the mostly rural communities near the conservation areas they patrol. Unlike the anonymity that city police may have, rural game wardens are more likely to be known to local residents in the community. This allows more scrutiny of their work and the potential for threats to be made against their families from offenders or those opposed to enforcement of conservation laws (Oliver and Meier 2006). This trait is shared with their African and Asian field ranger counterparts.

The Federal Agencies: U.S. Fish and Wildlife and U.S. Customs and Border Protection

The American public-sector system for controlling and preventing wildlife crimes also relies on federal agencies. Unique in the system is the U.S. Fish and Wildlife Service (USFWS), a federal agency dedicated to the enforcement of wildlife laws on federal lands, including those addressing the illegal trade, both native and non-native. Also involved in preventing wildlife offenses, including the illegal trafficking of foreign species into the country, is the U.S. Customs and Border Protection (CBP), which is within the Department of Homeland Security. Both USFWS and CBP have a role at the U.S. borders, the primary location for international trafficking to and from the United States. USFWS works with CBP on inspections of cargo shipments at all ports. As a result, these agencies represent the first and perhaps most important line of defense against smugglers importing or exporting illegal wildlife. If contraband wildlife enters the United States undetected and moves into the wholesale or retail markets, it becomes far more difficult to intercept.

USFWS employs specialists known as *wildlife inspectors,* individuals who are tasked with ensuring that imports and exports are in compliance with both U.S. and international laws. Given the large size of the U.S. consumer market for wildlife, the second largest in the world for both legal and illegal species, the task is extremely challenging for USFWS inspectors. Working at eighteen designated major urban ports and at the Canadian and Mexican border crossings, these individuals need to be able to identify a wide range of species of wildlife, verify the validity of permits used for their shipment, and determine if the actual contents of a shipment are in agreement with what is stated on the permits and shipping manifests (USFWS 2013). U.S. Customs and Border Protection, though not a dedicated wildlife conservation agency, has the dual role of protecting the borders of the United States while ensuring the smooth flow of travel and trade. This involves monitoring shipments via air, land, and sea. CBP officers who inspect cargo shipments are also charged with monitoring airline passengers for contraband items, including illegal wildlife they are transporting into the country, at three hundred ports of entry. With more than twenty-four million cargo containers entering the United States each year by truck, ship, and rail, and the large numbers of airline passengers, the task is daunting (U.S. Customs and Border Protection [hereafter USCBP] 2016).

Inspecting shipments for illegal wildlife by USFWS is further complicated by the relatively low number of inspectors. A report on this situation found only ten USFWS inspectors staffing the Port of Los Angeles, where an estimated 30 percent of all wildlife products enter the United States. Moreover, the detection of illegal narcotics was a higher priority than illegal wildlife for enforcement officials. Similarly, a news story on this issue found just six inspectors working at New York's JFK Airport, another major port of entry for international cargo (Fears 2014). According to the report, overall there were fewer than three hundred thirty USFWS inspectors working in the nation's ports, about the same number as in 1984. This was partly a function of law enforcement priorities. Though efforts had been made to enhance interagency cooperation at the federal level to reduce smuggling, staffing was not increased.

A second challenge stems from the sheer volume of shipments in transit at any one time, preventing comprehensive inspections. The shipments are electronically scanned, but the objective is typically to find narcotics or weapons rather than wildlife. USFWS inspectors will inspect cargo if they have sound intelligence that it contains contraband. Otherwise, they commonly rely on a spot-checking system of shipments for contraband, which is deemed to be more efficient. Given the volume of cargo and the low number of inspectors, one may conclude that the likelihood of successfully smuggling illegal wildlife shipments is good. Darryl Fears (2014) notes that when

USFWS inspectors arrest a smuggler for the first time, the subsequent investigation of his or her travel history may reveal that the same individual transported previous shipments through the same port, sometimes over several years. This is not to imply that smugglers move illegal wildlife with impunity into and out of the United States but that the task of interdiction is challenging. These federal agencies have made many notable recent large-scale seizures of illegal wildlife. One case, known as Operation Crash, carried out by the USFWS and U.S. Department of Justice, culminated in twenty-four arrests, resulting in at least twelve convictions of individuals for wildlife smuggling and related offenses. Included among them where two prolific South African rhinoceros horn smugglers who allegedly sold nearly four hundred horns (EIA 2015a).

International Contributions

INTERPOL, the international police organization established in 1923 as the International Criminal Police Commission, was created to foster cross-border cooperation between police agencies and to prevent international organized crime. Interpol has one hundred ninety member countries, each maintaining a National Central Bureau staffed by law enforcement officers. These bureaus are networked to allow for cooperation on international crime matters. INTERPOL focuses on a range of offenses, one of which is environmental crimes. Within this category is wildlife crime, which includes the exploitation of flora and fauna. INTERPOL recognizes that wildlife crime is in part the domain of criminal syndicates and that the offense represents a threat to a nation's economy and security. As a result, the organization offers assistance to national police agencies in investigations and operations against these networks (INTERPOL 2016).

INTERPOL also provides assistance to nongovernmental organizations dedicated to wildlife conservation, including combating the illegal trade. In response to the current wave of elephant poaching, in 2005 the International Fund for Animal Welfare (IFAW) began working with INTERPOL's Environmental Crime Program. IFAW was able to provide funding via a grant to establish a position of Criminal Intelligence Officer for Wildlife Crime at INTERPOL, a position that focuses strictly on establishing programs to end wildlife trafficking. Other interesting joint efforts between INTERPOL and IFAW include the large-scale Project Wisdom and Operation Worthy. These programs have been directed at enhancing law enforcement's capacity to prevent poaching of elephants and rhinoceros and carrying out operations against criminal networks in more than a dozen African nations, resulting in over two hundred arrests and the confiscation of ivory and rhino horn (IFAW n.d.[a]).

Militarization of African Field Rangers

A contemporary subject recently addressed in the research is the practice of militarizing field ranger units in response to the increasing threat of poaching (Lunstrum 2014). The term *green militarization* describes the adoption of military equipment, tactics, and leadership models designed to meet the threat of the heavily armed poaching units that operate in some African nations. These criminal units include insurgency, terror, and paramilitary groups poaching wildlife in Central Africa and East Africa. One may recognize the concept of militarization, since it has been used of late to refer to changes in some police departments in the United States that have received surplus military equipment from the Department of Defense. This equipment may include armored vehicles formerly used in overseas conflicts, military firearms, surveillance gear, and tactical clothing. Some observers have been highly critical of this development, arguing that police departments begin to look more like occupying armies than public safety agencies. This unease, in turn, serves to increase tension, as occurred with the British Army's occupation of Northern Ireland from the 1970s to the 1990s.

Elizabeth Lunstrum's (2014) study of green militarization focused on the enhanced security efforts in South Africa's Kruger National Park in response to significantly increased rhinoceros poaching. Kruger is unique among South Africa's national parks because it shares a border with Mozambique, the location from which poachers often enter the park. I found not only that KNP's ranger force incorporated military hardware, including manned and unmanned aircraft, and tactics in its anti-poaching efforts but also that the South African Defense Forces were involved in attempting to prevent illegal hunting. The green militarization of ranger forces has been questioned with regard to its unintended consequences. These include environmental damage to the park from operations of military units, higher levels of violence when security forces encounter poachers, deaths of immigrants from Mozambique illegally transiting the park to South Africa, and changing the park's dynamic to a battlefield. Lunstrum points out that the militarization of park security did not appear to have much effect on reducing poaching. The counter-argument to critics of militarizing ranger forces is that well-armed poaching groups, including military units and terrorist groups, are now actively involved in poaching in some parts of Africa, though not South Africa. Traditional ranger units offer little or no deterrence to this type of threat. This was acknowledged by former KWS director Richard Leakey when he advocated for improving the firearms issued to park ranger units to effectively confront well-armed poaching gangs (Leakey and Morrell 2001). Yet this practice goes well beyond providing modern weapons to ranger forces to match those of poachers. The long-term effectiveness of green militarization in reducing poaching and the militarization's impact on the parks remain to be seen. Whether the Kruger National Park security model should become a standard for other parks in Africa under severe poaching threat is also at issue.

Prosecuting Conservation Cases

Preventing wildlife crimes requires appropriate legislation, effective policing of the resources, and prosecution of the offenders in the court system (Nurse 2015). A significant body of legislation exists to protect wildlife in many nations. The United States, for example, is a party to CITES and has enacted major federal legislation and a myriad of state laws to protect wildlife and its habitats. Other nations rich in wildlife also have long-standing and extensive legal codes to protect and preserve these natural resources. Added to this equation as discussed previously is the need for wildlife conservation law enforcement agents, whether they are game wardens in the United States or field rangers in Africa or Asia. Finally, it is necessary to have trained prosecutors familiar with conservation violations and a court system that is willing to adjudicate the offenses. With this combination of resources, there can be an improvement in the conviction of wildlife offenders that can, in turn, reduce poaching and smuggling and serve as a deterrent to offenders, both current and future.

While there is a considerable amount of legislation at both the international and national level addressing wildlife offenses, the enforcement of these laws varies considerably, owing in part to national priorities, funding, and even the effects of corruption, especially in some developing nations. Even with well-written legislation, if the enforcement is lax or inefficient, the laws can do little to protect wildlife (Schneider 2012; Warchol and Kapla 2012). In nations with well-staffed and funded enforcement agencies, proper arrests of suspects followed by well-prepared case files still leave another hurdle to clear. Wildlife offenses are niche crimes that are not very common in the court systems of most nations. Prosecutors may have little or no familiarity with conservation laws or past experience in trying these cases. Furthermore, it may simply not be a priority for the prosecutors in a given jurisdiction where rates of violent or property crime are high and filling the court's docket. In other instances, in southern Africa, some wildlife offenses may be viewed as either not very important or not even a crime. Finally, prosecutors might sympathize with offenders who are impoverished subsistence poachers or be unwilling to proceed with a case because they lack a background in wildlife conservation law (SANParks field rangers, personal communication, 2005).

Angus Nurse (2015) found that a lack of knowledge by both prosecutors and judges would certainly hinder the process of adjudicating wildlife crime

offenses. Obvious solutions to the problem include training of court personnel in the nature of conservation violations and the application of the law, or
the expansion of prosecutorial staff and needed resources to manage these
cases in jurisdictions that also have high numbers of violent and property
offenses. Another solution found in South Africa was for field rangers to
work closely with local prosecutors in an effort to build a relationship. The
rangers staffing a private game farm that was regularly targeted by poachers
worked to educate local prosecutors on the conservation laws. Concurrently,
the prosecutors instructed the rangers on what they required in a case for a
successful outcome. The belief was that building this relationship would
make it more likely for the local prosecutor to agree to file the case with the
court (Herbig and Warchol 2011). While this may not lead to a dramatic
increase in prosecutors accepting cases, it can help increase the number of
convictions, benefiting both the game owners and the prosecutors.

The Role of the Courts

The next potential hurdle for prosecuting wildlife offenders lies with the
court system. In some jurisdictions in Africa and Asia, the courts can be
overburdened with other types of crimes considered more serious or have
judges unfamiliar with or not interested in wildlife offense cases. This was a
common complaint made to me during fieldwork in southern Africa. Frus-
trated rangers, in both the public and the private sector, often reported that
they arrested poachers and worked with prosecutors to prepare the case only
to have it declined by the local court (private game farm field rangers, personal communication, 2004; SANParks section rangers, personal communication, 2008). Reasons that local magistrates provide to justify their
decisions included the explanations that poaching cases are trivial compared
to more serious and common violent crimes, that it is of little value to prosecute an indigent subsistence hunter, and that their own knowledge of wildlife conservation laws was limited. It is important to note that these cases
generally involve low-level offenders—typically small-scale subsistence or
for-profit hunters. Major poaching or trafficking cases involving large
amounts of wildlife products were more likely to be prosecuted because of
the seriousness of the offense. However, if this situation becomes the norm,
rangers may feel little incentive to make arrests for cases that have slight
chance of making it onto the local court's docket.

When wildlife crime cases are heard by the court, a conviction is certainly not guaranteed even if the case involves endangered or threatened species. Research by the EIA in Southeast Asia found that the results of wildlife
offense prosecutions in Vietnam were inconsistent at best. According to the
group's investigation, even though offenders trafficking in ivory, rhino horn,

and tiger parts were convicted, oftentimes the court chose to impose a fine, probation, or even a suspended sentence. These light sentences limit the deterrent effect on the offenders and on aspiring offenders (EIA 2015a). Furthermore, the EIA (2014) found instances in which there was a lack of judges available to hear the cases and, more seriously, evidence of attempted bribery of officials, resulting in high numbers of lost wildlife offense cases. The end result is fewer prosecutions and convictions. The other issue was the all too common focus on low-level operators in the illegal wildlife trade. EIA investigations determined that too many wildlife crime arrests were of lower-level members of the supply chain. Because the wildlife trade is transnational and involves various types of criminal syndicates, the leaders of these organizations were not easily targeted or apprehended. Low-level workers lost through convictions were easily replaced with new willing participants. While targeting the head of criminal syndicates is of course more time-consuming and difficult, the apprehension and conviction of a syndicate leader can have a far greater impact on the enterprise than that of a low-level worker.

Green Courts

Solutions have been offered to better ensure that wildlife crime cases are at least heard by courts. One unique approach is the concept of a *green court*. This term refers to a court of limited jurisdiction dedicated to handling environmental law violations, which would include conservation crimes. This concept is similar to the use of dedicated probate, juvenile, or traffic courts commonly found in the United States. In developing countries experiencing significant challenges with wildlife crimes, the lack of dedicated green or environmental courts has detracted from the ability to consistently handle cases brought forward by investigators and prosecutors. My research in South Africa revealed a need for this institution to prosecute wildlife crimes, alleviating pressure on the criminal courts and perhaps deterring current and aspiring offenders. In the green courts, judges or magistrates and prosecutors would specialize in hearing only environmental crime cases. Such cases would be exclusively directed to these courts, which would allow the concentration of expertise in specialized areas of environmental law.

The idea of environmental courts is not new. In more than forty nations, dedicated environmental courts process green crimes that involve both criminal and civil offenses (White 2013). The majority of these courts direct their efforts at policing and regulating the environment (Walters and Westerhuis 2013). China, for example, has dedicated environmental courts with jurisdiction over offenses in this area of law (Zhang and Zhang 2012). These courts have also been established in India in an effort to concentrate on environmental crimes (Desai and Balraj 2010). In New South Wales, Australia, green courts were established to hear cases involving a range of environmental harms. The cases adjudicated in these courts come under the broad category of ecological justice cases, a concept that "upholds the importance of all living creatures as well as inanimate objects . . . and provides useful insights for guiding future economic and developmental decisions" (Walters and Westerhuis 2013, 280). When environmental courts are established and staffed with trained judicial personnel, there is a better chance of prosecuting offenders (White 2013). While this is a sound starting point, one issue detracting from their effectiveness is that environment courts commonly handle a wide range of cases involving both criminal and civil law violations. These may include air and water pollution, land use and development, and natural resources. Wildlife offenses, which require a specialized area of legal knowledge, are just one of many types of offenses within the category of environmental crimes. Furthermore, establishing dedicated environmental crimes courts comes with a price, which can prevent their implementation in some nations. Yet this type of court remains a positive step toward increasing the rates of prosecution of wildlife crime offenders. The ideal solution, though not necessarily the most feasible given resource constraints, would be dedicated green courts with exclusive jurisdiction over wildlife crimes.

Summary: Natural Resource Protection Efforts

The need to protect the natural resource of wildlife has long been recognized by nations and private enterprises. This concern resulted in the development of a variety of specialized law enforcement agencies that work directly in the protected areas and at nations' borders and ports to intercept illegal wildlife shipments. The American approach to wildlife conservation law enforcement included the creation of fish and game or natural resource departments at the state level. These agencies typically include a police force employing conservation officers or game wardens who enforce fish and game laws. Unique among state game wardens is that many have full police power with jurisdiction that goes beyond enforcing conservation laws. State conservation officers may be called on to assist local law enforcement or enforce federal laws. Wildlife law enforcement in the United States at the national level involves one dedicated federal agency—the U.S. Fish and Wildlife Service, whose mission includes enforcing federal wildlife laws, protecting endangered species, managing refuges, and assisting in international conservation efforts. Though wildlife law enforcement is not its primary mission, U.S. Customs and Border Protection is also involved through its efforts at cargo and passenger inspections at national ports and borders.

The first line of defense for wildlife in Africa and Asia is the field ranger in the public parks and, in some countries, the private parks. While American and African rangers share both the responsibility of biodiversity monitoring and protection and the burden of operating in difficult and often dangerous environments, there are very distinct differences between the two. The type and duration of their training, daily operations, general responsibilities, and level of violence from poachers vary considerably. Many African rangers rely on a paramilitary model that focuses on armed patrol, military tactics, surveillance, and interdiction of poachers. This is a function of the higher likelihood of violent encounters with well-armed poaching gangs in some reserves. To improve their effectiveness, ranger forces in some African nations, including South Africa and Uganda, are embracing new technologies for surveillance, accountability, and patrol. Of these, the trend toward predictive analysis models may provide a greatly improved technique to maximize the effectiveness of ranger patrols.

Field rangers are not exclusive to the public sector in Africa. Supporting the need among private, for-profit game reserves and farms for wildlife protection are private anti-poaching ranger training academies and anti-poaching units. The private ownership and management of game in several southern African nations, with South Africa being the most notable, led to the development of this industry. These private forces, which work on a contractual basis with the different types of for-profit game reserves, can be similar to their public-sector counterparts in terms of appearance, training, and operations. Mostly relying on the same paramilitary model, they lend support to the view that game protection in parts of Africa is becoming more militarized in response to increased poaching.

While game wardens and field rangers commonly apprehend poachers, the immediate hurdle they encounter is ensuring that suspects will be prosecuted in the courts. The lack of prosecution of poaching cases is a long-standing issue in parts of Africa and Asia. Court systems are overwhelmed by the more serious violent and property crimes; there is a lack of interest in trying poaching offenders, owing to a view that the crimes are of little importance; and prosecutors and judges often have inadequate knowledge of conservation law. Arresting offenders only to have them released without prosecution not only inhibits the deterrent effect of the law but also decreases morale among rangers, who often risk their lives to apprehend offenders. Solutions to this problem have included efforts by game departments to educate and work with prosecutors on poaching law to improve the likelihood the case will proceed. The other solution is the development of dedicated environmental or green courts. While environment courts exist in dozens of nations, they handle a wide range of environmental law violations of which poaching is just one. Green courts dedicated to wildlife crime violations, though a luxury, can assist with the appropriate adjudication of offenders.

7

Future Issues
and Developments

Trends and Developments in Wildlife
Crime and Conservation

A thorough look at the state of the illegal trade in wildlife described in previous chapters often paints a dark picture of the situation and the prospects for the long-term survival of many endangered or threatened species. Recent trends include a dramatic increase in rhinoceros poaching in southern Africa, beginning in 2008, threatening to erase the remarkable recovery efforts of the last few decades that saved the species from possible extinction. This trend is driven by additional demand for the product in certain Asian nations, the result of increasing prosperity and a new set of beliefs in the perceived curative powers of the horn. Also contributing to the problem is the presence of well-organized and difficult-to-penetrate criminal syndicates controlling the majority of the trade in rhino horn, which since 2008 has cost the lives of nearly 6,000 animals (Orenstein 2013; Save the Rhino 2015). Similarly, evidence of the presence of other Asian criminal syndicates operating in southern Africa to poach marine species indicates how extensive the threat has become in the last decade (Warchol and Harrington 2016). Another recent emerging problem is the involvement of armed militias and terrorist groups in extensive elephant poaching in Central Africa and East Africa to raise revenue to fund their operations. Linked to criminal groups in Asia that provide ivory for the consumer market, this contemporary model of militarized poaching has fostered a surge in the loss of elephants in the region. The ongoing problem of tiger poaching in Asia and Russia has put significant pressure on the species, whose long-term survival is in doubt. The loss of these animals is the result of consumer demand for decorative objects or ingredients for traditional medicines. One current government response to the problem of heavy poaching has been referred to as *green militarization*. This concept refers to the practice at some African national parks of transforming their field ranger forces into paramilitary forces with new equipment, training, and tactics and reinforcing them with actual military units. Recent research has questioned the efficacy of this practice, noting the possible unintended negative consequences (Lunstrum 2014). Another area of concern is the increasing human population in developing nations, which can put additional pressure on wildlife as a food source, with corresponding habitat destruction. Yet the fact that human populations are increasing should not automatically correspond with negative impacts on ecosystems and their wildlife. Proper resource management via sound conservation programs should help mitigate the problems. Unfortunately, in many developing nations with sought-after wildlife, this type of resource management is not always the case. The combination of entrenched government corruption, poverty, resource exploitation by local and foreign business interests, and ineffective game and/or environmental departments creates a perfect storm for the loss of wildlife and habitat.

However, even with severe problems currently threatening a wide range of species around the globe, there have been many very positive developments in conservation that illustrate how wildlife populations can be protected, recover, and eventually prosper. These include various types of successful programs for protecting wildlife and their habitats; new approaches to enforcement for protected conservation areas; initiatives by governments, private enterprises, and NGOs to control and prevent the illegal trade; campaigns to reduce demand for wildlife products; and new legislation and agreements. Involved in these efforts are nongovernmental organizations, academic researchers, private-sector businesses, and national governments, at times forming public/private partnerships. Another positive development is the steadily increasing body of scholarly research that describes the illegal trade and offers numerous strategies that may protect endangered and threatened species and foster their survival for the long term. A growing body of scholarship is applying criminological theories once generally confined to explaining violent, property, and public order crimes to the problem of wildlife crimes. A portion of this research is being applied in the field to implement and assess the effectiveness of new conservation techniques.

This chapter describes a selection of programs and efforts designed to control or prevent the illegal trade in different regions of the world and reduce consumer demand for these products. In much of this book we have examined the structure and effects of the illegal trade in Africa—a region that is heavily exploited for not only its charismatic megafauna but also a wide range of common species. In response, conservation programs have been implemented on the continent in an effort to protect wildlife and its habitat. These include *community-based conservation programs* that allow the local residents living near protected areas to benefit from the wildlife. One of the most distinctive is Zimbabwe's CAMPFIRE program. This decentralized conservation program allows the sustainable for-profit use of protected lands by people who live in the nation's communal areas. A goal of the program is to give an economic value to the wildlife, which, in turn, benefits the local community and the wildlife, thereby fostering its protection. A somewhat similar program was begun in 2005 via a partnership between the nongovernmental organization International Fund for Animal Welfare (IFAW) and the Kenya Wildlife Service (KWS) at Tsavo National Park, which made a joint effort to improve the quality of the park, protect the wildlife from poaching, and benefit local residents. A different and more traditional supply reduction conservation program is one that focuses on protecting one or several different species from losses to poaching. Known as the Carnivore Programme, it was instituted in Zambia in an effort to protect the population of large predators—lion, leopard, wild dog, hyena, and cheetah—in its reserves. To illustrate the unique attributes and value of these programs, each is described in more detail later in this chapter.

Other recent supply reduction conservation efforts have emerged from national governments in major consumer nations of wildlife. In 2014, President Barack Obama announced a formal U.S. National Strategy for Combating Wildlife Trafficking. This strategy was an outgrowth of increasing concern over the problem of the illegal trade by both the Obama and Bush administrations. The administration noted that illegal trade not only harms wildlife and ecosystems but also contributes to the destabilization of the countries that are suffering from the poaching and trafficking and their corrupting influences. This, in turn, results in a national security threat in the region. Across the Atlantic in 2015, a new conservation effort was announced in the United Kingdom called the Buckingham Palace Declaration, which focuses on the illegal trade from the source countries into the United Kingdom. Uniquely, this effort involves private-sector shipping companies and conservation groups working together on one essential component that the illegal trade requires—the ability to transport its contraband.

At one time, much of the scholarly research on wildlife poaching and species loss was found in the literature on biology and environmental conservation. In the last fifteen years, an increasing number of scholars have begun to examine aspects of the illegal wildlife trade through the lens of criminology. One result of this approach is contemporary research applying situational crime prevention theory, routine activities theory, and GIS crime mapping techniques to the problem of poaching. Recent studies examined the concept of creating data-driven mathematical models to improve ranger effectiveness in the game reserves. The goal was to collect a range of data on poaching, terrain, and human and wildlife activity to create a model for developing the best patrol routes for rangers to increase their likelihood of intercepting poachers. A predictive analysis computer application based on this research is being used regularly in Malaysia to protect its tiger populations.

Another aspect of wildlife conservation and controlling the illegal trade is the role of the private sector. While nongovernmental organizations have a long history of working to prevent the illegal wildlife trade, for-profit entities are also involved in conservation. This chapter examines the role of the privatization of wildlife for commercial hunting and tourism in supporting conservation and preventing poaching. The view is that when wildlife is given an economic value for hunting or photographic safaris, an incentive is created to protect the animals. The concept of *conservation by the gun* is used to describe hunting as a form of conservation, oftentimes derisively. Yet many African nations allow trophy hunting, and some of the fees paid by hunters are transferred to game departments for wildlife conservation (S. Chen 2016). Most notable among these is South Africa, which has developed a prosperous trophy hunting industry. Up until 2015, limited attention has been paid to the role of hunting in conservation. When Zimbabwe's *Cecil the lion* hunting case attracted the attention of the mass media, the issue of hunting as conservation became a hotly debated subject.

Part of privatization is allowing the sale of wildlife products from endangered species into consumer markets to generate revenue for conservation. As noted earlier in this work, this is not a new concept. So-called *one-off* sales of ivory have been approved by CITES and conducted by African elephant range states to obtain needed funds for game departments. In 2015, South Africa proposed selling its stockpile of confiscated rhinoceros horns, which had an estimated value of $1 billion USD. The revenue from the sale would be used to fund conservation. Both proponents and critics of the problem offered their views as to the benefits and negative consequences of this market-involved approach to controlling the illegal trade.

Finally, this chapter examines some notable efforts at reducing consumer demand for wildlife and influencing changes to policy. As in the illegal narcotics trade, if demand were reduced, it is presumed that less of the product would be produced and smuggled to the consumer market. Attempting to influence public opinion to avoid wildlife products from threatened and endangered species has long been a component of conservation groups. The Asian-based WildAid produces sophisticated public relations campaigns to raise awareness among consumers about the impact of the illegal trade. Another, more dramatic, public relations strategy, focused in part on demand reduction, has been the staging of public ivory burns. First begun in Kenya in 1989 under the guidance of Richard Leakey of the Kenya Wildlife Service and Kenyan president Daniel Moi, ivory burns and crushes have been done in several nations, including the United States, to focus public attention on the problem of elephant poaching and to reduce the supply of ivory on the market. On April 30, 2016, Kenya conducted the largest one in history, destroying 105 tons of ivory and another 1.5 tons of rhinoceros horn. While the well-publicized event attracts the attention of the public and media, another goal was to use it to push for a complete global ban on ivory sales. The benefits and liabilities of this practice are examined in this chapter.

Conservation Programs

Community Involvement and Public-Private Efforts

Contemporary solutions to poaching and trafficking wildlife go beyond strictly focusing on the law enforcement component. While effective game ranger forces are necessary, this alone will not solve the problem. Rather, more comprehensive resource management practices need to be considered and implemented (Hauck and Sweijd 1999). These management practices include programs that foster relationship building between park administrators, rangers, and local residents. People living near game reserves should be aware that the protected areas are more than a holiday place. They need to know why the park is there—to protect a valuable resource (SANParks section ranger, personal communication, 2010). Furthermore, the concerns of local residents about the reserve need to be addressed along with ways they are able to benefit from the area through employment opportunities or sustainable use of the resources. The sought-after end result is for local communities to value the reserve and its resources and therefore become involved in its protection. This is a main goal of community-based or grassroots conservation programs.

CAMPFIRE

One of the most well-known conservation programs is CAMPFIRE (Communal Areas Management Program for Indigenous Resources), implemented in the southern African nation of Zimbabwe in 1989. It is a community conservation program that falls within the Payment for Environmental Services model. This type of conservation program allows local communities to access their wildlife resources at sustainable levels as a source of revenue (Frost and Bond 2007). Zimbabwe began this program in an effort to both conserve natural resources and alleviate rural poverty (Logan and Moseley 2002). The CAMPFIRE

Project is mostly decentralized, with the program management authority delegated to the rural district councils (RDC) in communal agricultural areas or lands that are adjacent to protected areas. Unlike other centralized programs administered from a national government, the CAMPFIRE Project allows the RDCs to manage their local resources, including the game animals. They have the right to contract with trophy hunting and safari tourism companies to access the lands and game, cull selected species for use as bushmeat, sell excess animals, and collect other useful or valuable wildlife resources, such as timber, insects, river sand, and some eggs (Frost and Bond 2007).

CAMPFIRE was specifically developed to benefit the residents of Zimbabwe's communal farming lands (Martin 1986). While CAMPFIRE is primarily a conservation program, it is also designed to help alleviate the severe poverty found in many rural communal land areas (Logan and Mosley 2002). The program functions by placing an economic value on the natural resources, including animals, and by allowing residents of the adjacent communal lands to market these for profit. Previously, residents in these areas, having been denied access to the protected lands and their wildlife, considered these resources to be of little value and not worthy of protecting. An objective of this program was to instill an economic interest in the resource that can be accessed by the local residents to their benefit. They derive revenues both from the sale of access to the area and from the proceeds of the wildlife, along with being allowed to consume some of the resource for their own needs at sustainable levels (Gibson 1999). The most profitable component of CAMPFIRE is trophy hunting. Fees paid to purchase rights for hunting generates the most revenue for the participating communal lands (Frost and Bond 2007). The revenue goes to the agricultural communities and is managed by the local rural district councils.

Another rationale for the program was the need to erase the colonial conservation legacy that had moved some communities off their lands to establish protected areas and then subsequently prohibited or limited the communities' access to their former lands (Alexander and McGregor 2000). CAMPFIRE's origins are found in a 1978 program called Wildlife Industries New Development for All, or WINDFALL, which focused on allowing local communities living adjacent to game reserves to benefit from elephant culling operations. Though not considered successful, this older program allowed rural residents to benefit from the wildlife that they were previously prohibited from using and commonly viewed as a nuisance. The deficiencies of WINDFALL were addressed in CAMPFIRE so that local communities would now not only benefit financially but also have a say in the management of the resource (Gibson 1999). By so doing, it was hoped, the illegal use of the resources would be reduced, thus protecting the wildlife. This model allows the RDCs to negotiate with the lucrative trophy hunting companies for access to game, and the profits go directly to the councils for redistribution to the community, at times in the form of direct payments. Though CAMPFIRE employs a largely decentralized model, the wildlife is considered the property of the state and therefore Zimbabwe's Department of National Parks establishes the quotas for hunting and culling (Gibson 1999).

The Zambian Carnivore Programme

One area of concern in sub-Saharan Africa has been the slow decline of some of the large carnivore species because of a combination of poaching, disease, and habitat loss due to human encroachment (Watson et al. 2015). For example, current estimates of the population of the best-known carnivore, the African lion, are between 30,000 and 35,000 remaining animals in the wild (WWF n.d.). The southern African nation of Zambia is well known for its large and diverse wildlife populations, including the major predators. Concern over the loss of these species owing to human-wildlife conflict, poaching, or disease led to the development and establishment of the Zambian Carnivore Programme (ZCP) by a nonprofit Zambian trust (Zambian Carnivore Programme [hereafter ZCP] 2016). This more traditional conservation program was implemented with the goal of protecting selected carnivore species considered currently or potentially at risk. It primarily focuses on the protection of the large cat species (lion, leopard, and cheetah), the African wild dog and hyena, their prey species, and their ecosystem.

Zambia presents unique challenges for conservation efforts given the extent of its protected areas (national parks, game management areas, and wildlife sanctuaries), which encompass about 40 percent of the nation's land mass, and the problems faced by wildlife. Wildlife populations and their ecosystems are under pressure from poaching, commonly including indiscriminant snaring for bushmeat, human settlements, encroachment of subsistence agriculture on wildlife habitat, and commercial development. The situation is made more difficult by weak enforcement and management of the lands by the national government and limited economic opportunities for Zambian citizens to improve their situation (Lindsey et al. 2006).

By focusing on the current threats to carnivores' survival, ZCP attempts to protect designated species while also improving the data collection necessary for effective management of the program, something that was previously lacking in other conservation programs. One aspect of the program was to address threats to carnivores from the use of snares for illegal bushmeat hunting. Set in large numbers by poachers in search of game meat, snares are indiscriminately injuring and killing all types of prey animals as well as the large cat species (Becker et al. 2013). In response, ZCP includes a snare removal component to reduce and eliminate this threat to the wildlife. A second focus of the project is to reduce the transmission of disease between wildlife and domestic dogs. Africans own canines not as family pets but for security and hunting, as crucial working members of the family. When wildlife comes into close contact with dogs, diseases can be transmitted from one species to another with potentially fatal results. Program managers, realizing that the contacts between the species cannot be prevented, instead turned to a vaccination program for the domestic dogs. A third component of the program is mitigating human-carnivore conflicts. Referred to as conflict or problem animals, large carnivores represent a serious threat to the safety of humans and livestock residing in close proximity to protected areas. Efforts at reducing these conflicts are included in the program's major goals. Finally, the last part of the ZCP involves the reintroduction of carnivore species into selected areas where they have disappeared (ZCP 2016). This may be the most challenging aspect of the program, given that local residents near these areas must be willing to accept the return of dangerous wildlife. To measure progress toward these four objectives, it is key to assess the effectiveness of the program. This is accomplished through data collection, which is used to guide management decisions. Included in the program is active field research done year-round in selected ecosystems in an effort to obtain data on the wildlife, the environment, and the threats to the carnivores' survival (ZCP 2016). The creation of solutions based on continuous research can allow a more proactive approach to protecting the designated species.

The KWS and IFAW Partnership

In 2005, a new wildlife conservation program was established via a public-private partnership in Kenya's Tsavo National Park. Located in southeastern Kenya, Tsavo was established in 1948; it covers more than sixteen thousand square miles and makes up about 3 percent of the total land mass of the country (IFAW 2011). The park is well known for its biodiversity, including elephant and rhino populations along with more common plains game. Concerns about improving Tsavo and reducing poaching led to a partnership between the nongovernmental organization International Fund for Animal Welfare and the Kenya Wildlife Service with the goal of developing a conservation program. The unique, comprehensive, five-year program that resulted from an analysis of the park identified six distinct problem areas that needed improvement: anti-poaching, infrastructure and operations improvement, human-wildlife conflict mitigation, community conservation, ecological research, and conservation education for local communities (IFAW 2011). This program also incorporated continuous data collection and analysis to assess progress in attaining the sought-after improvements and to guide decision making by administrators.

Part of the program's uniqueness is its creation of a comprehensive strategy rather than just a concentration on the common problem of poaching. While protecting wildlife was certainly important, the other components of the program focused on enhancing the park's infrastructure and operations and working with local residents adjacent to the park to address their concerns, which included the frequent presence of large or dangerous animals that damaged crops or threatened residents. Other critical issues were providing economic opportunities for residents and establishing educational programs focused on the value of conservation (IFAW 2011; IFAW Nairobi staffer, personal communication, March 2011). IFAW worked to provide funding for the project to help ensure its long-term success beyond its completion of date of 2009.

Supply Reduction Efforts

The 2014 U.S. National Strategy and China's 2017 Ban on Ivory

As the international wildlife trade has persisted and even expanded in some geographic areas, initiatives have been implemented by consumer nations to address the problem. In the United States, President Obama announced an effort in February 2014 to reduce the illegal trade in wildlife, including elephant poaching. This initiative is known as the U.S. National Strategy for Combating Wildlife Trafficking. The document establishes the U.S. government's primary objectives or guiding principles for the control and prevention of the illegal trade in wildlife (White House 2014; WWF 2014b). Furthermore, it includes the strategy for strengthening both domestic and international enforcement efforts, reducing demand for illegal wildlife both in the United States and abroad, and improving partnerships with nongovernmental organizations, private businesses, communities, and international parties (U.S. Department of State 2015). The second major component included a ban on the commercial trade in elephant ivory in the United States. This would restrict the domestic sale and prohibit the commercial import and export of elephant ivory. The ultimate goal is to end the U.S. commercial market for ivory and ivory products. This would be accomplished by changes to the rules of the federal departments and administrative agencies, including the U.S. Fish and Wildlife Service (White House 2014). However, there are still exceptions carved out in the national strategy. For example, antique ivory verified at being over one hundred years old and hunting trophies would still be allowed on the U.S. domestic market and would be legal to export. The announcement of this strategy was based on the realization that in part the illegal trade in elephant ivory represents both a conservation issue and a national security threat

(White House 2014). The Obama administration also sought to obtain commitments on preventing the illegal trade in the series of new trade agreements being negotiated, such as the Trans-Pacific Partnership, involving Asia and the Pacific, and the Transatlantic Partnership Agreement, which involves the European Union (U.S. Department of State 2015). However, the Trump administration's opposition to these trade agreements may result in a different approach.

In a follow-up to the announcement of the National Strategy, in February 2015 an implementation plan for the strategy was introduced by the Presidential Task Force on Wildlife Trafficking. This group comprises seventeen federal agencies and departments, led by State, Interior, and Justice. The implementation plan provides the process for meeting the main objectives of the National Strategy, designation of the agencies and their tasks, and progress measurement efforts. The role of the U.S. Department of Justice is carried out through its Environmental and Natural Resources Division, along with the Offices of the U.S. Attorney in the ninety-four federal districts. Their jurisdiction is based on the Lacey Act of 1900 and the Endangered Species Act of 1973, as well as the various statutes that define the crimes commonly used to facilitate the illegal trade in wildlife. These include money laundering, smuggling, and wire fraud (U.S. Department of Justice 2015b).

In December 2016, a major development for elephant conservation occurred in China when the government announced a ban on ivory, to take full effect by the end of 2017. The ban started with an end to the commercial processing and sale of ivory by March 31, followed by the phasing out of all commercial traders by the end of the year, thereby completing the halting of China's domestic trade ("China announces ban on ivory trade by end of 2017" 2016). With China's status as the world's largest market for ivory, the nation is considered the biggest driver of elephant poaching in Africa. While the international trade in ivory was prohibited in 1990, the domestic trade was legal in both China and the United States. Elephant conservationists have argued that the existence of a legal ivory trade contributes to the illegal trade because poached tusks are smuggled to legal carving operations (Bale 2017b). This policy should yield considerable benefits for elephant conservation.

The United Kingdom's Buckingham Palace Declaration

Concern over the illegal wildlife trade and its impact on selected species, the exploitation of legitimate shipping companies, and weaknesses in customs controls in the United Kingdom resulted in a successful one-year effort of the United for Wildlife (UFW) task force to establish an agreement known as the Buckingham Palace Declaration. This initiative takes a different approach than the U.S. National Strategy in attempting to control the illegal trade. The Declaration is focused on the trafficking or transportation component of the trade, which is key to moving illegally obtained wildlife from its source nations across international borders to its end user countries. What makes this agreement unique is that it involves private enterprises—that is, shipping companies working with the legal authorities to help stop the trafficking of wildlife (Zoological Society of London 2016).

The Declaration is a commitment by the signatories to address vulnerabilities in the transportation industry critical for wildlife traffickers to move contraband, specifically focusing on the weaknesses in the shipping and customs systems (TRAFFIC 2016a). The agreement was signed by more than thirty parties in a commitment to support private businesses in combating the illegal trade (Airports Council International 2016). The signatories include the leaders of shipping companies, airlines, customs agencies, nongovernmental organizations, and port operators. It incorporates information sharing from the parties about likely smuggling routes accessible to law enforcement and customs. It also provides for the companies to notify the authorities in the event of the discovery of a suspect cargo shipment (United for Wildlife 2016). The approach is designed to cut the crucial line between suppliers and consumers by targeting the trafficking or shipment of illegally obtained wildlife—the operations of the smuggler, who represents the essential middleman between the poacher and the consumer. A prime goal is to raise the standards for shippers to prevent wildlife smugglers from taking advantage of critical vulnerabilities in transportation systems to move their illegal cargos. It is important to note that the Buckingham Palace Declaration is simply a formal commitment that must be implemented by the parties that agreed to the effort. Future efforts are needed to ensure that it is functioning as designed and that the signatories are adhering to their commitments. Yet it represents a unique conservation initiative in that it involves end user or consumer nations and focuses on the trafficking of wildlife.

Anti-poaching via Predictive Analysis Models

In recent years, one of the more innovative approaches to protecting wildlife from poaching has emerged from field research in Asia and Africa that focused on maximizing the effectiveness of ranger operations (Fei et al. 2016; Lemieux et al. 2014). Realizing that wildlife law enforcement shares a common operational characteristic with conventional urban policing—reactive rather than proactive—researchers employed criminological theory to determine how rangers can best stop poachers, ideally before they succeed in taking the wildlife. These projects relied on contemporary technologies to develop a proactive and efficient approach for ranger operations in Africa and Asia (Mailley 2014).

A standard feature of daily ranger operations in protected areas is the patrol (Warchol and Kapla 2012). Routes for daily ranger patrols are commonly designated on the basis of intelligence gathered about poachers or the experience of supervisory rangers as to where poaching is likely to occur in the park at a given time of the day or month (Eloff and Lemieux 2014; KNP section ranger, personal communication, May 2004; Lemieux et al. 2014). Rangers have gathered intelligence from informants or investigations about the location of a poaching operation or rely on their past knowledge that poachers will set up snares near certain water sources or game trails or will track animals as they migrate through the park. Yet the result may be a hit-or-miss strategy that fails to make the most efficient use of the patrols. Given the large size of game parks, difficult terrain, and wide variety of access points for poachers to enter a protected area, the chances of rangers intercepting the poachers with a conventional method of patrol are very slim, resulting in the inefficient use of the law enforcement resource (Fei et al. 2016)

The solution, derived from contemporary urban policing, was to identify and focus on the poaching hotspots (Fei et al. 2016) and allocate resources to those areas accordingly. This is accomplished by the ongoing collection of data on poaching incidents, locations of snares, carcasses, evidence of entry points into the reserve, periods of full moon, and spoor/ human tracks from trespassers. These data are continuously recorded and analyzed, and the results are used to establish ranger patrols on the most likely locations to intercept poachers. A preliminary effort at examining the efficacy of this technique was done in South Africa's Kruger National Park with a focus on rhinoceros poaching. The researcher identified the temporal distribution of poaching, factoring in month, location, physical features of the terrain, and poacher techniques over a five-month period. The results revealed patterns and hotspots that could be used to identify patrol routes for the best deployment of the ranger force. Similarly, in a subsequent study in a Ugandan national park, the researchers applied a data-driven model with a basis in situational crime prevention theory to develop the most efficient ranger patrol routes. A spatial analysis model of patrol intensity and effectiveness was developed and used to assess the areas of the park that yielded the best returns in preventing poaching (Lemieux et al. 2014). Data were recorded on GPS units, a practice implemented previously in some South African national parks, though with a different initial intent of documenting the patrol activity and observations (TMNP section ranger, personal communication, May 2011).

A recent project by the National Science Foundation (2016) supported field researchers by using artificial intelligence and game theory to develop a patrol strategy to prevent poaching. The strategy for ranger operations relies on computer models of the behavior of poachers to determine patrol operations for best effect. According to the originator of the model, this approach had previously been successfully used in the United States by the Transportation Security Administration and U.S. Coast Guard. It relies on gathering and analyzing data to give ranger patrols the best opportunity to intercept poachers and prevent the loss of wildlife. The application is based in part on previous work in Africa and has been fully implemented in Malaysia. The Protection Assistant for Wildlife Security (PAWS) application employs a "game theoretical" decision aid to make the best use of ranger patrols. Regularly applied in an effort to protect tiger populations in Malaysia, the PAWS application relies on data about animal and human activity and terrain that are continuously input to create a model for an effective patrol strategy (Fei et al. 2016). PAWS is considered the first green security game application being regularly used in Malaysia. The contemporary technologies described in Chapter 6 are being employed to collect data for these predictive analysis models. These include the aforementioned handheld ranger GPS units, such as Cyber Tracker, drone aircraft, GPS collars on wildlife, and game cameras.

Private-Sector and Market-Based Conservation Efforts

Funding Conservation with Trophy Hunting

The concept of privatizing wildlife is viewed negatively by a range of groups that adhere to the view that wildlife is a natural public resource and should remain subject to government management. However, privatization of natural resources is far from uncommon and has resulted in both notable successes and problems in southern Africa (Spenceley 2003). While wildlife populations have increased substantially in South Africa, where the private ownership of game is allowed along with trophy hunting, they have declined in Kenya, where hunting was prohibited in 1977, and in Tanzania, which allows trophy hunting.

It has long been argued in the United States that sport hunting can play a positive role in wildlife conservation. This view is premised on the idea that hunters place a value on game species and are willing to support the protection and management of these species to ensure the ability to hunt in the future (Posewitz 2004). Conservation programs are funded in part by the fees paid by hunters to purchase licenses and permits from states' natural resource or fish and game departments. Businesses in local communities that benefit from money spent by hunters may also become aware of the value of conserving not only the wildlife but also the ecosystem they inhabit. In a sense, the wildlife becomes a valued commodity for the hunter, private businesses, and the state.

Research on African trophy hunting reveals that it offers both benefits and liabilities (Lindsey, Roulet, and Romanach 2007). The view that hunting can support wildlife conservation emerged in the 1980s and is commonplace in about two dozen African nations that allow trophy hunting operations (Adams 2004). Unique among these nations is South Africa, which is well known for its national and provincial parks but also has nearly ten thousand private game reserves for conventional tourism (photo safaris), game breeding, and trophy hunting (Cousins, Sadler, and Evans 2008; Lindsey, Roulet, and Romanach 2007). South Africa's overall tourism industry contributed more than 103 billion Rand (about $7 billion USD) to the nation's economy in 2013 (Statistics South Africa 2015). Of this amount, $744 million USD came from its overall hunting industry, and trophy hunting had become the most profitable type of commercial land use in the country (Voice of America News [hereinafter VOA News] 2014). These figures are cited by advocates of using hunting to support conservation, who argue that it is necessary to give an economic value to wildlife, including CITES-listed species such as rhinoceros and elephant, in order to provide an incentive for its protection. The view is supported by data showing that wildlife populations have increased fourfold in South Africa (Aguilar 2015). The South African approach is based on privatization of wildlife. Private landowners were allowed the right to own wildlife and use the game for hunting (Lindsey, Roulet, and Romanach 2007). This resulted in the development of a commercial hunting industry that included agricultural farms converted into game farms and breeding facilities (Bond et al. 2004). What developed was the largest hunting industry in Africa, along with the creation of private game reserves for photo safaris or traditional tourism. In addition, as described in Chapter 6, the private tourism and hunting industry led to the development of private anti-poaching units and training schools for game protection on these reserves.

The commercialization of wildlife for trophy hunting is not limited to South Africa. Other East African and southern African nations allow this business, though with a different model with regard to land and game ownership. In other nations, where private game ownership is not permitted, hunting businesses rely on leasing a hunting concession or block from the government that allows them a quota of wildlife. The lease revenue is used by the state in part to support its game department and the local communities living adjacent to the concessions (Owner of Miombo Safaris Tanzania, personal communication, May 2005). Furthermore, the hunting companies provide employment to a range of staff, including professional hunters, their assistants, drivers, cooks, and mechanics. Their salaries and taxes, in turn, help support the local economy. Some hunting companies also conduct anti-

poaching operations and/or provide logistical and material support to national game departments on the concession in order to protect the game they
need for their businesses (Miombo Safaris Ltd. 2005).

Proponents of this model assert that it offers several benefits, one being
that the majority of the hunting in South Africa does not involve threatened
species. Rather, the more common plains game species are typically taken in
trophy hunting. Those who hunt elephant, rhinoceros, or lion, for example,
represent a small portion of the trophy hunters in South Africa but also pay
significantly higher fees for these animals and for the services of the professional hunting company. Another argument in support of wildlife conservation via trophy hunting is that with well-managed operations incorporating
sustainable limits on the number of animals taken, the resource will be pre-
served for the future. Furthermore, proponents note that hunting operations
can utilize private land or leased concessions that are unused or not suitable
for photo safaris or agricultural development. Advocates also point out that
legal hunting provides a way to reduce poaching by allowing hunters to take
conflict animals threatening local communities (Lindsey et al. 2006). It is
presumed that by eliminating this problem, local residents benefit from trophy hunting and will, in turn, be more inclined to avoid poaching. Finally,
proponents argue that hunting operations have a less damaging environmental footprint than tourist operations (Lindsey, Roulet, and Romanach 2007).
Land developed for private tourist-oriented reserves requires extensive infrastructure, including lodges, restaurants, administration buildings, utilities,
and roads, to support hundreds or even thousands of guests each year. However, hunting properties may require only tented camps and primitive roads
for safaris of mere dozens of clients per year (professional hunter Natasha
Illum Berg, Robin Hurt Safaris, personal communication, May 2005).

The concept of using trophy hunting to support conservation is not without its critics. IFAW, which contends that the practice is not sustainable in
some nations for the long term (VOA News 2014), notes that while trophy
hunting generates revenue, it may not be significant to a nation's economy.
While South Africa's total revenue from tourism in 2013 may seem impres-
sive, it constituted only 2.9 percent of its total GDP (Statistics South Africa
2015), and trophy hunting contributed just a small portion of the total tourism dollars. IFAW (2013b) further notes that hunting contributed only a
fraction of a percent of GDP and very little of that money ever reached the
rural communities. IFAW's analysis, conducted in nine African nations,
concluded that trophy hunting revenues constituted only 1.8 percent of tourism monies and that only 3 percent of those proceeds went to local communities where the hunting took place. IFAW advocates what is referred to as
nonconsumptive tourism in place of trophy hunting. The view is that a hunted animal is used only once, while that same animal may be viewed and

photographed hundreds of times over its lifetime, thus generating more revenue for conservation. An analysis by renowned African wildlife conservationists Dereck and Beverly Joubert found that one male lion would perhaps provide $15,000 in revenue if taken as a hunting trophy, while that same animal, if protected, could provide as much as $2 million USD in tourist dollars during an estimated ten-year lifetime (Africa Geographic 2015).

A critical focus on trophy hunting developed in the wake of the *Cecil the lion* case in Zimbabwe. In this publicized case, an American trophy hunter killed a well-known male lion that lived in the Hwange National Park in what was claimed to be an illegal operation. The trophy hunter and his professional hunter were accused of using bait to lure the animal out of the national park, where hunting was prohibited, and into a neighboring privately owned game farm, where it was shot. The lion also happened to be a radio-collared research subject, which further angered some conservationists. This incident contributed to a critical look at trophy hunting and wildlife conservation. It also resulted in several U.S. air carriers refusing to ship hunting trophies from Africa into the United States ("Cecil the lion" 2015).

The concept of *conservation by the gun* is sometimes derisively used to describe the model of using sport or trophy hunting to fund conservation (Howley 2013). The Jouberts contend that this model serves only to reduce wildlife populations over the long term, with prized species such as the African lion being especially harmed. They argue that it is questionable about how much money is actually returned for conservation efforts and note that trophy hunting eliminates the genetic best from the wildlife population rather than the way nature works to eliminate the old, sick, or weak. The Jouberts question the effectiveness of hunting companies' anti-poaching work, pointing out that the hunting season is not year-round (Africa Geographic 2015). Tanzania's season, for example, runs from July 1 to December 31 (Miombo Safaris Ltd. 2005). As a result, the concession may not be patrolled for about half the year, making it susceptible to poaching. In some cases, trophy hunting operations are also inefficiently managed, resulting in overharvesting of wildlife, improper gender selection, canned hunting, and corruption (Lindsey, Roulet, and Romanach 2007).

Funding Conservation with Rhino Horn Sales

In response to a wave of rhinoceros poaching in South Africa beginning in about 2008, the South African government became concerned about its inability to solve the problem. One proposed solution was a one-time sale of the stockpile of rhinoceros horn in the private consumer market. Valued at about $1 billion USD on the legal market, the money would be used in part to fund conservation efforts for the animals. The proposed sale was premised on the belief that it would flood the market with rhinoceros horn, thereby driving down the price. This, in turn, would reduce demand and subsequently reduce poaching (IFAW n.d.[b]; Save the Rhino 2015). The government of South Africa would need to submit a proposal to CITES for the sale. Critics charged that this plan would likely backfire, for several reasons. One claim was that illegally obtained rhinoceros horn would ultimately be commingled with the government stockpiles. A second criticism was that the flood of horn into the consumer markets would only stimulate demand for the product and remove the stigma that buying and owning the horn was harmful. Given that this is a one-time-only sale, poaching would eventually increase due to higher demand, further devastating the limited population of rhinoceros in Africa. Furthermore, WWF, which supports sustainable use of wildlife, noted that the sale of the horns should not take place until the criminal syndicates involved in the illegal horn trade were incapacitated (WWF 2016a). In the spring of 2016, the South African government declined to move forward with the sale. However, partly in response to lobbying from private rhino breeders, in 2017 South Africa's constitutional court reauthorized the regulated domestic buying and selling of rhino horn, which had been prohibited with a moratorium in 2009. The private ownership of wildlife in South Africa has resulted in game farmers owning about a third of the nation's population of 20,000 rhino ("South Africa lifts ban on domestic rhino horn sales" 2017) and amassing stocks of rhino horns potentially worth hundreds of millions of dollars. The private breeders argue that the legal sale of horns, which can be removed from a sedated animal only to regrow, will help reduce poaching by increasing the supply with a renewable source. Protections to prevent their illegal trade include a permit issued by the provincial government that will be required for those trading in, possessing, or transporting the horns. Detractors contend that these *domestic-trade-only* horns will eventually be commingled with legal hunting trophies destined for Asia. Given the lack of domestic market for the horn in South Africa, the concern is that the domestic trade will ultimately result in more horn being smuggled to these markets (Bale 2017a). Furthermore, it could increase demand for the horns, which will ultimately lead to even more poaching with illegal horns sold at below government-set prices.

Demand Reduction Efforts

Public Relations

Supply reduction efforts are based on the premise that a decrease in the availability of a product will result in price increases and a subsequent decline in demand and use by consumers (Abadinsky 2001). While anti-poaching and trafficking efforts are often the first response to wildlife crimes to reduce the supply, they do not necessarily result in less demand, especially among wealthy buyers of ivory, rhino horn, or tiger parts, whose purchasing habits are less affected by price changes, or those unfamiliar with the true impact of poaching. At the Kasane Conference on the Illegal Wildlife Trade in 2015, it was acknowledged that combating the trade requires eradicating both supply and demand (Kasane Statement on the Illegal Wildlife Trade 2015). Therefore, additional programs specifically designed to reduce the demand for wildlife products have been employed to alter consumer behavior as part of a balanced approach to controlling wildlife crime. Proponents of this approach note that past public relations efforts to reduce the use of bird feathers and animal fur in the clothing industry by changing consumer attitudes have been successful (Fauna & Flora International 2015).

Advocates of demand reduction programs have stated that some consumers of wildlife products may not be aware of the extent of the killing (IFAW n.d.[b]). In response to this lack of information, public relations campaigns in consumer nations sometimes feature local and international celebrities and show the true impact of the trade through graphic images. The Asian-based NGO WildAid (2016), which concentrates on reducing consumption and enhancing enforcement efforts via a powerful media campaign, contends that its message reaches one billion people each week. Demand reduction public relations campaigns are generally useful, but an effective program goes beyond just running print or television advertisements. The campaigns must be based on research that identifies the drivers of the market for illegal wildlife products and must be continuously monitored for their effectiveness (Kasane Statement on the Illegal Wildlife Trade 2015). The Wildlife Conservation Society (WCS 2016a) developed a demand reduction strategy that is "evidence based, measurable, strategic and culturally appropriate for the relevant consumers (rather than just a generic awareness)." The NGO Wildlife Act (2014) reported on its unique demand reduction program. While acknowledging the value of other public relations programs, Wildlife Act argued that one aspect was missing. This was a focus on wealthy business owners in Asia, who are the most prolific consumers of wildlife, especially elephant and rhinoceros. Wildlife Act's objective was to educate this group of Asian end users about the impact of the crime, the value of Africa's heritage, and the African buyers of their goods and services. It was hoped that these companies would incorporate the message of wildlife conservation into their corporate culture and spread the message to their customers.

Bonfires of the Vanities: Burning Rather Than Selling Ivory

Some of the most visible and dramatic efforts intended to reduce demand are public ivory destructions. These high-profile events serve a symbolic purpose, to show the extent of the killing and to advocate for the intrinsic value of live elephants (IFAW n.d.[b]). On April 30, 2016, Kenya conducted the largest destruction of confiscated ivory in history (EIA 2016a). The public burning of multiple pyres of neatly arranged tusks weighing 105 tons in Nairobi National Park was one of a succession of ivory burns carried out in an effort to increase awareness of the illegal trade, end elephant poaching, and ban the legal sale of ivory. The public destruction of elephant ivory was first enacted in Kenya by President Daniel Moi in 1989 on the basis of the advice of the head of the Kenya Wildlife Service at that time, Richard Leakey. The 1989 burn included ivory from over 2,000 poached elephants with an estimated value of about $3 million USD (Leakey and Morrell 2001). Leakey, the originator of the concept, believed that the burn would be the impetus for an effort to push for a formal ban on the ivory trade. A ban was established the following year. However, not all African elephant range states agreed with the practice, and exemptions to the ban were provided for several African nations that were not facing excessive poaching (Narula 2014). South Africa and Zimbabwe, for example, which later sold parts of their stockpiles in CITES-approved sales to fund conservation, criticized the burn as mere public relations (Perlez 1989). Ivory crushes and burns were later conducted in the United States, France, Belgium, Philippines, Dubai, and China (Born Free Foundation 2015). Since 2013, eight other African nations with stockpiles of ivory, including raw tusks and finished products worth potentially millions if legal sales were held, have destroyed ivory by burning or crushing in an effort to attract public interest to the problem and permanently remove the product from the market (EIA 2016a). Together, nineteen ivory burns or crushes were done between 1989 and 2015, destroying a combined 130 tons (WWF 2016c).

The ivory marked for destruction comes from confiscations by the police and customs services and from deceased animals whose tusks remained intact. This practice is not without criticism. Opponents argue that it is little more than a grand publicity stunt that is the equivalent of burning money. If the ivory were legally sold, as in past one-off auctions, it could potentially generate millions of dollars for financially strapped wildlife departments in the elephant range states that are experiencing heavy elephant poaching (Spence 2015). Opponents also noted concern over the need to keep very accurate records of the ivory marked for destruction and monitor its disposal to prevent some of the stocks from being diverted into the illegal market (WWF 2016c). The counter-argument offered by proponents of destroying ivory is that if sold into the legal market, this ivory would only stimulate demand for additional product, thus leading to additional poaching. With nearly 50,000 elephants being lost to poaching each year (Born Free Foundation 2015), the results could be disastrous.

Summary: What Can Be Done?

The illegal trade in wildlife is a global crime involving a wide range of species sought after for diverse uses. Given the demand for wildlife products, increasing human populations, entrenched poverty in some developing nations with desired species, and the complications of corruption and weak law enforcement, the illegal trade is a problem that cannot be solved, but it can be managed. The purpose of this chapter has been to examine a selection of conservation programs, government initiatives, private-sector solutions, and demand reduction efforts focused on reducing the loss of wildlife from the illegal trade. While the illegal trade is extensive, progress is being made at mitigating its negative impact on wildlife and its ecosystems. One well-tested effort involves the use of community conservation programs, which serve to protect the wildlife, provide financial benefits to those people who live near game reserves, and foster awareness that wildlife merits protection. These programs have evolved from the more traditional conservation efforts that focus strictly on conserving the species with little regard for other factors. One of the more contested approaches to conservation, the role of the private sector in wildlife conservation via private game ownership for both conventional tourism and hunting, also warranted discussion.

Some of the most promising developments were announcements by the United States, China, and the United Kingdom of new strategies and efforts to prevent the illegal trade; these are positive steps in the right direction by consumer nations. The U.S. and Chinese approach targets the overall illegal trade, including a ban on ivory, while the United Kingdom's public-private efforts focus on the role of the transportation industry in wildlife crimes. These programs are based on a realization of the impact of this crime not just on wildlife but on national security, and they acknowledge that the private sector has a key role to play in combating these offenses. Finally, one of the most exciting developments is the blending of criminology with crime mapping technologies to develop predictive analysis methods that enhance ranger effectiveness. As this outgrowth of modern urban policing is applied to wildlife conservation, it moves research from the theoretical to the applied to help alleviate the challenges of wildlife law enforcement.

References

Abadinsky, H. 2001. *Drugs: An introduction.* 4th ed. Belmont, CA: Wadsworth/Thomson.

Adams, J., and T. McShane. 1992. *The myth of wild Africa.* New York: W. W. Norton.

Adams, W. 2003. Nature and the colonial mind. In *Decolonizing nature: Strategies for conservation in the post-colonial era,* ed. W. Adams and M. Mulligan, 16–50. London: Earthscan.

———. 2004. Good hunting. In *Against extinction,* ed. W. Adams, 19–23. London: Earthscan.

Africa Geographic. 2015. Dereck Joubert responds to a hunter on the economics of hunting. August 28. Available at http://africageographic.com/blog/dereck-joubertresponds-to-a-hunter-on-the-economics-of-hunting/. Accessed April 2, 2016.

African Wildlife Foundation. 2005. *Annual report: Lands sustaining life.* Washington, DC: AWF.

Aguilar, R., producer. 2015. Your call: What's the most effective way to fund wildlife conservation? Audio podcast. August 15. Available at http://kalw.org/post/your-call-whats-most-effective-way-fund-wildlife-conservation#stream/0. Accessed April 18, 2017.

Airports Council International. 2016. Airports Council International signs United for Wildlife Declaration at Buckingham Palace. March 16. Available at http://www.aci.aero/News/Releases/Most-Recent/2016/03/15/Airports-Council-International-signs-United-for-Wildlife-Declaration-at-Buckingham-Palace. Accessed May 3, 2016.

Albanese, J. 2003. Organized crime: A perspective from South Africa. In *Challenges for the future,* ed. J. Albanese, D. Das, and A. Vermer, 438–459. Upper Saddle River, NJ: Prentice Hall.

———. 2011. *Transnational crime and the 21st century: Criminal enterprise, corruption and opportunity.* New York: Oxford University Press.

Alexander, J., and J. McGregor. 2000. Wildlife and politics: CAMPFIRE in Zimbabwe. *Development and Change* 31:605–627.

Alves, R., J. Lima, and H. Arujo. 2013. The live bird trade in Brazil and its conservation implications: An overview. *Bird Conservation International* 23 (1): 53–65.

Animal Defenders International. 2016. ADI takes a stand for wild animals at the CITES CoP17. Available at http://www.ad-international.org/conservation/go.php?id=4197&ssi=14. Accessed October 2, 2016.

Asibey, E. 1972. Ghana's progress. *Oryx* 11:470–475.

Associated Press (AP). 2014. Two Vietnamese arrested with rhino horns in South Africa anti-poaching operation. *Fox News*, November 1. Available at http://www.foxnews.com/world/2014/11/01/2-vietnamese-arrested-with-rhino-horns-in-south-africa-anti-poaching-operation.html. Accessed June 15, 2016.

———. 2015. Suspected poachers target elephants in Congo park. *Fox News*, November 8. Available at http://www.foxnews.com/world/2015/11/08/rangers-in-congo-garamba-park-fight-die-in-skirmishes-with-heavily-armed.html?intcmp=hplnws. Accessed June 11, 2016.

Bachman, R., and R. Schutt. 2014. *The practice of research in criminology and criminal justice*. 5th ed. Los Angeles: Sage.

Bale, R. 2015. With ivory ban imminent, what will happen to China's legal stockpile? *National Geographic*. Available at http://news.nationalgeographic.com/2015/11/151112ivory-china-elephants-poaching-wildlife-trafficking-conservation/. Accessed May 31, 2016.

———. 2017a. Rhino horn trade to return to South Africa. *National Geographic*. Available at http://news.nationalgeographic.com/2017/04/wildlife-watch-rhino-horn-ban-overturned-south-africa/. Accessed April 17, 2017.

———. 2017b. World's biggest ivory market shutting down: What it means. *National Geographic*. Available at http://news.nationalgeographic.com/2017/03/wildlife-watch-china-elephant-ivory-trafficking-ban/. Accessed April 18, 2017.

Barosso, M. 2012. Twenty years of peace in Mozambique. *Deutsche Welle*, April 10. Available at http://www.dw.com/en/20-years-of-peace-in-mozambique/a-16280820. Accessed June 11, 2016.

Beccaria, C. 1963. *Of crimes and punishment*. Trans. H. Paulucci. Indianapolis: Bobbs-Merrill. Originally published 1764.

Becker, M., R. McRobb, F. Watson, E. Droge, B. Kanyembo, J. Murdoch, and C. Kakumi. 2013. Evaluation of wire-snare poaching trends and the impacts of by-catch on elephants and large carnivores. *Biological Conservation* 158:26–36.

Beirne, P., and N. South. 2013. *Issues in green criminology: Confronting harms against environments, humanity and other animals*. New York: Routledge.

Bernard, T., J. Snipes, and A. Gerould. 2010. *Vold's theoretical criminology*. 6th ed. New York: Oxford University Press.

Bond, I., B. Child, D. de la Harpe, B. Jones, J. Barnes, and H. Anderson. 2004. Private land contribution to conservation. In *Parks in transition*, ed. B. Child, 29–61. London: Earthscan.

Born Free Foundation. 2015. Ivory destruction. Available at http://www.bornfree.org.uk/campaigns/elephants/campaign-action/ivory-trade/ivory-destruction/. Accessed April 18, 2017.

Broad, S., T. Mulliken, and D. Roe. 2005. The nature and extent of the legal and illegal trade in wildlife. In *The trade in wildlife: Regulation for conservation*, ed. S. Oldfield, 3–22. Sterling, VA: Earthscan.

Burgener, M., N. Snyman, and M. Hauck. 2001. *Towards a sustainable wildlife trade*. Cape Town, South Africa: Institute of Criminology, University of Cape Town.

Bushmeat Crisis Task Force (BCTF). 2008. Bushmeat: A wildlife crisis in West and Central Africa and around the world. Available at http://www.bushmeat.org/sites/default/files/BCTFBRIE.pdf. Accessed June 4, 2016.

Bushmeat trade threatens African wildlife. 2006. *Pretoria News*, June 18. Available at http://www.iol.co.za/index.php?art_id=vn20060617090728812C429589&set_id1&click_id=68&sf=. Accessed March 4, 2008.

Carter, T. 2006. Police use of discretion: A participant observation study of game wardens. *Deviant Behavior* 27 (6): 591–627.

Caruthers, J. 1995. *The Kruger National Park: A social and political history*. Pietermaritzburg, South Africa: University of Natal Press.

———. 2007. Conservation and wildlife management in South African national parks, 1930s–1960s. *Journal of the History of Biology* 41 (2): 203–236.

———. 2008. Police boys and poachers: Africans, wildlife protection and national parks, the Transvaal 1902 to 1950, Koedoe—African Protected Area. *Conservation and Science, North America* 36 (September): 11–22.

Cecil the lion: Zimbabwe will not charge US dentist over killing. 2015. *The Guardian*, October 12. Available at http://www.theguardian.com/environment/2015/oct/12/zimbabwe-will-not-charge-us-dentist-killing-cecil-lion. Accessed May 3, 2016.

Chaber, A., S. Allebone-Webb, Y. Lignereux, A. Cunningham, and J. Rowcliffe. 2010. The scale of illegal meat importation from Africa to Europe via Paris. *Society for Conservation Biology* 3 (5): 317–321.

Chamley, S. 2005. From nature tourism to eco-tourism? The case of Ngorongoro Conservation Area, Tanzania. *Human Organization* 64 (1): 75–88.

Chen, S. 2016. Conservation by the gun: Trophy hunting in Africa. *The Contour*, February 5. Available at http://www.thecontournews.org/2016/02/05/conservationby-the-gun-trophy-hunting-in-africa/. Accessed May 2, 2016.

Chen, T. 2012. Easy pickings for abalone smugglers. *Wall Street Journal, China Real Time*, March 30. Available at http://blogs.wsj.com/chinarealtime/2012/03/30/easy-pickings-for-abalone-smugglers.

China announces ban on ivory trade by end of 2017. 2016. *BBC News*, December 30. Retrieved April 14, 2017. Available at http://www.bbc.com/news/world-asia-china-38470861.

Chng, S., J. Eaton, K. Krishasamy, C. Shepherd, and V. Nijman. 2015. *In the market for extinction: An inventory of Jakarta's bird markets*. September. Selangor, Malaysia: TRAFFIC Southeast Asia.

Christy, B. 2008. *The lizard king: The true crimes and passions of the world's greatest reptile smugglers*. New York: Twelve.

Church, P. 2015. Rhino horn smuggling thwarted at OR Tambo. *The South African*, December 28. Available at http://www.thesouthafrican.com/rhino-horn-smuggling-thwarted-at-or-tambo/. Accessed June 15, 2016.

CITES. 2016a. CITES at work. Available at https://www.cites.org/eng. Accessed June 4, 2016.

———. 2016b. Convention on the International Trade in Endangered Species of Wild Fauna and Flora. Geneva, Switzerland. Available at https://www.cites.org/. Accessed May 10, 2016.

Clarke, R. 1997. *Situational crime prevention*. Albany, NY: Criminal Justice Press.

———. 1999. *Hot products: Understanding, anticipating and reducing demand for stolen goods*. Police Research Paper 112. Policing and Reducing Crime Unit, Research Development and Statistics Directorate. London: Home Office.

Cohen, L., and M. Felson. 1979. Social change and crime rate trends: A routine activity approach. *American Sociology Review* 44 (August): 588–608.

Cornish, D., and R. Clarke. 1987. Understanding crime displacement: An application of rational choice theory. *Criminology* 25:933–947.

Cousins, J., J. Sadler, and J. Evans. 2008. Exploring the role of private wildlife ranching as a conservation tool in South Africa: Stakeholder perspectives. *Ecology and Society* 13:2. Available at http://www.ecologyandsociety.org/vol13/iss2/art43/. Accessed May 4, 2016.

Davies, B. 2005. *Black Market: Inside the endangered species trade in Asia.* San Rafael, CA: Earth Aware Editions.

Denyer, S. 2015. China to ban ivory trade within a year or so as pressure mounts on Hong Kong. *Washington Post,* October 21. Available at https://www.washingtonpost.com/world/china-to-ban-ivory-trade-within-a-year-or-so-as-pressure-mounts-on-hong-kong/2015/10/21/4c96c5e4-7683-11e5-a5e2-40d6b2ad18dd_story.html. Accessed May 31, 2016.

Desai, B., and S. Balraj. 2010. On the quest for green courts in India. *Journal of Court Innovation* 3:79–110.

Donovan, D. 2013. Shooting wildlife in the heart of Africa: In some places now only with a camera. *Africa Watch Discussion Papers,* March 18. Available at http://www.polity.org .za/article/shooting-wildlife-in-the-heart-of-africa-in-some-places-now-only-with-a-camera-2013-03-19. Accessed April 12, 2017.

Eliason, S. 2003a. Illegal hunting and angling: The neutralization of wildlife law violations. *Society and Animals* 11:225–243.

———. 2003b. Throwing the book versus cutting some slack: Factors influencing the use of discretion by game wardens in Kentucky. *Deviant Behavior* 24:129–152.

———. 2008. Wildlife crime: Conservation officers' perceptions of elusive poachers. *Deviant Behavior* 29 (2): 111–128.

———. 2011a. Patrolling the peaks and the plains: An analysis of big sky game wardens. *Criminal Justice Studies* 24 (4): 409–418.

———. 2011b. Trophy poaching: A routine activities perspective. *Deviant Behavior* 33 (1): 72–87.

Eliason, S., and R. Dodder. 1999. Techniques of neutralization used by deer poachers in the western United States: A research note. *Deviant Behavior* 20:233–252.

Ellis, K. 2013. *Tackling the demand for rhino horn.* London: Save the Rhino.

Eloff, C., and A. Lemieux. 2014. Rhino poaching in Kruger National Park, South Africa: Aligning analysis, technology and prevention. In *Situational prevention of poaching,* ed. A. Lemieux, 19–43. New York: Routledge.

Emslie, R., and M. Brooks. 1999. *African rhino: Status survey and conservation action plan.* Cambridge, UK: International Union for Conservation of Nature.

Endangered Species Act (ESA). 1973. 16 U.S.C. § 1531 et seq.

Environmental Investigation Agency (EIA). 1993. *Taiwan kills rhinos with your money.* London: EIA.

———. 1998. *The state of the tiger: India's tiger crisis.* London : EIA.

———. 2000. *Lethal experiment: How the CITES-approved ivory sale led to increased elephant poaching.* London: EIA.

———. 2002a. *Back in business: Elephant poaching and the ivory black markets of Asia.* London: EIA.

———. 2002b. *Scourge of corruption threatens Indonesia's forests.* London: EIA.

———. 2006. *Skinning the cat: Crime and politics of the big cat skin trade.* London: EIA.

———. 2014. *In cold blood: Combating organized wildlife crime.* Washington, DC: EIA.

———. 2015a. *High profit/low risk: Reversing the wildlife crime equation.* Washington, DC: EIA.

———. 2015b. *The role of corruption in wildlife and forest crime.* London: EIA.

———. 2016a. Kenya ivory burn a beacon to the end of all ivory trade. Available at https://eia-international.org/kenya-ivoryburn-beacon-road-end-ivory-trade. Accessed April 30, 2016.

———. 2016b. U.S. Lacey Act. Available at http://eia-global.org/lacey/. Accessed May 11, 2016.

European Association of Zoos and Aquaria (EAZA). 2011. EAZA and IUCN SSN Southeast Asia Conservation Fund. Amsterdam, Netherlands. Available at http://www.eaza.net/conservation/campaigns/. Accessed April 18, 2017.

Falcone, D. 2004. America's conservation police: Agencies in transition. *Policing: An International Journal of Police Strategies and Management* 27 (1): 56–66.

Fauna & Flora International. 2015. Confronting demand reduction in illegal wildlife trade. November. Available at http://www.fauna-flora.org/confronting-demand-reduction-in-illegal-wildlife-trade/. Accessed September 29, 2016.

Fay, M. 2011. Ivory wars: Last stand in Zakouma. *National Geographic* 211 (3): 34–65.

Fears, D. 2014. Overwhelmed U.S. port inspectors unable to keep up with the illegal wildlife trade. *Washington Post,* October 17. Available at https://www.washingtonpost.com/national/health-science/overwhelmed-us-port-inspectors-unable-to-keep-up-with-illegal-wildlife-trade/2014/10/17/2fc72086-fe42-11e3-b1f4-8e77c632c07b_story.html. Accessed May 19, 2016.

Fei, F., T. Nguyen, R. Pickles, W. Lam, G. Clements, B. An, A. Singh, M. Tambe, and A. Lemieux. 2016. Deploying PAWS: Field optimization of the Protection Assistant for Wildlife Security. Available at http://teamcore.usc.edu/papers/2016IAAI16_PAWS.pdf. Accessed May 1, 2016.

Felson, M. 2006. *Crime and nature.* London: Sage.

Felson, M., and L. Cohen. 1980. Human ecology and crime: A routine activity approach. *Human Ecology* 8:389–406.

Forsyth, C. 1993a. Chasing and catching bad-guys: The game warden's prey. *Deviant Behavior* 14:209–226.

———. 1993b. Factors influencing game wardens in their interaction with poachers: The use of discretion. *Free Inquiry in Creative Sociology* 21:1.

Forsyth, C., and Y. Forsyth. 2009. Dire and sequestered meetings: The work of game wardens. *American Journal of Criminal Justice* 34 (3–4): 213–223.

Forsyth, C., and T. Marckese. 1993. Thrills and skills: A sociological analysis of poaching. *Deviant Behavior* 14:157–172.

Freeland. 2013. Thailand launches elite wildlife ranger team. Available at http://www.freeland.org/press-releases/elite-wildlife-ranger-team/. Accessed May 21, 2016.

Frost, P., and I. Bond. 2007. The CAMPFIRE program in Zimbabwe: Payments for wildlife services. *Ecological Economics* 65:776–787.

Gastrow, P. 1999. Main trends in the development of South Africa's organized crime. *African Security Studies* 8 (6): 58–69.

———. 2001. *Organized crime in the SADC region: Police perceptions.* Cape Town, South Africa: Institute for Security Studies.

———. 2003. Introduction. In *Penetrating state and business: Organized crime in southern Africa*. Vol. 1, ed. P. Gastrow, 1–17. Cape Town, South Africa: Institute for Security Studies.

Gettlemen, J. 2012. Elephants dying in epic frenzy as ivory fuels wars and profits. *New York Times,* September 3. Available at http://www.nytimes.com/2012/09/04/world/africa/africas-elephants-are-being-slaughtered-in-poaching-frenzy.html?_r=0. Accessed June 11, 2016.

Gißibl, B. 2006. German colonialism and the beginnings of international wildlife preservation in Africa. *German Historical Institute Bulletin, Supplement 3*. Washington, DC: GHI.

Gibson, C. 1999. *Politicians and poachers: The political economic of wildlife policy in Africa.* Cambridge: Cambridge University Press.

Gilbertson, T. 2006. Alcohol-related incident guardianship and undergraduate college parties: Enhancing the social norms approach. *Journal of Drug Education* 36 (1): 73–90.

Goitom, H. 2013. Wildlife trafficking and poaching: Tanzania. Available at http://www.loc.gov/law/help/wildlife-poaching/tanzania.php. Accessed October 4, 2016.

———. 2014. Kenya: Implementation of new wildlife law expedited. Available at http://www.loc.gov/law/foreign-news/article/kenya-implementation-of-new-wildlife-law-expedited/. Accessed October 4, 2016.

Goodrich, J., A. Lynam, D. Miquelle, H. Wibisono, K. Kawanishi, A. Pattanavibool, S. Htun, T. Tempa, J. Karki, Y. Jhala, and U. Karanth. 2015. *Panthera tigris*. The IUCN Red List of Threatened Species 2015: e.T15955A50659951. Available at http://dx.doi.org/10.2305/IUCN.UK.2015-2.RLTS.T15955A50659951.en. Accessed May 28, 2016.

Grobler, J. 2003. Namibia. In *Penetrating state and business: Organized crime in southern Africa*. Vol. 1, ed. P. Gastrow, 18–43. Cape Town, South Africa: Institute for Security Studies.

Guest, R. 2004. *The shackled continent: Africa's past, present and future*. London: Macmillan.

Guynup, S. 2014. Illegal tiger trade: Why tigers are walking gold. *National Geographic Voices*, February 12. Available at http://voices.nationalgeographic.com/2014/02/12/illegal-tiger-trade-why-tigers-are-walking-gold/.

Hagan, F. 2017. *Introduction to criminology*. 9th ed. Los Angeles: Sage.

Hauck, M., and N. Sweijd. 1999. A case study of abalone poaching in South Africa and its impact on fisheries management. *ICES Journal of Marine Science* 56 (6): 1024–1032.

Herbig, F, and G. Warchol. 2011. South African conservation crime and routine activities: A causal nexus? *Southern African Journal of Criminology* 24 (2): 1–16.

Herman, S. 2013. *Elite Thai rangers conduct first operation to nab poachers*. Bangkok, Thailand: Voice of America News.

Hess, K., and C. Hess-Orthmann. 2010. *Criminal Investigation*. 9th ed. New York: Delamar.

Hewson, M. 1998. Traditional healers in southern Africa. *Annuals of Internal Medicine* 128:1029–1034.

Howley, A. 2013. The end of safari hunting in Botswana. *National Geographic Voices*, September 17. Available at http://voices.nationalgeographic.com/2013/09/17/the-end-of-safari-hunting-in-botswana/. Accessed February 6, 2016.

Huang, H., and E. Valoi. 2013. Ivory poaching in Mozambique. *Le Monde diplomatique*, November. Available at http://mondediplo.com/blogs/ivory-poaching-in-mozambique. Accessed June 11, 2016.

International Fund for Animal Welfare (IFAW). 2011. *Tsavo: Challenges, solutions, hopes, July 2005–June 2011*. Nairobi, Kenya: IFAW East Africa.

———. 2013a. *Criminal nature: The global security implications of the illegal wildlife trade*. Yarmouth Port, MA: IFAW.

———. 2013b. New report: Economics of trophy hunting in Africa are overrated and overstated. Available at http://www.ifaw.org/united-states/news/new-report-economics-trophy-hunting-africa-are-overrated-and-overstated. Accessed April 18, 2016.

———. 2016. Reducing markets for wildlife products in China. Available at http://www.ifaw.org/international/our-work/wildlife-trade/reducing-markets-wildlife-products-china. Accessed May 27, 2016.

———. n.d.(a). IFAW and INTERPOL, working together to fight wildlife crime. Available at http://www.ifaw.org/united-states/our-work/wildlife-trade/ifaw-and-interpol-working-together-fight-wildlife-crime. Accessed June 30, 2016.

———. n.d.(b). Reducing demand for wildlife products. Available at http://www.ifaw.org/international/our-work/wildlifetrade/reducing-demand-wildlife-products. Accessed May 2, 2016.

International Union for Conservation of Nature (IUCN). 2013. About IUCN Viet Nam. Available at http://www.iucn.org/about/union/secretariat/offices/asia/asia_where_work/vietnam/about/. Accessed May 13, 2016.

———. 2014. Rising murder toll of park rangers calls for tougher laws. July 14. Available at http://www.iucn.org/content/rising-murder-toll-park-rangers-calls-tougher-laws. Accessed June 11, 2016.

———. 2015a. About IUCN. Available at http://www.iucn.org/about/. Accessed May 13, 2016.

———. 2015b. *Panthera tigris*. Available at http://www.iucnredlist.org/details/15955/0. Accessed June 15, 2016.

INTERPOL. 2016. Environmental crime. Available at http://www.interpol.int/Crime-areas/Environmental-crime/Environmental-crime. Accessed June 30, 2016.

Irish, J., and K. Qhobosheane. 2003. South Africa. In *Penetrating state and business: Organized crime in southern Africa*. Vol. 2, ed. P. Gastrow, 71–135. Cape Town, South Africa: Institute for Security Studies.

Ishihara, A., K. Kanari, T. Saito, and A. Takahashi. 2010. *The state of the wildlife trade in Japan*. Tokyo: TRAFFIC East Asia.

Ives, M. 2015. Smooth operators: Southeast Asia is a haven for ivory smugglers; for now, government efforts to stop the flow of contraband fall short. *Earth Island Journal* 30 (2): 39–43.

Jachmann, H., and M. Billiouw. 1997. Elephant poaching and law enforcement in the Central Luangwa Valley, Zambia. *Journal of Applied Ecology* 34:233–244.

Jackson, P. 2003. *Elephants*. London: Quantum Publishing.

Jenkins, M. 2008. Who murdered the Virunga gorillas? *National Geographic* 214, no. 1 (July): 34–65.

Jones, D. 1979. The poacher: A study in Victorian crime and protest. *Historical Journal* 22 (4): 825–860.

Kasane Statement on the Illegal Wildlife Trade. 2015. Kasane Conference on the Illegal Wildlife Trade. Kasane, Botswana. Available at http://www.mofa.go.jp/mofaj/files/000074311.pdf.

Knecht, G. 2006. *Hooked: Pirates, poaching and the perfect fish*. Emmaus, PA: Rodale.

Koch, E. 1996. South Africa—environment: Military implicated in poaching. IPS Press Service News Agency, January 22.

Kofi-Tsekpo, M. 2003. Institutionalization of African traditional medicine in health care systems in Africa. *African Journal of Health Sciences* 11 (1–2): i–ii.

Lawson, H. 2003. Controlling the wilderness: The work of wilderness officers. *Society and Animals* 11 (4): 329–351.

Leakey, R., and V. Morell. 2001. *Wildlife wars: My fight to save Africa's natural treasures*. New York: St. Martins-Griffin.

Leberatto, A. 2016. Understanding the illegal trade of live wildlife species in Peru. *Trends in Organized Crime* 19 (1): 42–66.

Lee, S. 1999. *Trade in traditional medicines using endangered species: An international context*. Selangor, Malaysia: TRAFFIC East Asia.

Lemieux, A., ed. 2014. *Situational prevention of poaching*. London: Routledge.

Lemieux, A., W. Bernasco, A. Rwetsiba, N. Guma, M. Driciru, and H. Kirya. 2014. Tracking poachers in Uganda: Spatial models of patrol intensity and patrol efficiency. In *Situational prevention of poaching*, ed. A. Lemieux, 102–119. London: Routledge.

Library of Congress. 2015a. Wildlife trafficking and poaching: Kenya. Available at http://www.loc.gov/law/help/wildlife-poaching/kenya.php. Accessed October 4, 2016.

———. 2015b. Wildlife trafficking and poaching: South Africa. Available at http://www.loc.gov/law/help/wildlife-poaching/southafrica.php. Accessed October 4, 2016.

Lindsey, P., R. Alexander, L. Frank, A. Mathieson, and S. Romañach. 2006. Potential of trophy hunting to create incentives for wildlife conservation in Africa where alternative wildlife-based land uses may not be viable. *Animal Conservation* 9:283–298.

Lindsey, P., P. Roulet, and S. Romanach. 2007. Economic and conservation significance of the trophy hunting industry in sub-Saharan Africa. *Biological Conservation* 134 (4): 455–469.

Lo, C., and G. Edwards. 2015. *The hard truth: How Hong Kong's ivory trade is fueling Africa's elephant poaching crisis*. Hong Kong: World Wildlife Fund.

Logan, B., and W. Moseley. 2002. The political ecology of poverty alleviation in Zimbabwe's Communal Areas Management Programme for Indigenous Resources (CAMPFIRE). *Geoforum* 33:1–14.

Lowry, W. 2016. Ring of elephant poachers broken up by Tanzanian authorities. *New York Times*, February 8. Available at https://www.nytimes.com/2016/02/09/world/africa/ring-of-elephant-poachers-broken-up-by-tanzanian-authorities.html. Accessed April 11, 2017.

Lunstrum, E. 2014. Green militarization: Anti-poaching efforts and the spatial contours of Kruger National Park. *Annals of the Association of American Geographers* 104:816–832.

Lusaka Agreement Task Force. 2016. Lusaka agreement on cooperative enforcement operations directed at the illegal trade in wild fauna and flora. Available at http://lusakaagreement.org/?page_id=24. Accessed May 10, 2016.

MacKenzie, J. 1988. *The empire of nature: Hunting, conservation and British imperialism*. Manchester, UK: Manchester University Press.

Magill, R. 2003. The cheetah challenge: The world's fastest cat races for survival in South Africa. *Wildlife Conservation* 106 (5): 28–35.

Mailley, J. 2014. Can the Problem Analysis Module (PAM) help us imagine new preventative solutions to a specific tiger poaching issue? In *Situational prevention of poaching*, ed. A. Lemieux, 63–81. New York: Routledge.

Manning, R. 1993. *Hunters and poachers: A social and cultural history of unlawful hunting in England, 1485–1640*. Oxford: Oxford University Press.

Mannon, J. 1998. Domestic and intimate violence: An application of routine activities theory. *Aggression and Violent Behavior* 2 (1): 9–24.

Marshall, L. 2002. Poaching, smuggling threaten abalone colonies in South Africa. *National Geographic News*, April 3. Available at http://news.nationalgeographic.com/news/2002/04/0402_020402_abalone.html.

Martin, R. 1986. *Communal areas management programme for indigenous resources (CAMPFIRE)*. Harare, Zimbabwe: Department of National Parks and Wildlife Management.

McConnell, T. 2015. The end for elephants? Gangsters use poachers to make a killing in the ivory trade. *Earth Island Journal* 30 (2): 30–38.

McMullan, J., and D. Perrier. 1997. Poaching vs the law: The social organization of illegal fishing. In *Crime, laws and communities*. Halifax, Canada: Fernwood.

———. 2002. Poaching and the ironies of law enforcement. *Law and Society Review* 36 (4): 679–718.

Meduna, A., A. Ogunjinmi, and S. Onadeko. 2009. Biodiversity conservation problems and their implications on ecotourism in Kainji Lake National Park, Nigeria. *Journal of Sustainable Development in Africa* 10:59–73.

Meithe, T., and R. Meier. 1994. *Crime and its social context: Toward an integrated theory of offenders, victims, and situations.* Albany: State University of New York Press.

Meredith, M. 2003. *Elephant destiny: Biography of an endangered species.* New York: Public Affairs.

Messer, K. 2000. The poacher's dilemma: The economics of poaching and enforcement. *Endangered Species Update* 17 (3): 50–56.

Messner, S., and K. Tardiff. 2006. The social ecology of urban homicide: An application of the "routine activities approach." *Criminology* 23 (2): 241–267.

Miller, W. 1958. Lower-class culture as a generating milieu of gang delinquency. *Journal of Social Issues* 14 (3): 5–19.

Milliken, T., and J. Shaw. 2012. *The South Africa–Vietnam rhino horn trade nexus: A deadly combination of institutional lapses, corrupt wildlife industry professionals and Asian crime syndicates.* Cambridge, UK: TRAFFIC.

Mills, J. 1999. The symbiotic match of traditional medicine and wildlife conservation. Paper presented at the meeting of the Healthy People, Healthy Planet International Conferences on Traditional Chinese Medicines and Endangered Wildlife Conservation. Beijing, China.

Milner-Gulland, E., and N. Williams. 1992. A model of incentives for the illegal exploitation of black rhinos and elephants: Poaching pays in the Luangwa Valley, Zambia. *Journal of Applied Ecology* 28:388–401.

Ministry of Natural Resources and Tourism. 2016. Wildlife division. Available at http://www.mnrt.go.tz/sectors. Accessed October 4, 2016.

Miombo Safaris Ltd. 2005. *Classic hunting safaris in Tanzania.* Dar es Salaam, Tanzania: Miombo.

Mitchell, J. 2006. George Schaller Parks: Where the spirit soars. *National Geographic,* October, 33–41.

Moreto, W. 2015. Occupational stress among law enforcement rangers: Insights from Uganda. *Oryx,* FirstView. Available at http://dx.doi.org/10.1017/S0030605315000356.

Moreto, W., R. Brunson, and A. Braga. 2015. "Such misconducts don't make a good ranger": Examining law enforcement ranger wrongdoing in Uganda. *British Journal of Criminology* 55:359–380.

Moreto, W., and A. Lemieux. 2015. Poaching in Uganda: Perspectives of law enforcement rangers. *Deviant Behavior* 36 (11): 853–873.

Moreto, W., A. Lemieux, A. Rwetsiba, N. Guma, M. Driciru, and H. Kirya. 2014. Law enforcement monitoring in Uganda: The utility of official data and time/distance based ranger efficiency measures. In *Situational prevention of poaching,* ed. A. Lemieux, 82–101. London: Routledge.

Moyle, B. 2005. Regulation, conservation and incentives. In *The trade in wildlife: Regulation for conservation,* ed. S. Oldfield, 41–51. London: Earthscan.

Murombedzi, J. 2003. *Precolonial and colonial conservation practices in southern Africa and their legacy today.* Washington, DC: International Union for Conservation of Nature.

Muth, R., and J. Bowe. 1998. Illegal harvest of renewable natural resources in North America: Toward a typology of the motivations for poaching. *Society and Natural Resources* 11:9–24.

Narula, S. 2014. Crush and burn: A history of the global crackdown on ivory. *The Atlantic*, January 27. Available at http://www.theatlantic.com/international/archive/2014/01/crush-and-burn-a-history-of-the-global-crackdown-on-ivory/283310/. Accessed April 26, 2016.

National Public Radio. 2003. Confronting Central Africa's poaching crisis: International efforts target abuses of "bushmeat trade." Available at http://www.npr.org.display_pages/features/feature_912962.html. Accessed January 2, 2003.

National Science Foundation. 2016. Outwitting poachers with artificial intelligence. Press release, April 21. Available at http://www.eurekalert.org/pub_releases/201604/nsf-opw042116.php. Accessed May 21, 2016.

Neme, L. 2015a. Elephant killings in Chad's signature park cause alarm. *National Geographic*, September 1. Available at http://news.nationalgeographic.com/2015/09/150901-elephants-poaching-chad-zakouma-national-park-ivory/. Accessed June 11, 2016.

———. 2015b. Will mobilization of military forces stop elephant poaching in Cameroon? *National Geographic*, February 14. Available at http://voices.nationalgeographic.com/2015/02/14/will-mobilization-of-military-forces-stop-elephant-poaching-in-cameroon/. Accessed June 11, 2016.

Nkala, G. 2003. Botswana. In *Penetrating state and business: Organized crime in South Africa*. Vol. 2, ed. P. Gastrow, 53–70. Cape Town, South Africa: Institute for Security Studies.

Nurse, A. 2015. *Policing wildlife: Perspectives on the enforcement of wildlife legislation*. Hampshire, UK: Palgrave/Macmillan.

Nyerere, J. 1961. *Arusha manifesto speech*. Arusha, Tanzania.

Nyschens, I. 1997. *Months of the sun*. Long Beach, CA: Safari Press.

Ogunjinmi, A., K. Umunna, and K. Ogunjinmi. 2008. Factors affecting job satisfaction of rangers in Yankari Game Reserve, Bauchi, Nigeria. *Journal of Agriculture and Social Research* 8 (2): 37–53.

Olindo, P. 1997. The success of Appendix I in conserving African elephants. In *Proceedings of the African Elephant Conference*, ed. A. Thornton, 6–9. London: Environmental Investigation Agency.

Oliver, W., and A. Meier. 2006. "Duck cops," "game wardens" and "wildlife enforcement": Stress among conservation officers. *Applied Psychology in Criminal Justice* 2 (1): 1–25.

Orenstein, R. 2013. *Ivory, horn and blood*. Buffalo, NY: Firefly Books.

Payne, O. 2015. Drones can curb poaching, but they're much costlier than alternatives. *National Geographic*, May 23. Available at http://voices.nationalgeographic.com/2015/05/23/drones-can-curb-poaching-but-theyre-much-costlier-than-alternatives/. Accessed May 23, 2016.

Peace Parks Foundation. 2016. Great Limpopo Transfrontier Park. May 5. Available at http://www.peaceparks.org/tfca.php?pid=19&mid=1005. Accessed June 11, 2016.

Perlez, J. 1989. Kenya, in gesture, burns ivory tusks. *New York Times*, July 18. Available at http://www.nytimes.com/1989/07/19/world/kenya-in-gesture-burns-ivory-tusks.html. Accessed April 25, 2016.

Petrossian, G., and R. Clarke. 2013. Explaining and controlling illegal commercial fishing: An application of the CRAVED theft model. *British Journal of Criminology*. Available at https://doi.org/10.1093/bjc/azt061.

Pillinger, S. 2003. *The illicit bushmeat trade: Northern KwaZulu Natal*. Durban, South Africa: Strategic Research Consultants.

Pires, S. F., and R. V. Clarke. 2011. Sequential foraging, itinerant fences and parrot poaching in Bolivia. *British Journal of Criminology*. Available at https://doi.org/10.1093/bjc/azq074.

———. 2012. Are parrots CRAVED? An analysis of parrot poaching in Mexico. *Journal of research in crime and delinquency* 49 (1): 122–146.

Pires, S. F., J. Schneider, and M. Herrera. 2016. Organized crime or crime that is organized: The parrot trade in the neo-tropics. *Trends in Organized Crime* 19 (1): 4–20.

Plaganyi, E., D. Butterworth, and M. Burgener. 2011. Illegal and unreported fishing of abalone: Quantifying the extent using a fully integrative assessment model. *Fisheries Research* 107 (1): 221–232.

Poole, C., and C. Shepherd. 2016. Shades of grey: The legal trade in CITES-listed birds in Singapore, notably the globally threatened African grey parrot *Psittacus erithacus*. *Oryx*. Available at https://doi.org/10.1017/S0030605314000234.

Posewitz, J. 2004. *Rifle in hand: How wild America was saved*. Helena, MT: Riverbend.

Puffer, F. 1982. *Informal markets: Smuggling in East Africa; A preliminary discussion*. International Development Program, Clark University.

Rademeyer, J. 2012. *Killing for profit: Exposing the illegal rhino horn trade*. Cape Town, South Africa: Zebra Press.

———. 2015. North Korean diplomat kicked out of South Africa for smuggling rhino horn. Available at http://www.timeslive.co.za/scitech/2015/12/23/North-Korean-diplomat-kicked-out-of-SA-for-smuggling-rhino-horn. Accessed June 14, 2016.

Raemaekers, S., and P. Britz. 2009. Profile of the illegal abalone fishery in the Eastern Cape Province, South Africa: Organized pillage and management failure. *Fisheries Research* 97 (3): 183–195.

Redpath, J. 2001. *The hydra phenomenon, rural sitting ducks and other recent trends around organized crime in the Western Cape*. Technikon, South Africa: Institute for Human Rights and Criminal Justice Studies.

Reilly, T. 2004. *The Kingdom of Swaziland's big game parks*. Malkerns, Swaziland: Big Game Parks.

Republic of Korea. 2014. The fifth national report to the convention on biological diversity. April. Available at https://www.cbd.int/doc/world/kr/kr-nr-05-en.pdf. Accessed May 11, 2016.

Reuters. 2015. Tanzanian court jails four Chinese men for rhino horn smuggling. December 18. Available at http://www.reuters.com/article/us-tanzania-poaching-idUSK-BN0U11NG20151218. Accessed June 15, 2016.

Revkin, A. 2012. A closer look at Gibson Guitar's legal troubles. *New York Times*, August 12. Available at http://dotearth.blogs.nytimes.com/2012/08/10/a-closer-look-at-gibson-guitars-legal-troubles/. Accessed May 12, 2016.

Robinson, J., and D. Bennett. 2004. Having your wildlife and eating it too: An analysis of hunting sustainability across tropical ecosystems. *Animal Conservation* 7:397–408.

Robinson, J., K. Redford, and D. Bennett. 1999. Wildlife harvested in logged tropical forests. *Science* 284 (5414): 595–596.

Rogers, G. 2010. Poachers act with impunity. *The Herald*, South Africa, May 24. Available at http://www.environment.co.za/environmental-issues-news/perlemoen-poachers-act-with-impunity.html.

Root, G. 2005. *Roots of a game ranger*. Pietermaritzburg, South Africa: The Roots.

Save the Rhino. 2013. Mozambique's role in the poaching crisis. Available at https://www.savetherhino.org/rhino_info/thorny_issues/mozambiques_role_in_the_poaching_crisis. Accessed June 11, 2016.

———. 2015. One-off sale of rhino horn stockpiles. Available at https://www.savethe rhino.org/rhino_info/thorny_issues/legalising_the_horn_trade/one off_sale_of_rhi no_horn_stockpiles. Accessed April 23, 2016.

————. 2016a. Poaching statistics. Available at https://www.savetherhino.org/rhino_info/poaching_statistics. Accessed June 11, 2016.

————. 2016b. The transportation industry and the illegal wildlife trade. Available at https://www.savetherhino.org/rhino_info/thorny_issues/the_transportation_industry_and_the_illegal_wildlife_trade. Accessed June 15, 2016.

Schneider, J. 2012. *Sold into extinction: The global trade in endangered species.* Santa Barbara, CA: Praeger.

Shelly, L. 1996. Transnational organized crime: An imminent threat to the nation state. *Journal of International Affairs* 48 (2): 463–489.

Shepherd, C., J. Compton, and S. Warne. 2007. *Transport infrastructure and wildlife trade conduits in the GIMS: Regulating the illegal and unsustainable wildlife trade.* Selangor, Malaysia. TRAFFIC Southeast Asia.

Shepherd, C., and L. Shepherd. 2010. The poaching and trade of Malayan sun bears in Peninsular Malaysia. *Traffic Bulletin* 23 (1): 49–52.

South Africa lifts ban on domestic rhino horn sales. 2017. *The Guardian,* April 6. Available at https://www.theguardian.com/environment/2017/apr/06/south-africa-lifts-ban-on-domestic-rhino-horn-sales. Accessed April 17, 2017.

South African National Parks (SANParks). 2016. SANParks Corporate Investigation Services (CIS). Available at https://www.sanparks.org/conservation/investigations/. Accessed May 21, 2016.

Spence, J. 2015. The history of burning ivory: Powerful anti-poaching message or PR stunt? Aardvark Safaris, April 27. Available at http://www.blog.aardvarksafaris.com/blog/the-history-of-burning-ivory/. Accessed April 27, 2016.

Spenceley, A. 2003. *Tourism, local livelihoods and the private sector in South Africa: Case studies on the growing role of the private sector in natural resources management.* Sustainable Livelihoods in Southern Africa, Research Paper 8. Brighton, UK: Institute of Development Studies.

Statistics South Africa. 2015. Tourism satellite account for South Africa, final 2011 and provisional for 2012 and 2013. Report 04-05-07. Pretoria, South Africa, March 26. Available at http://www.statssa.gov.za/publications/Report-04-05-07/Report-0405-072013.pdf. Accessed April 3, 2016.

Steinberg, J. 2005. *The illicit abalone trade in South Africa.* ISS Paper No. 5. Pretoria, South Africa: Institute for Security Studies.

Steinhart, E. I. 1989. Hunters, poachers and gamekeepers: Toward a social history of hunting in colonial Kenya. *Journal of African History* 30 (2): 247–264.

Sustainable management of bark harvesting for traditional medicine. 2011. *SA Forestry Magazine,* August. Available at http://saforestryonline.co.za/articles/non_timber_forest_products/sustainble_management_of_bark_harvesting_for_traditional_medicine/. Accessed May 29, 2016.

Swails, B., and D. Magnay. 2014. Anti-poaching "war" to save rhinos whose horns are more valuable than gold. December. Available at http://www.cnn.com/2014/11/30/world/africa/rhino-poaching-kruger-national-park/index.html?hpt=iaf_t2. Accessed June 3, 2016.

Sykes, G., and D. Matza. 1957. Techniques of neutralization: A theory of delinquency. *American Sociology Review* 22 (6): 664–670.

Thornton, A. 1997. *Proceedings of the African elephant conference, Johannesburg, South Africa:* London: Environmental Investigation Agency.

————. 2015. Wildlife groups urge Japanese PM to end ivory trade. April. Available at http://wildaid.org/news/wildlife-groups-urge-japanese-pmhalt-domestic-ivory-trade. Accessed May 31, 2016.

Tilsley, P. 2015. "Queen of ivory": Africa's infamous poaching mastermind nabbed. *Fox News*, October 8. Available at http://www.foxnews.com/science/2015/10/08/queen-ivory-africas-infamous-poaching-mastermind-nabbed.print.html#. Accessed June 16, 2016.

Tobias, M. 1998. *Nature's keepers: On the front line of the fight to save wildlife in America.* New York: John Wiley and Sons.

Toit, J., K. Rogers, and H. Biggs. 2003. *The Kruger experience: Ecology and management of savanna heterogeneity.* Washington, DC: Island Press.

TRAFFIC. 1995. *The bear facts: The East Asian market for bear gall bladder.* Cambridge, UK: TRAFFIC.

———. 1998. *The medicinal wildlife trade in East and southern Africa.* Nairobi, Kenya: TRAFFIC East/Southern Africa.

———. 1999. *Time to act on traditional medicine and wild resources: A challenge to the health and wildlife heritage of Africans.* Lilongwe, Malawi: TRAFFIC East/Southern Africa.

———. 2002a. *Food for thought: The utilization of wild game meat in eastern and southern Africa.* Nairobi, Kenya: TRAFFIC East/Southern Africa.

———. 2002b. *Searching for a cure: Conservation of medicinal wildlife resources in East and southern Africa.* Nairobi, Kenya: TRAFFIC: East/Southern Africa.

———. 2002c. *Time to act on traditional medicine and wild resources: A challenge to the health and wildlife heritage of Africans.* Johannesburg, South Africa: TRAFFIC.

———. 2008. European Union wildlife trade initiative. Available at http://www.traffic.org/eu-wildlife-trade/. Accessed May 30, 2016.

———. 2014a. *Briefing paper: Wildlife trade in the European Union.* Cambridge, UK: TRAFFIC.

———. 2014b. Europe needs to rid itself of wildlife products. Available at http://www.traffic.org/home/2014/1/15/europe-needs-to-rid-itself-of-illegal-wildlife-products.html. Accessed May 30, 2016.

———. 2014c. Experts discuss EU response to global wildlife trafficking crisis. Available at http://www.traffic.org/home/2014/4/16/experts-discuss-eu-response-to-global-wildlife-trafficking-c.html. Accessed May 30, 2016.

———. 2014d. France to destroy ivory stockpiles. Available at http://www.traffic.org/home/2014/2/6/france-to-destroy-ivory-stockpiles.html. Accessed May 30, 2016.

———. 2015a. Asian Songbird Trade Crisis Summit calls on regional governments to shut down illegal bird markets. Available at http://www.traffic.org/home/2015/10/2/asian-songbird-trade-crisis-summit-calls-on-regional-governm.html. Accessed May 8, 2016.

———. 2015b. New study throws light on South Africa's lion bone trade. Available at http://www.traffic.org/home/2015/7/16/new-study-throws-light-on-south-africas-lion-bone-trade.html. Accessed June 5, 2016.

———. 2015c. UK boosts global efforts against wildlife crime. Available at http://www.traffic.org/home/2015/8/5/uk-boosts-global-efforts-against-wildlife-crime.html. Accessed May 30, 2016.

———. 2016a. Global transport leaders sign historic declaration in fight to shut down illegal wildlife trafficking routes. Available at http://www.traffic.org/home/2016/3/15/global-transport-leaders-sign-historic-declaration-in-fight.html. Accessed April 9, 2016.

———. 2016b. Pangolin trade; synthetic wildlife substitutes; China's botanicals market; lizards: spiny-tailed and sungazers. *TRAFFIC Bulletin* 28, no. 1. Cambridge, UK: TRAFFIC.

———. 2016c. Wildlife trade: What is it? Available at from http://www.traffic.org/trade/. Accessed June 3, 2016.

———. n.d. *Wildlife trade in South-East Asia.* Selangor, Malaysia: TRAFFIC, Southeast Asia.

Tynon, J., D. Chavez, and J. Baur. 2010. Crime in the woods: Role of law enforcement officers in national forests. *Managing Leisure* 15 (4): 251–263.

United for Wildlife. 2016. The Buckingham Palace Declaration. Available at http://www.unitedforwildlife.org/#!/our-partners. Accessed April 21, 2016.

United Nations. 2016. Convention on Biological Diversity. Available at https://www.cbd.int/. Accessed June 21, 2016.

United Nations Environment Programme. 2014. Illegal wildlife trade. Available at http://www.unep.org/yearbook/2014/PDF/chapt4.pdf. Accessed June 3, 2016.

United Nations Office on Drugs and Crime (UNODC). 2016. The illegal wildlife trade in East Asia and the Pacific: A threat assessment. Available at https://www.unodc.org/toc/en/reports/TOCTA-EAPacific.html. Accessed May 27, 2016.

U.S. Customs and Border Protection (USCBP). 2016. Cargo security and examinations. Available at https://www.cbp.gov/border-security/ports-entry/cargo-security. Accessed May 19, 2016.

U.S. Department of Justice. 2015a. Operation Chameleon. Available at https://www.justice.gov/enrd/operation-chameleon. Accessed June 16, 2016.

———. 2015b. Wildlife trafficking. Available at https://www.justice.gov/enrd/wildlife-trafficking. Accessed May 3, 2016.

U.S. Department of State. 2015. Presidential task force releases implementation plan for the National Strategy for Combating Wildlife Trafficking. February 11. Available at http://www.state.gov/r/pa/prs/ps/2015/02/237399.htm. Accessed April 11, 2016.

U.S. Fish and Wildlife Service (USFWS). 2001. *Rhinoceros and Tiger Conservation Act: Summary report, 1999–2000.* Washington, DC: U.S. Department of the Interior.

———. 2004. *Rhinoceros and Tiger Conservation Act: Summary report, 2001–2003.* Washington, DC: U.S. Department of the Interior.

———. 2012. Snake smuggler busted in Orlando. August 24. Available at https://www.fws.gov/southeast/news/2012/043.html. Accessed June 16, 2016.

———. 2013. About service wildlife inspectors. Available at http://www.fws.gov/le/wildlife-inspectors.html. Accessed May 19, 2016.

———. 2015. ESA basics: 40 years of conserving endangered species. Available at http://www.fws.gov/endangered/esa-library/pdf/ESA_basics.pdf. Accessed May 13, 2016.

———. 2016. Illegal wildlife trade. Available at https://www.fws.gov/international/travel-and-trade/illegal-wildlife-trade.html. Accessed June 3, 2016.

———. n.d. Lacey Act. Available at https://www.fws.gov/international/laws-treaties-agreements/us-conservation-laws/laceyact.html. Accessed June 21, 2016.

Vallery, A. 2015. Three plants we are losing to poachers . . . Yes, plant poaching exists! February 18. Available at http://www.onegreenplanet.org/environment/plant-poaching/. Accessed June 6, 2016.

Van Song, N. 2003. *Wildlife trading in Vietnam: Why it flourishes.* Economy and Environmental Program for Southeast Asia. Research Report 2003-RR6. Hanoi, Vietnam: Hanoi Agricultural University.

van Uhm, D., and D. Siegel. 2016. The illegal trade in black caviar. *Trends in Organized Crime* 19 (1): 67–87.

Venter, C. 2003. Organized crime: A perspective from South Africa. In *Organized crime: World perspectives,* ed. J. Albanese, D. Das, and A. Vermer, 379–391. Upper Saddle River, NJ: Prentice Hall.

Vira, V., and T. Ewing. 2014. *Ivory's curse: The militarization and professionalization of poaching in Africa*. Washington, DC: Born Free Foundation USA.

Voice of America News. 2014. Trophy hunting is big business in South Africa. Available at http://learningenglish.voanews.com/content/trophy-hunting-south-africa/2412610.html. Accessed April 18, 2016.

von Lampe, K. 2015. *Organized crime: Analyzing illegal activities, criminal structures and extra-legal governance*. Thousand Oaks, CA: Sage.

Walsh, A., and L. Ellis. 2007. *Criminology: An interdisciplinary approach*. Thousand Oaks, CA: Sage.

Walters, R., and D. Westerhuis. 2013. Green crime and the role of environmental courts. *Crime, Law and Social Change* 59 (3): 279–290.

Warchol, G., and M. Harrington. 2016. Exploring the dynamics of South Africa's illegal abalone trade via routine activities theory. *Trends in Organized Crime* 19 (1): 21–41.

Warchol, G., and B. Johnson. 2009. Wildlife crimes in the game reserves of South Africa: A research note. *International Journal of Comparative and Applied Criminal Justice* 33 (1): 143–154.

Warchol, G., and D. Kapla. 2012. Policing the wilderness: A descriptive study of wildlife conservation officers in South Africa. *International Journal of Comparative and Applied Criminal Justice* 36 (2): 83–102.

Warchol, G., L. Zupan, and W. Clack. 2003. Transnational criminality: An analysis of the illegal wildlife market in southern Africa. *International Criminal Justice Review* 13:1–27.

Watson, F., M. Becker, J. Milanzi, and M. Nyirenda. 2015. Assessing human encroachment trends in protected area networks using land use change data: Implications for large carnivore conservation. *Regional Environmental Change* 15 (2): 415–429.

Wells, M. 1996. The social role of protected areas in the new South Africa. *Environmental Conservation* 23:322–331.

White, R. 2013. Environmental crime and problem-solving courts. *Crime, Law and Social Change* 59 (3): 267–278.

White House. 2014. Fact sheet: National strategy for combating wildlife trafficking and commercial ban on trade in elephant ivory. February 11. Available at https://www.whitehouse.gov/the-press-office/2014/02/11/fact-sheet-national-strategy-combating-wildlife-trafficking-commercial-b. Accessed March 24, 2016.

WildAid. 2003. *First half report—January/June 2003*. Bangkok, Thailand: WildAid.

———. 2004. *Thailand Report: Six-month report, January–June 2004*. Bangkok, Thailand: WildAid.

———. 2015a. *Ivory demand in China, 2012–2014*. San Francisco: WildAid.

———. 2015b. Wildlife groups urge Japanese PM to halt ivory trade. Available at http://wildaid.org/news/wildlife-groups-urge-japanese-pm-halt-domestic-ivory-trade. Accessed June 11, 2016.

———. 2016. The WildAid difference. Available at http://wildaid.org/about-wildaid. Accessed September 29, 2016.

Wildlife Act. 2014. Rhino horn—education, conservation and demand reduction. August 14. Available at http://wildlifeact.com/blog/rhino-horn-education conservation-demand-reduction/. Accessed September 29, 2016.

Wildlife Conservation Society (WCS). 2005. *Africa program*. New York: WCS.

———. 2016a. Stopping illegal wildlife trade. Available at http://www.wcs.org/our-work/solutions/illegal-wildlife-trade. Accessed September 29, 2016.

———. 2016b. We stand for wildlife. Available at http://www.wcs.org/our-work. Accessed May 14, 2016.

Wildlife Direct. 2010. The African wildlife police: Lusaka task force. Available at http://
banivory.wildlifedirect.org/tag/lusaka-agreement-task-force/. Accessed May 10, 2016.

Williams, F., and M. McShane. 2010. *Criminological theory.* 5th ed. Upper Saddle River,
NJ: Prentice Hall.

Williams, P. 1984. Transnational criminal organizations and international security. *Survival* 36 (1): 96–11.

———. 1997. Transnational organized crime and national and international security: A
global assessment. *Society under Siege* 1. Available at https://issafrica.s3.amazonaws
.com/site/uploads/SWILLIAMS.PDF.

Winslow, R., and S. Zhang. 2008. *Criminology: A global perspective.* Upper Saddle River,
NJ: Prentice Hall.

World Bank. 2013. Africa development indicators, 2013. Available at http://data.world-
bank.org/data-catalog/africa-development-indicators. Accessed June 3, 2016.

World Wildlife Fund (WWF). 2003. Cactus poaching, legal harvesting a growing threat
to Chihuahuan desert cacti. January. Available at http://wwf.panda.org/wwf_
news/?5402/Cactus-poaching-legal-harvesting-a-growing threat-to-Chihuahuan-
Desert-cacti. Accessed June 6, 2016.

———. 2007. South African abalone to come under international trade controls. Available
at http://wwf.panda.org/?94101/south-african-abalone-to come-under-international-
trade-controls. Accessed June 9, 2016.

———. 2014a. Kenya finally gets a new wildlife law. Available at http://wwf.panda.org/
wwf_news/?216350/Kenya-finally-gets-a-new-wildlife-law. Accessed October 4, 2016.

———. 2014b. National strategy for combatting wildlife trafficking. Available at http://
www.worldwildlife.org/publications/national-strategy-for-combating-wildlife-traf
ficking?_ga=1.155799867.1655311738.1459626695. Accessed March 7, 2016.

———. 2015a. CITES: Ensuring that species are not threatened by international trade.
Available at http://wwf.panda.org/what_we_do/how_we_work/policy/conventions/
cites/. Accessed June 11, 2016.

———. 2015b. Greater Mekong. Available at http://www.worldwildlife.org/places/greater-
mekong. Accessed May 7, 2016.

———. 2015c. Major successes for largest ever global operation against wildlife crime.
Available at http://wwf.panda.org/wwf_news/?248311/Major-successes-for-largest-
global-operation ever-against-wildlife-crime. Accessed May 11, 2016.

———. 2016a. African rhinos. Available at http://wwf.panda.org/what_we_do/endan
gered_species/rhinoceros/african_rhinos/. Accessed June 11, 2016.

———. 2016b. Asian rhinos. Available at http://wwf.panda.org/what_we_do/endangered_
species/rhinoceros/asian_rhinos/. Accessed June 4, 2016.

———. 2016c. Crush and burn: Destroying illegal ivory. Available at http://www.world-
wildlife.org/stories/crush-and-burn-destroying-illegal-ivory. Accessed May 3, 2016.

———. 2016d. Species that suffer from illegal activities on the ocean. Available at http://
www.worldwildlife.org/stories/species-that-suffer-from-illegal-activities-on-the-
ocean. Accessed June 6, 2016.

———. 2016e. Species: Tiger. Available at http://www.worldwildlife.org/species/tiger. Accessed June 5, 2016.

———.n.d. African lions. Available at http://www.wwf.org.uk/wildlife/african-lions/. Accessed May 2, 2016.

Wright, R., and S. Decker. 1994. *Burglars on the job: Streetlife and residential break-ins.*
Boston: Northeastern University Press.

Wrong, M. 2009. *It's our turn to eat: The story of a Kenyan whistle-blower.* New York: Harper.

Yamagiwa, J. 2008. Bushmeat poaching and the conservation crisis in Kahuzi-Biega National Park, Democratic Republic of Congo. *Journal of Sustainable Forestry* 16 (3–4): 111–130.

Zambian Carnivores. 2016 Zambian Carnivore Programme. Available at http://www.zambiacarnivores.org/about-us/the-programme. Accessed February 3, 2016.

Zhang, M., and B. Zhang. 2012. Specialized environmental courts in China: Status quo challenges and responses. *Journal of Energy and Natural Resource Law* 30 (4): 361–390.

Zoological Society of London. 2016. Global transport leaders sign historic declaration at Buckingham Palace in fight to shut down illegal wildlife trafficking routes. March 16. Available at https://www.zsl.org/news/global-transport-leaders-sign-historic-declaration-at-buckingham-palace-in-fight-to-shut. Accessed April 18, 2016.

Index

Page numbers followed by the letter *f* refer to figures. Page numbers followed by the letter *t* refer to tables.

Greg L. Warchol is Professor of Criminal Justice
at Northern Michigan University.